THE CHRONICLERS

THE CHRONICLERS

By the Editors of

TIME-LIFE BOOKS

with text by

Keith Wheeler

TIME-LIFE BOOKS / ALEXANDRIA, VIRGINIA

Time-Life Books Inc.
is a wholly owned subsidiary of

TIME INCORPORATED

Founder: Henry R. Luce 1898-1967

Editor-in-Chief: Henry Anatole Grunwald
President: J. Richard Munro
Chairman of the Board: Ralph P. Davidson
Executive Vice President: Clifford J. Grum
Chairman, Executive Committee: James R. Shepley
Editorial Director: Ralph Graves
Group Vice President, Books: Joan D. Manley
Vice Chairman: Arthur Temple

TIME-LIFE BOOKS INC.

Managing Editor: Jerry Korn
Executive Editor: David Maness
Assistant Managing Editors: Dale M. Brown (planning),
George Constable, Thomas H. Flaherty Jr. (acting),
Martin Mann, John Paul Porter
Art Director: Tom Suzuki
Chief of Research: David L. Harrison
Director of Photography: Robert G. Mason
Assistant Art Director: Arnold C. Holeywell
Assistant Chief of Research: Carolyn L. Sackett
Assistant Director of Photography: Dolores A. Littles

Chairman: John D. McSweeney
President: Carl G. Jaeger
Executive Vice Presidents: John Steven Maxwell,
David J. Walsh
Vice Presidents: George Artandi (comptroller);
Stephen L. Bair (legal counsel); Peter G. Barnes;
Nicholas Benton (public relations); John L. Canova;
Beatrice T. Dobie (personnel); Carol Flaumenhaft
(consumer affairs); James L. Mercer (Europe/South
Pacific); Herbert Sorkin (production);
Paul R. Stewart (marketing)

THE OLD WEST

EDITORIAL STAFF FOR "THE CHRONICLERS"
Editor: George G. Daniels
Picture Editor: Mary Y. Steinbauer
Text Editors: Valerie Moolman, Joan S. Reiter,
Gerald Simons
Designer: Bruce Blair
Staff Writers: Don Earnest, Frank Kappler,
Gerry Schremp, Rosalind Stubenberg
Chief Researcher: June O. Goldberg
Researchers: Loretta Britten, Thomas Dickey,
Terry Drucker, Thomas Fitzharris, Harriet Heck,
Helen M. Hinkle, Jane Jordan, Thomas Lashnits,
Mary Leverty, Fred Ritchin, John Conrad Weiser,
Gretchen Wessels
Design Assistant: Joan Hoffman

EDITORIAL PRODUCTION
Production Editor: Douglas B. Graham
Operations Manager: Gennaro C. Esposito,
Gordon E. Buck (assistant)
Assistant Production Editor: Feliciano Madrid
Quality Control: Robert L. Young (director),
James J. Cox (assistant), Daniel J. McSweeney,
Michael G. Wight (associates)
Art Coordinator: Anne B. Landry
Copy Staff: Susan B. Galloway (chief),
Barbara H. Fuller, Celia Beattie
Picture Department: Marianne Dowell
Traffic: Kimberly K. Lewis

THE AUTHOR: A North Dakotan born and raised, Keith Wheeler began his own career as a chronicler in the South Dakota town of Huron, where, as one of a four-man staff on the *Daily Huronite,* he served as sports editor, assistant city editor, state editor, columnist and copy boy. After two years, he moved on to the Chicago *Times* as a rewrite man and later became a World War II correspondent in the Pacific campaigns. He joined LIFE in 1951 as a writer and continued there until 1970 when he became a freelance. He has authored four other volumes in the OLD WEST series.

THE COVER: Wittily commenting on his workaday routine in the wilderness, George Catlin shows himself painting Chief Mah-to-toh-pa (The Four Bears) in 1832 as awestruck Mandans look on. Catlin spent six years building up a comprehensive pictorial record of the Plains tribes before white settlement engulfed their culture. In the frontispiece photograph, taken in 1902, a lady of Leavenworth, Kansas, models a novel salute to journalism—an outfit bearing the impress of a local weekly, *Western Life.*

CORRESPONDENTS: Elisabeth Kraemer (Bonn); Margot Hapgood, Dorothy Bacon, Lesley Coleman (London); Susan Jonas, Lucy T. Voulgaris (New York); Maria Vincenza Aloisi, Josephine du Brusle (Paris); Ann Natanson (Rome). Valuable assistance was also provided by: Robert Kroon (Geneva); Judy Aspinall, Karin B. Pearce (London); Carolyn T. Chubet, Miriam Hsia, Christina Lieberman (New York); Mimi Murphy (Rome); Janet Zich (San Francisco).

Other Publications:

LIBRARY OF HEALTH
CLASSICS OF THE OLD WEST
THE EPIC OF FLIGHT
THE GOOD COOK
THE SEAFARERS
THE ENCYCLOPEDIA OF COLLECTIBLES
THE GREAT CITIES
WORLD WAR II
HOME REPAIR AND IMPROVEMENT
THE TIME-LIFE LIBRARY OF BOATING
HUMAN BEHAVIOR
THE ART OF SEWING
THE EMERGENCE OF MAN
THE AMERICAN WILDERNESS
THE TIME-LIFE ENCYCLOPEDIA OF GARDENING
LIFE LIBRARY OF PHOTOGRAPHY
THIS FABULOUS CENTURY
FOODS OF THE WORLD
TIME-LIFE LIBRARY OF AMERICA
TIME-LIFE LIBRARY OF ART
GREAT AGES OF MAN
LIFE SCIENCE LIBRARY
THE LIFE HISTORY OF THE UNITED STATES
TIME READING PROGRAM
LIFE NATURE LIBRARY
LIFE WORLD LIBRARY
FAMILY LIBRARY:
  HOW THINGS WORK IN YOUR HOME
  THE TIME-LIFE BOOK OF THE FAMILY CAR
  THE TIME-LIFE FAMILY LEGAL GUIDE
  THE TIME-LIFE BOOK OF FAMILY FINANCE

For information about any Time-Life book, please write:
Reader Information
Time-Life Books
541 North Fairbanks Court
Chicago, Illinois 60611

CONTENTS

Artist Sanford Gifford sketches Wyoming's Chugwater valley in this photograph by William H. Jackson.

1|Capturing the image of the frontier

In 1832, when the immense wilderness beyond the Mississippi was inhabited by fewer than 20,000 Americans, the novelist Washington Irving headed west on horseback. His purpose was to observe and write of "those great Indian tribes, which are now about to disappear as independent nations."

In the next few decades, many daring chroniclers followed Irving: journalists like the famed Horace Greeley of the *New-York Tribune* and Samuel Bowles of the *Springfield* (Massachusetts) *Republican* toured the West to satisfy their readers' hunger for reliable information about the vast terrain. Tough small-town reporters and editors — a veteran reporter called them "pistol-packin' pencil pushers" — went west to start publishing newspapers in cow towns and mining camps. Artists and photographers added their vivid pictures to the swelling annals of frontier life.

These chroniclers were almost unanimous in predicting the rapid settlement of the West. It was a self-fulfilling prophecy. Their reports on rich lands and richer opportunities helped persuade hundreds of thousands of emigrants to move out — and to create what editor Bowles termed "the broadest, freest, most active and aggressive society that the world has yet developed."

The Union Pacific's official photography car, decorated with elk antlers and proudly advertising its wares, halts for its own portrait in 1869.

U.P.R.R. PHOTOGRAPH CAR.

J.B. SILVIS,

GEMS.

STEREOSCOPIC & LANDSCAPE VIEWS of NOTABLE POINTS On LINE of PACIFIC R.R. ALWAYS on HAND.

PHOTOGRAPHER.

Covering the Modoc Indian war, William McKay of the San Francisco *Bulletin* hunkers down by a rock-ringed rifle pit to write a dispatch.

11

12

A New Mexico weekly is put to bed in 1886. Over the years, some 10,000 small papers sprouted — and mostly withered — in the West.

13

Perched on the lip of the Grand Canyon around 1900, Henry G. Peabody prepares to capture the scene with an enormous camera.

Big-time boosters from the Eastern press

At dusk on June 1, 1859, almost 400 miles out from the Missouri River along the Denver trail, the Leavenworth & Pike's Peak Express stage started to negotiate a steep and tricky descent into a dry creek bed. At that moment three Indians galloped up on the opposite slope, and the four stagecoach mules were so startled by the sudden appearance of the intruders that they bolted. As the stage careened off the track and slewed sideways down the declivity, one of the two passengers leaped clear and stood aside to watch succeeding events.

This man was Albert Deane Richardson, correspondent for the *Boston Journal.* "Our mules broke a line, ran down a precipitous bank, upsetting the coach which was hurled upon the ground with a tremendous crash," he wrote of the incident. "From a mass of cushions, carpet-sacks and blankets soon emerged my companion, his head rising above the side of the vehicle like that of an advertising boy from his frame of pasteboard. Blood was flowing profusely from cuts in his cheek, arm and leg; but his face was serene and benignant as a May morning."

Here was a second vision that might have frightened the mules even more, except that they were already out of sight across the creek bed. The blood was dripping from a most unusual head: pale, round as a bowling ball, and fringed across the pate, down the sides

Greeley's *Tribune* announces the boss's trip.

and under the chin with a fluff of whitish hair. Through wire-rimmed glasses, light-blue eyes peered down a long pointed nose with a look of wistful inquiry.

Severely abraded as he was — enough to keep him limping and bone sore for many weeks — the passenger was still functioning. And this was singular good fortune for the American West, indeed, for the whole nation. The injured man was Horace Greeley, editor of the *New-York Tribune* and far and away the most influential journalist of his era.

Greeley and Richardson were fellow passengers by happenstance, but they were bent upon the same general errand. Each was there to inspect the West at firsthand and to report what he found to Eastern readers. The East had been in need of harbingers like these ever since the Lewis and Clark expedition of 1804-1806 had opened the way to the Pacific. Since then, though a number of traveling writers had sent back reports on their excursions to the West, information had tended to be sparse and sporadic, usually limited to the travelers' own special interests, and sometimes fatally inaccurate — as testified by the fate of the Donner party, which arrived at its cannibalistic denouement via a loudly advertised "shortcut."

By now, in 1859, the need for straight, informative reporting had grown into a pressing national concern. The country was about to split, North and South, with each side reaching for every available instrument of political, economic or, if the worst came, military advantage. And war or no, America had begun to see its real destiny in a westward move; the people needed practical information to guide them. Which land was fertile? Where did timber grow, and where might gold, coal and other minerals truly lie? Where was

---

Mathew Brady made this portrait of Horace Greeley in 1858 shortly before the famed founder and editor of the *New-York Tribune* started forth "looking for the Far West." "And here it is!" Greeley exulted on his arrival in Atchison, Kansas.

17

water, where desert? Could a railroad one day cross that stupefying distance? On what line and grades, at what cost? The East's appetite for information was omnivorous and insatiable—not only the East's, the world's. One of history's grandest migrations stood waiting for the word. It would come from the likes of Greeley and Richardson.

These were the West's chroniclers. Joining hands with such distinguished journalists were historians, anthropologists, artists, illustrators and photographers, adventurous and inquiring Europeans, and illustrious men of letters. Together they accumulated a vast store of knowledge and created a fresh body of legend of their very own. They put forth in striking graphics the look of the West—its variety, majesty and sheer immensity. They studied the baffling sociological problem of the region's indigenous Indian population and foresaw its sad solution. And they set down for posterity a record of how life and the land were beyond the Missouri River before the white man—for better or for worse—changed them for all time.

They were by no means of one mind. Each of the men—and women—saw the West in the colors and shapes of his own special vision. Some were chroniclers of hard fact who described the region much as it really was and contributed substantially to its growth and population. Others were storytellers or troubadours, who wove fact into fantasy to sing the praises of the West or deride it according to their bent, spinning their tales to delight armchair adventurers. Some, such as the incomparable Mark Twain, were both. The one belief they all held in common was that the West was the biggest, most overwhelming entity any of them had ever seen.

Of all the chroniclers of the Old West, the journalists enjoyed the greatest professional advantages. They had an ever-ready platform from which to deliver what they saw, heard or thought, and an eager audience to absorb their every word.

Albert Deane Richardson and Horace Greeley were two particularly illustrious gentlemen of the press. Richardson, born on a Massachusetts farm, reared in an austere New England Congregationalist family and schooled in journalism in Ohio, was at 26 a veteran frontier reporter. He had first gone to eastern Kansas for the *Boston Journal* in 1857 as a young man of 23.

A bold Horace Greeley sits calmly beside stagecoach driver Hank Monk in this lithograph spoofing a hair-raising ride the editor experienced in California. Actually, Greeley was inside the coach, bouncing around like so much baggage and calling helplessly for the ebullient Monk to slow down.

Gold miners and wives stand by a sluice-way in Gregory Gulch, near Denver, where Horace Greeley and others confirmed a strike in 1859. Within weeks, 30,000 people had flooded into the area.

There he had lived at Sumner on the Missouri River, got involved with abolitionist politics, and served for a time as secretary to the territorial legislature. In those early days he was as much a participant in the booming frontier as a professional observer of it. "Making governments and building towns are the natural employments of the migratory Yankee," he reported. "He takes to them as instinctively as a young duck to water. Congregate a hundred Americans anywhere beyond the settlements, and they immediately lay out a city, frame a State constitution and apply for admission into the Union, while twenty-five of them become candidates for the United States Senate."

Once at Osawkee, Kansas, he borrowed $150 in order to make the down payment on a quarter section of land. But he left his homestead in the spring of 1859 when the "grand stampede for the mountains" lured him out of Kansas to find out the truth about the rumors of a great gold strike in the Rockies.

Somewhat the same combination of background, taste and circumstance had lured west the man who was Richardson's traveling companion. Horace Greeley, farm-born in New Hampshire, had become by 48 a man with two important roles to play. Not only was he the acknowledged dean of American journalism as the admired and feared editor of the *New-York Tribune,* but he was also a growing force in national politics. Three years before the stagecoach accident, he had been one of the founding fathers of the new Republican Party, which would soon perform the profoundly important act of nominating Abraham Lincoln for the Presidency.

It is hard to say which of the two roles Greeley regarded as the more vital. What is certain is that he had been planning his trip West for a decade, during which he had unendingly preached his famous dictum, "Go West, young man, go West." If he had not himself gone before, it was because his life had been ruled by work—lecturing, writing, politicking, opinion-making —and the tragedy of the early deaths of five of his seven children. At last, taking advantage of the political lull before the Presidential campaign of 1860, he had acted upon his own advice. He saw his specific mission as acting as advance scout for a railroad that would join the Atlantic to the Pacific Coast: "From the hour when, late in 1848, the discovery of rich gold placers in California had incited a vast and eager migration thither," Greeley wrote, "the construction of a great International Railway from the Missouri to the Pacific seemed to me to be imperative and inevitable. I resolved to make a journey of observation across the continent, with reference to the natural obstacles presented to, and facilities afforded for, its construction." And, of course, he reserved the general right to inform his readers about anything and everything else that struck him as important to their well-being.

He left New York by Erie Railroad on May 9, 1859; took steamer passage from St. Joseph, Missouri, to Atchison, Kansas; wound his way from Atchison to Lawrence via steamboat, two-horse wagon and stage; traveled by another stage from Lawrence to Leavenworth and thence to Manhattan, Kansas, where his western journey began in earnest. Thereafter, in slightly less than four months of often excruciatingly uncomfortable travel, he wrote, talked and jolted his way across the Great Plains to Denver and the Rockies, to Laramie, South Pass, Bridger and Salt Lake City, to Carson Valley and the Sierra Nevada, and down to California where he ended his odyssey in San Francisco early in September.

It was on the Leavenworth stage from Manhattan that he met the young newsman who would accompany him to the Rocky Mountains. "Thus far," wrote Albert Deane Richardson on May 27, "I had been the solitary passenger. But at Manhattan, Horace Greeley joined me for the rest of the journey. His overland trip attracted much attention. A farmer asked me if Horace Greeley had failed in business, and was going to Pike's Peak to dig gold! Another inquired if he was about to start a newspaper in Manhattan."

En route, Richardson observed with both amusement and some admiration that the great editor was not always recognized. At a creek crossing in Kansas on May 30 they came upon a party of Ohio emigrants whose mired wagon blocked the road. Without being asked, Greeley climbed down from the coach and lent a shoulder to the wheel of the stuck vehicle. During a pause for breath one of the emigrants asked Greeley what his business might be; the editor replied modestly that he was with a New York paper, the *Tribune.*

"That's old Greeley's paper, isn't it?" the emigrant asked. "Yes sir," Horace Greeley replied, and let it go at that. The passengers on the righted and repaired stagecoach sighted Pikes Peak on June 5, only one day out of Denver. It was the ideal time for the arrival of professionals of the stamp of Greeley and Richardson. The presence of gold had indeed been reported in the region. When the trail-worn newsmen pulled into town, they found a junior colleague in possession of a brand-new gold strike story that urgently needed confirmation. Greeley and Richardson would supply it, and the weight of journalism's word would make itself felt from one end of the country to the other.

The reporter Greeley and Richardson encountered in Denver was 24-year-old Henry Villard, who had come by devious pathways from his native Germany to represent the *Cincinnati Daily Commercial* in this remote American mountain hamlet. Villard had been born Ferdinand Heinrich Gustav Hilgard in the family of a German judge. He had fled from Bavaria to America in 1853 to escape military service. Now, with a new name and self-taught in English, he had been sent to Denver as a reporter assigned to learn whether the Pikes Peak gold rush was real or a hoax.

The rush had started in June of 1858 when small quantities of gold had been discovered at Cherry Creek, near Denver, and gathered momentum with reports of three more strikes in the early months of 1859—at Clear Creek, Black Hawk and Gold Run in the mountains west of Denver. Tales of these finds, told by excited prospectors, suppliers of mining equipment—and William N. Byers' brand-new, promotion-minded *Rocky Mountain News*—were seized upon and blazoned by the Eastern press. But bitter, debunking rumors soon began to drift around. Disappointed gold seekers returned from the digs empty-handed, angrily claiming that the whole thing was a fraud.

At first it had seemed to Villard, too, that the gold was nothing but a myth. He reported a westward flood tide of gold-bedazzled humanity bent upon tapping what they had heard was the new El Dorado. Equally, he reported an ebb tide of destitute prospectors straggling back eastward in threadbare disillusion. Villard was particularly moved by the fact that so few of the gold hunters had prepared themselves for the rigors of travel and life in the West. It was not uncommon for improvident journeyers "to meet death in its most aw-

ful form, by starvation," he told the *Daily Commercial's* readers. And some, he recounted with a shudder, "were driven by the maddening pangs of hunger to acts of cannibalism, such as living on human flesh."

By early May, a few weeks after his arrival, Villard reported that Denver, like nearby Auraria two-thirds deserted, was a dying town. Then, on the second Sunday of May, Villard and several companions were sitting gloomily in Denver's log-cabin express office when "a short, slender, heavily bearded individual, in miner's garb, entered the room and inquired for letters." In answer to questions, the stranger allowed that he had just come from the north fork of Clear Creek 30 miles to the west. There, in company with a man named John H. Gregory, he had been finding gold—as much as a dollar's worth to the pan, weighed out according to the delicate scales always to be found among the tools of any diggings. To back his story, he displayed a bottle which, he said, contained about $40 worth of gold dust, and a few chunks of decomposed quartz that he avowed to be veined with gold. But the men in the express office, grown skeptical of all such claims, were not impressed. Their disbelief irritated the stranger.

"He asserted most emphatically that he would warrant one dollar to the pan of dirt to any number of men that would follow him," Villard noted, "and added that they might bring a rope along and swing him up in case he should be found a liar."

A few prospectors decided to call the bluff and accompanied the miner—whose name was lost in the subsequent rush of events—back to the Gregory mine. Villard himself, still unbelieving, remained in Denver. Days passed without further news, and the faint flicker of hope sparked by the stranger dwindled away. Then, on the fifth day, reported Villard, "a Mr. Bates, late of Dubuque, Iowa, made his appearance with a vial full of gold, representing a value of about eighty dollars, which he claimed to have washed out of thirty-nine pans of dirt, obtained not far from the spot on which Gregory had made his discovery."

Mr. Bates, being known as a reliable man, stirred a new wave of excitement and a general race to the hills. Still skeptical, Villard dallied a few days more before climbing aboard a mule and riding out to see for himself. The young reporter spent several days in "Gregory Gulch," as the place was now called. Testing the

AN OVERLAND JOURNEY.

XXI.

TWO HOURS WITH BRIGHAM YOUNG.

SALT LAKE CITY, Utah, July 13, 1859.

My friend Dr. Bernhisel, M. C., took me this afternoon, by appointment, to meet Brigham Young, President of the Mormon Church, who had expressed a willingness to receive me at 2 P. M. We were very cordially welcomed at the door by the President, who led us into the second-story parlor of the largest of his houses (he has three), where I was introduced to Heber C. Kimball, Gen. Wells, Gen. Ferguson, Albert Carrington, Elias Smith, and several other leading men in the Church, with two full-grown sons of the President. After some unimportant conversation on general topics, I stated that I had come in quest of fuller knowledge respecting the doctrines and polity of the Mormon Church, and would like to ask some questions bearing directly on these, if there were no objection. President Young avowed his willingness to respond to all pertinent inquiries, the conversation proceeded substantially as follows:

H. G.—Am I to regard Mormonism (so-called) as a new religion, or as simply a new development of Christianity?

B. Y.—We hold that there can be no true Christian Church without a priesthood directly commissioned by and in immediate communication with the Son of God and Savior of mankind. Such a church is that of the Latter-Day Saints, called by their enemies Mormons; we know no other that even pretends to have present and direct revolations of God's will.

H. G.—Then I am to understand that you regard all other churches professing to be Christian as the Church of Rome regards all churches not in communion with itself—as schismatic, heretical, and out of the way of salvation?

B. Y.—Yes, substantially.

H. G.—Apart from this, in what respect do your doctrines differ essentially from those of our Orthodox Protestant Churches—the Baptist or Methodist, for example?

B. Y.—We hold the doctrines of Christianity, as revealed in the Old and New Testaments—also in the Book of Mormon, which teaches the same cardinal truths, and those only.

H. G.—Do you believe in the doctrine of the Trinity?

B. Y.—We do; but not exactly as it is held by other churches. We believe in the Father, the Son, and the Holy Ghost, as equal, but not identical—not as one person [being]. We believe in all the Bible teaches on this subject.

H. G.—Do you believe in a personal devil—a
[   ] being

One of Horace Greeley's journalistic coups for the *New-York Tribune* on his celebrated 1859 journey to the West was a lengthy interview with a man who at once fascinated and repelled Easteners: Mormon leader Brigham Young. Greeley quizzed the Prophet concerning his religious tenets, particularly the practice—shocking to most Victorian Americans—of polygamy, by which Young had acquired 15 wives. In addition, Greeley, a staunch abolitionist, asked Young's views on slavery. Young replied that while some people in the territory owned slaves, he believed it "the curse of the masters"; if and when Utah entered the Union it would do so as a free state.

diggings for himself, he washed many pans of dirt that variously yielded from $1.50 to $4.00 worth of precious dust, and held in his own hands the gold that other miners had gleaned from their sluices. Villard returned to Denver "thoroughly persuaded by this overwhelmingly ocular evidence, that gold actually existed to a large extent in at least a portion of the Rocky Mountains," and wrote a report to that effect for the *Cincinnati Daily Commercial.*

That was barely a week before Horace Greeley and Albert Richardson arrived. The newcomers rented sleeping space in the log-walled, tent-roofed Denver House, and a bruised and weary Greeley gave grateful thought to surcease for his wracked frame. However, it was not to be; Greeley's name was too renowned and Denver demanded a speech. Richardson reported on it: "On one side the tipplers at the bar silently sipped their grog; on the other the gamblers respectfully suspended the shuffling of cards and the counting of money from their huge piles of coin, while Mr. Greeley standing between them, made a strong anti-drinking and anti-gambling address, which was received with perfect good humor."

Greeley, a man of sterling fortitude and a strong sense of responsibility toward his reading public, insisted on starting for the gold diggings at dawn on the following morning to confirm or deny the strikes once and for all. "I shall state nothing at second-hand where I may know if I will," he declared. Villard, his own story already filed, graciously volunteered to go along and guide his new and more influential colleagues.

The trip, 25 miles as a single-minded crow might have flown it, was nearer twice that on muleback, mostly up and down steep ridges, and through mountain freshets so tumultuous that once Greeley's mule was pitched to her knees, "very nearly throwing me over her head; had she done it, I am sure I had not the strength left to rise and remount."

The day's ride ended a few miles from the diggings with Greeley so sore and worn that "I had to be tenderly lifted from my saddle and laid on a blanket." By morning, however, the editor was more or less ambulatory and the party pressed on to the gulch. They spent two days circulating among the 5,000 male prospectors — plus five white women and seven Indian ones — inspecting their labors and examining the results.

Richardson noted that, "In our presence one miner washed $2.50 from a pan-full of dirt, and told us another pan had just yielded him $17.87." Greeley at one point was shown a lump of solid gold estimated to be worth $510 at the going price, between $17 and $20 an ounce.

On the strength of such evidence, the journalistic trio decided to compile a joint report on the state of the strike in Gregory Gulch, and wrote it on June 9 while still at the diggings. Beginning with a disclaimer that they had any personal interest in mining, and asserting that their presence on the scene was solely for the "purpose of ascertaining and setting forth the truth with regard to a subject of deep and general interest," the journalists then declared: "We have this day personally visited nearly all the mines or claims already opened in this valley, have witnessed the operation of digging, transporting and washing the vein-stone, have seen the gold plainly visible in the riffles of every sluice, and in nearly every pan of the rotten quartz washed in our presence." The report continued with examples of the profits obtained:

"John H. Gregory, from Gordon County, Georgia. Worked five days with two helpers — result, $972." Gregory sold his two claims for $21,000; afterward he prospected for other parties on new claims that yielded a total of about $200 a day.

S. G. Jones of Kansas washed $225 a day. "Never seen a piece crushed that did not yield gold."

Zeigler, Spain & Co., of South Bend, Indiana: Four men sluiced $3,000 in three weeks, making from $21 to $495 a day.

Sopris Henderson & Co., Farmington, Indiana: Four men sluiced $607 in four days.

The three journalists carried their report back to Denver — a trip during which Villard was thrown from his mule and painfully dragged along when his foot caught in the stirrup. Signed in order by Greeley, Richardson and Villard, the story testifying to the existence of the riches of Gregory Gulch so overjoyed Editor Byers of the *Rocky Mountain News* that he got out an extra — on brown wrapping paper, since he had run out of newsprint.

"Extra — Greeley's Report," proclaimed the headline; and, beneath it, four columns of hastily set type gave the journalists' dispatch in full. In a brief introduction, Byers observed that the report would "give satisfaction to the public mind, and at once set at rest the cry of 'humbug' reiterated by the returning emigration from this region. The names of the gentlemen signed to this report," he added, "are sufficient to give it credence without further comment from us."

There is no doubt about it; the report was the saving of Denver. Trumpeted locally, it immediately stemmed the tide of disheartened "go-backs." Reprinted in Greeley's *Tribune,* Richardson's *Journal* and Villard's *Daily Commercial* — and in other papers all over the country — it electrified the nation and set the Rocky Mountain mining region on the road to its ultimate development. Capital started pouring in, along with the heavy machinery and technical knowledge necessary for large-scale processing of the "mother of gold," as the mineral-bearing quartz of the mountains was called.

But Greeley and his colleagues were not satisfied simply to attest to the presence of treasure. Their journalistic duty, as they saw it, was also to render a humane service by stressing the hardships of mining for individuals, and the need for the vital element of luck: "We cannot conclude this statement without protesting most earnestly against a renewal of the infatuation which impelled thousands to rush to this region a month or two since. Gold mining is a business which eminently requires of its votaries, capital, experience, energy, endurance, and in which the highest qualities do not always command success. Great disappointment, great suffering, are inevitable. We beg the press generally to unite with us in warning the whole people against another rush to these gold-mines, as ill-advised as that of last Spring — a rush sure to be followed like that by a stampede, but one far more destructive of property and life."

In separate dispatches of his own to the *Tribune,* Greeley was even more emphatic. "I adhere to my long-settled conviction," he wrote, "that, next to outright and indisputable gambling, the hardest way to obtain gold is to mine for it; that a good farmer or mechanic will usually make money faster, and of course immeasurably easier, by sticking to his own business than by deserting it for gold-digging."

Such cautionary and pedagogic sentiments from Greeley's pen probably neither surprised nor offended his regular readers. They were accustomed to the idea that Greeley would not hesitate to advise what was good for them, and, now that he was far away in the West, they knew that he was using his eyes and mind to perceive it in their behalf. Clearly, he was a man to be trusted. But just as clearly, he was not always heeded. In the wake of his reports thousands descended upon the Pikes Peak area — and thousands found nothing but the disappointment he had warned of.

Meanwhile, Greeley proceeded with his fact-finding tour. His curiosity embraced everything great and small; but, as the great West's untiring advocate, he kept certain large themes uppermost in his observations. One, of course, was the land itself for, as a devout weekend farmer in his own right (he owned a 75-acre farm in Chappaqua, New York), he had an almost religious conviction that the future depended on the soil. Consequently nothing so engaged his view from the coach windows as the fertility of the land, or the possibility of improving it by scientific husbandry.

Way back in eastern Kansas he had written, "We left the smart village of Olathe and struck off nearly due south, over high prairies sloped as gently and grassed as richly as could be desired, with timber visible along the watercourses on either hand. If the Garden of Eden exceeded this land in beauty or fertility, I pity Adam for having to leave it."

Greeley saw here the ideal destination for the young he had urged westward. Nonetheless, even at the apex of his enthusiasm, Greeley was honest and he would not praise the land where it disappointed him by being barren. Some 400 miles deeper into the prairie he felt obliged to report that "for more than a hundred miles back, the soil has been steadily degenerating. Of grass there is little, and that little of miserable quality — either a scanty furze or coarse alkaline sort of rush, less fit for food than physic. The dearth of water is fearful. Even the animals have deserted us."

His good opinion of his surroundings revived in the Rocky Mountains, which "with their grand, aromatic forests, their grassy glades, their frequent springs, and dancing streams of the brightest, sweetest water, their pure elastic atmosphere, and their unequalled game and fish, are destined to be a favorite resort and home of civilized man."

But he was roused to censure again farther westward; after crossing the Utah desert, he observed that

"if Uncle Sam should ever sell that tract for one cent per acre, he will swindle the purchaser outrageously." When he came to the valley of the Carson River and its palatable, although still relatively scant, waters, it struck him that the barren vistas were intrinsically fertile and would prove fruitful if only the pioneers would apply intelligence to the job. "The time will ultimately come when two or three great dams over the Carson will render the irrigation of these broad, arid plains on its banks perfectly feasible. The vegetable food of one million people can easily be grown here."

In California he found the climate's habit of drying the vegetation to brown in summer objectionable and said so. "I dislike to look for miles across so rich and beautiful a valley as this of San José and see paralysis and death the rule, greenness and life the exception." Still, despite the rarity of rain in summer, he felt obliged to attest to the state's boundless underlying fertility and its promise of even greater abundance when better managed. "All the fruits of the temperate zone are grown here in great luxuriance and perfection. No other land on earth produces wheat, rye and barley so largely with so little labor."

The roving editor outspokenly scolded Westerners who tended to ignore or squander their paradisaic surroundings. He did not hesitate to advise them to mend their ways and to point out specific steps to be taken in that direction.

"There are too many idle, shiftless people," he reported testily in one dispatch. "How a man located in a little squalid cabin on one of these rich 'claims' can sleep moonlit nights passes my comprehension. I should

A DRAMATIC ARCHEOLOGICAL DISCOVERY

Reporter Ernest Ingersoll (*sitting*) of the *New-York Tribune* and his guide lounge against a prehistoric Indian cliff dwelling they found in Colorado's Mancos Canyon in 1874. Ingersoll had been traveling the West with geological surveyors when his party met miners who told of the remnants of an ancient civilization nearby. The journalist promptly sought out the ruins, joined by survey leader William Jackson, who took this picture. Ingersoll's *Tribune* story electrified archeologists in the East, and led to expeditions that uncovered a series of cliff cities, including the complex at Mesa Verde where the ancient Pueblos had built a 200-room cliff palace and 300 other dwellings.

want to work moderately but resolutely, at least fourteen hours of each secular day."

He tried his hand at civilizing the native population but, in evident disgust, admitted failure. Meeting an Arapaho chief named Left Hand, he urged the Indian leader to initiate a communal tribal farm. He got nowhere because, he wrote, the Indian warriors "are disinclined to any such steady, monotonous exercise of their muscles. Squalid and conceited, proud and worthless, lazy and lousy, they will strut out or drink out their miserable existence, and at length afford the world a sensible relief by dying out of it."

Then, having let off steam, he tackled the problem from another angle—and saw hope. The Indian's redemption, he concluded, rested with the women who "are neither too proud nor too indolent to labor. The squaw accepts work as her destiny from childhood. I urge, therefore, that in future efforts to improve the condition of the Indians, the women be specially regarded and appealed to."

It was always thus with Greeley. He saw his role in the West—and obviously reveled in fulfilling it—as much more than a mere reporter. The eager recipient of new vistas and new ideas, he went well beyond merely transmitting them. He was teacher, leader, corrector, conscience, and bellwether for the population and prosperity of this great new land.

As he advanced, he harped relentlessly on the themes that seemed to him urgently important for the fulfillment of the West's potential. Addressed both to the Americans already there and the great flood still to come, these exhortations called for roads and railways, schools for the young and, in California, rectification of the old Spanish and Mexican land grant systems that left in doubt title to thousands upon thousands of acres of real estate. As one of the West's earliest and most outspoken conservationists, he demanded improvement in the techniques of miners whose scarred hillsides, miles-long flumes and unlovely slag heaps demonstrated

Invited by mail companies to tour the West in 1865, Speaker of the House Schuyler Colfax (second from right) chose journalists (from left) Samuel Bowles, William Bross and Albert Richardson to accompany him. The three newspapermen later reported on the journey in letters and books.

that while "mining is a necessary art, it does not tend to beautify the face of nature."

It had been his intention to give the West more time than the four months it took him to reach and examine California. But in the course of his grueling cross-country journey he came down with a plague of boils whose torments made it impossible to sit any longer in a saddle and rendered a return trip across the continent in a rocking, jolting stagecoach a prospect of pure torture. Reluctantly he surrendered to this common ailment of Western travelers, and went home by ship via the Isthmus of Panama. He never saw the West again except for a brief visit to Texas in 1871, the year before his unsuccessful run for the Presidency.

But he was not finished with attending to the West's future. His peregrination complete, he at last turned to the subject he had set forth as the principal reason for his overland journey: the absolute, imperative necessity of a transcontinental railroad and the feasibility of building it. His final dispatch on the Western journey, written after he got back to New York, was a reasoned argument for the railroad, complete with estimates of potential traffic and revenue. He opened his argument with Greeleyesque forthrightness, advising his readers of what he was about to tell them and why it was important for them to pay heed. "I propose to present such considerations as seem to me pertinent and feasible, in favor of the speedy construction of a railroad. Let facts be submitted to, and pondered by, considerate, reflecting men."

Piling up his facts—consisting largely of official figures available to any inquiring newsman—Greeley reported that 381,107 persons had reached San Francisco by sea in the years from 1849 to 1857, and that $370,986,599 in gold had left California for the East in the same period. Venturing into reasoned conjecture, he calculated that a transcontinental railroad would carry 50,000 westbound and 30,000 eastbound passengers annually for an income of $6 million; and $50 million in gold eastbound and $20 million worth of westbound freight for an additional income of $3.5 million. He reckoned annual revenue from movement of troops and their supplies at $3 million, another $3 million for freight and passenger service to Kansas and the Rocky Mountain gold region, $1 million for carrying mail between the Missouri and

California, and—a special category—$500,000 for furnishing freight and passenger service to the Mormons of Utah. Altogether, he calculated, the railroad could anticipate annual revenues of no less than $17 million.

"Men and brethren!" he concluded his final dispatch in best Greeley style. "Let us resolve to have a railroad to the Pacific—to have it soon. It will add more to the strength and wealth of our country than would the acquisition of a dozen Cubas. It will prove a bond of union not easily broken, and a new spring to our national industry, prosperity and wealth. My long, fatiguing journey was undertaken in the hope that I might do something toward the early construction of the Pacific railroad; and I trust that it has not been made wholly in vain."

Clearly, it had not. Greeley not only helped convince the public that the railroad was necessary and practicable but helped to determine the mid-continent route that was eventually chosen. On May 10, 1869, the last spikes linking up the Union and Central Pacific railroads were driven home at Promontory in Utah, and the East and West coasts of the United States were finally joined by 3,000 miles of iron rail. Two years later the combined gross revenues of the two railroads reached $17,046,000—almost exactly what Greeley had estimated.

With his keen eye for journalistic talent, Greeley staffed his *Tribune* with many of the best editors and writers of the day. Among the men he hired as correspondents were his two companions on his trip to the Colorado gold mines. Albert Richardson continued his work as a roving reporter in the West. But Henry Villard, sharing Greeley's enthusiasm for a transcontinental railroad, eventually left journalism for a career as railroad promoter. In the early 1880s, he played a key role in the development of the Northern Pacific.

Almost without exception, anyone whom Greeley offered a job snapped at the chance to work for the rich and mighty *Tribune.* A notable exception was Samuel Bowles, a cantankerous, opinionated Yankee who became one of the most influential boosters of the West. Bowles had inherited from his father a small Massachusetts newspaper, the *Springfield Republican;* and, working tirelessly with a staff of three, had transformed it into what Greeley called "the best and ablest country journal ever published on this continent." Naturally Greeley offered Bowles a job—as editorial writer and head of the *New-York Tribune's* Washington bureau. Just as naturally, the independent-minded Bowles turned him down flat.

Bowles made two journeys through the West, both at the invitation of his powerful friend, politician Schuyler Colfax. On a trip to California in 1865, the Colfax party also included the peripatetic Richardson, who described Bowles as "a companionable gentleman of forty; a close observer; a pointed, suggestive, 'meaty' writer." Three years later, shortly before Colfax was elected Vice President under Ulysses S. Grant, Bowles accompanied him as far as Colorado. Bowles published two books based on his reports for the *Republican,* one on each of his trips, and then combined them under the title *Our New West,* further disseminating his outspoken—and sometimes outrageous—opinions.

Essentially, Bowles was a fervent apostle of America's Manifest Destiny—a destiny that, he felt, should be achieved without interference or delay. He was also convinced of the superiority of the white race. It was no wonder, then, that Bowles looked with extreme disfavor upon American Indians occupying Western lands—particularly after the Indians threw a scare into him while he was passing through the Colorado mountains. Bowles' camping party was sent into near-panic by the arrival of "a grim messenger from Denver," as the editor put it, bearing news that the Indians of the Plains were on the warpath and warning that the camp was in imminent danger of attack. No attack developed, but a night of fretful waiting gave Bowles a chance to think deeply—and later write at length—upon "the whole Indian question."

In a series of advisories that came all too completely to realization, he suggested first that Indian affairs should be concentrated in the hands of a single department in Washington—the war office. "Then we should stop making treaties with tribes, cease putting them on a par with ourselves. We know they are not our equals; we know that our right to the soil, as a race capable of its superior improvement is above theirs; and let us act openly and directly our faith."

This, continued Bowles, meant telling the Indian that "We want your hunting-grounds to dig gold from, to raise grain on, and you must 'move on.' Here is a

A legendary career launched in the West

Journalistic giant Henry M. Stanley and his wife, Dorothy, peer from a window of his personal Pullman car at Monterey, California.

One of the world's most renowned journalist-explorers made a triumphal lecture tour of the United States in the winter of 1890-1891, traveling in grand style aboard a lavishly appointed Pullman car. He was Henry Morton Stanley, famed for tracking down the long-lost missionary to Africa, Dr. David Livingstone. For Stanley, the junket was not his first visit to America, but a sentimental return to the foster home of his youth. He had arrived in New Orleans in 1859, a penniless 17-year-old by the name of John Rowlands, after working his way across from Liverpool as a cabin boy on a passenger vessel. A kindly merchant named Henry Morton Stanley took in young Rowlands, and became so fond of the boy that he gave him his own name. The adventurous youngster soon went off on his own—first to fight in the Civil

War (on both sides as it turned out). And at the same time he started his career as a newsman by sending back to various newspapers vivid accounts of the campaigns he witnessed.

Heading west after the war, Stanley got a job on the *Missouri Democrat,* for which he covered General Winfield Scott Hancock's 1867 expedition against the Kiowa and Comanche Indians. He was on hand when Congress dispatched an emergency peace commission to Medicine Lodge, Kansas. The Indians roused deep sympathy in Stanley: "They move us by their pathos and mournful dignity. But half a continent could not be kept as a buffalo pasture and hunting ground."

In 1869, Stanley won an overseas assignment from the *New-York Tribune.* His date-lined stories poured in from such places as India, Persia, Tur-

key—and Africa, where on November 10, 1871, he doffed his helmet to a frail, white-haired old man in the Tanganyikan village of Ujiji, and uttered the immortal phrase, "Doctor Livingstone, I presume?"

For the next two decades, Stanley stood as a colossus among journalists. And when he returned to the United States on his lecture tour, he was lionized from one end of the country to the other. He responded in kind, but reserved his greatest accolades for the Americans he regarded as the noblest of them all, nobler even than the Indians: the simple, hard-working Midwestern and Western farmers. "Milton's description of Adam 'the great Sire of all' a little altered would fit the typical American farmer," eulogized Stanley. "I never see one but I feel inclined to say 'Good and honest man, all blessings attend thee.'"

home for you. You must not leave this home we have assigned you. When the march of our empire demands this reservation of yours, we will assign you another" —using force, if necessary—"but so long as we choose, this is your home, your prison, your playground."

Bowles was not finished with his lethal admonitions. Segregate the Indian from civilization, he continued. Let him have adequate food and clothing, the means to raise stock and till the soil, and "such education as he will take. Then let him die—as die he is doing and die he must—under his changed life. This is the best and all we can do. His game flies before the white man; we cannot restore it to him if we would; we would not if we could; it is his destiny to die. All we can do is to smooth and make decent the pathway to his grave."

Bowles also found objectionable a number of things about the Mormons of Utah—but with far less impact on these stubborn, economically powerful people. Visiting Salt Lake City in 1865, he roundly disapproved of "the Mormon and polygamous rule of Brigham Young," which, he said, kept the city "out of sympathy with the grand free movement of American life." Nowhere had the *Republican's* editor encountered a more absolute religious autocracy, nowhere less respect for the United States government. "There is no sympathy here with the federal government," wrote Bowles, "only a hollow, cheating recognition of it."

Bowles was intrigued by the status of the Mormon women, a condition, he was convinced, that the women disliked and the men didn't want the women to talk about. "Our Mormon hosts took us, one day, on a picnic excursion to Salt Lake—a 'stag' picnic, be it noted —so we could bathe *au naturel,* our friends said—so we should not ask their 'women' how they liked polygamy, we thought." One Mormon woman who managed to find a brief moment to express her views to Bowles said, "with bated breath and almost hissing fury, 'Polygamy is tolerable enough for the men, but it is hell for the women.'"

As for Brigham Young, no one seemed to know exactly how many wives he had and he himself was vague on the subject. But Bowles, who had a journalist's insatiable zest for juicy gossip, guessed that Young had as many as 20, and proceeded to examine the subject in delicious detail. "Considering his op-

portunities," commented the editor, "he seems to have made a rather sorry selection of women on the score of beauty. The oldest or first is a matronly-looking old lady, serene and sober; the youngest and present pet is comely but common-looking, while all between are very 'or'nary' indeed. Handsome women and girls, in fact, are scarce among the Mormons of Salt Lake."

Borrowing for his book from the reports of one Charles Carleton Coffin, a Boston journalist who also had paid a visit to Salt Lake City, Bowles found racy tidbits to add to his own observations. He quoted Coffin's description of Brigham Young's home life: "A passage leads to the private office of Brigham—back of which is his private bedroom, where his concubines wait upon him—Amelia to-day, Emeline to-morrow, Lucy the day after.

"Brigham's lawfully wedded wife was Mary Ann Angell. She married the prophet while he was a young

32

man, before he was a prophet. She lives in a large stone building in the rear of the harem. Brigham does not often visit her now." Lucy Decker was the lawful wife of Isaac Seely and mother of two children; but Brigham Young, Coffin said, "could make her a queen in heaven, and so, bidding good-bye to Isaac, she became first concubine, and has added eight children to the prophet's household." Harriet Cook indulged in tantrums and did not hesitate to consign Brigham to the realm of evil spirits; Lucy Bigelow was affable and ladylike. Miss Twiss had borne no children and therefore ranked low in the prophet's esteem. "She looks after his clothes, sews buttons on his shirts, and acts the part of a housewife." Like Lucy Decker, Harriet Barney had deserted her husband to become a concubine so that she might be exalted in heaven, but, having failed to add any children to the household, was not even honored in the harem. Mary Bigelow had been a member of the harem for several years, "but Brigham became tired of her and sent her away."

Emeline Free was the apple of the prophet's eye. "The favor shown her brought on a row. The other concubines carried this jealousy to such a pitch that the prophet had a private passage constructed from his bed-room to Emeline's room, so that his visits to her and hers to him could be made without observation." She had produced eight children. Amelia Folsom, another favorite but apparently a less tractable one, "has things pretty much her own way—private box at the theater, carriage of her own, silks, satins, a piano, parlor elegantly furnished. If the prophet slights her, she pays him in his own coin."

Thus wrote Charles Carleton Coffin as quoted by Bowles. Upon his conclusion of this discourse on Brigham Young's wives, Bowles confidently predicted the end of polygamy and the Mormon social system, which he regarded as barbaric, monarchical, and antagonistic to everything that was American. Polygamy, a form of slavery, was doomed to fall, sooner or later, "before the influences of emigration, civilization and our democratic habits."

That was not to say the Mormons were all bad. In material matters they were outstanding, and Samuel Bowles was quick to commend Brigham Young and his followers for their achievements in pioneering the barren wastelands of Utah. They had built a city that he found surpassingly lovely, and for which he did not hesitate to predict a future as "the great central city of this West"; and with unflagging diligence and skill they had irrigated the desert and caused it to bloom into productive farmland. "All our experience and observation in Utah tended," Bowles summed up, "to increase our appreciation of the value of its material progress and development to the nation; to justify congratulations to the Mormons and to the country for the wealth they have created and the order, frugality, morality and industry that have been organized in this remote spot on our Continent."

While Bowles was thus scolding and rhapsodizing, Albert Deane Richardson was continuing his eyewitness saga of the West's leap into the future. Throughout his odyssey fast-growing Denver remained the touchstone of his incisive reports to the Eastern press. When he first saw Denver with Greeley, it had been a sprawling shantytown. Revisiting it just four months later, Richardson was impressed to see that "frame and brick edifices were displacing mud-roofed log-cabins. Two theaters were in full blast"—and gold dust was the medium of exchange.

A year later Richardson, by now a correspondent on Greeley's *Tribune,* noted that Denver boasted three dailies, a drugstore that distributed New York and Chicago papers only 10 days old, a functioning mint, door-to-door milk delivery, a new Catholic church, thrice-weekly express and coach service to the Missouri, building lots selling as high as $1,200 each, and a well-populated cemetery of whose inmates "a large majority met violent deaths."

This dispatch was among Richardson's last from Denver for some years. Shortly after the Civil War erupted he was commissioned by Greeley to organize a *Tribune* news service in the border areas of the West, and then assigned to cover the action with Union forces in Mississippi. In 1863 Richardson was captured in a daring attempt to reach Union headquarters at Grand Gulf on the Mississippi by running past the Confederate batteries at Vicksburg in a tugboat. He spent 20 months in various Southern prisons before escaping from Salisbury, North Carolina, and walking almost 350 miles through Confederate territory until he reached the Union lines at Knoxville, Tennessee. ◉

The prairie town planted by the "Tribune"

A dazzling testimonial to the power of the press — and to one journalist's word in particular — was the establishment in 1870 of an agricultural community on the empty plains of Colorado, 50 miles north of Denver. Its name: Greeley, after the redoubtable Horace, editor of the famed *New-York Tribune*.

The idea for the settlement came from Nathan C. Meeker, the *Tribune*'s agriculture editor. With his boss's blessings, Meeker announced the project in a *Tribune* article on December 4, 1869, and Greeley added a ringing editorial endorsement maintaining that Meeker was "eminently qualified for leading and founding such a colony."

Greeley's imprimatur was enough to bring 750 inquiries tumbling in, 20 times what Meeker had expected. Even when the list was pared to those able to pay their $155 share of the land purchase, the colony counted 444 members. In deference to the teetotaling Greeley, the settlers agreed to include in their bylaws the commandment: "Thou shalt not sell liquid damnation" within town boundaries.

In May 1870, when the first recruits arrived, they were aghast at the bleak surroundings. A number departed, snarling that the scheme was "a delusion, a snare, and a swindle." It turned out to be none of the three. Neither the upright Greeley nor the visionary Meeker had ever planned to make a dime on the deal. Nor did they; in the early days, Meeker went into debt to keep his community afloat.

But float it did, thanks to hard work, enduring patience — and an innovative irrigation system of Meeker's design that allowed crops to bloom in the Great American Desert. At the end of a decade, Greeley boasted a population of 1,200 and a viable wheat economy. Nathan Meeker, alas, did not live to see it. In 1879 he was killed by the Utes, whom he was teaching to farm.

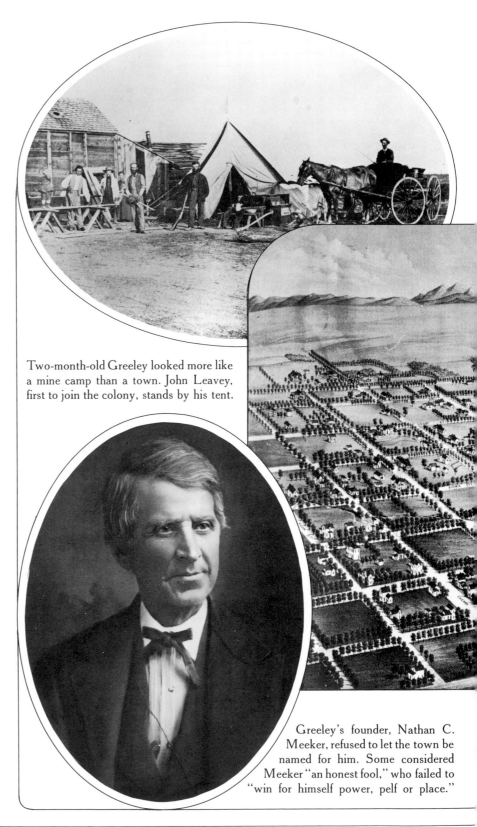

Two-month-old Greeley looked more like a mine camp than a town. John Leavey, first to join the colony, stands by his tent.

Greeley's founder, Nathan C. Meeker, refused to let the town be named for him. Some considered Meeker "an honest fool," who failed to "win for himself power, pelf or place."

Stark buildings dot the featureless plain that was Greeley in late 1870. Forlorn Luna Lake *(right)* had been scooped out as the focal point of the town's prospective Lincoln Park.

BIRD'S EYE VIEW OF
GREELEY, COLO.
COUNTY SEAT   OF WELD CO.
1882.

The houses and the streets of 12-year-old Greeley — as they finally looked after Nathan Meeker's death — were rendered in this overview. The inset shows the first-class Oasis Hotel, which was built in 1881.

OASIS HOTEL

Fever, scurvy, dysentery and near-starvation in prison left their mark upon Richardson, and for some time he was in precarious health. Nevertheless, with the courage often born into men in his craft, he was determined to get back to his beat in the West. And Greeley, his boss, was equally eager to have him there. Richardson managed to return in 1865.

For much of that year he traveled with noted companions — Colfax and Bowles. "The mail companies," he explained, "had proffered to the Hon. Schuyler Colfax, speaker of the national House of Representatives, special coaches for crossing the continent, and unusual facilities for studying the vast and varied interests of the West. He invited as companions Messrs. William Bross of the *Chicago Tribune,* Samuel Bowles of the *Springfield* (Massachusetts) *Republican,* and myself."

The trip included a stop at Denver, and Richardson was pleased to note that his touchstone city had become a bustling protometropolis. Its population had climbed to 5,000; building lots were now up to $12,000. Six or seven daily newspapers were now being published, and "hotel bills-of-fare did not differ materially from those in New York or Chicago."

"I did not readily recover from my surprise," wrote Richardson, "on seeing libraries and pictures, rich carpets and pianos, silver and wine. Keenly we enjoyed the pleasant hospitalities of society among the quickened intelligences and warmed hearts of the frontier."

He pressed on to Salt Lake City and was fascinated when one of his companions, the *Chicago Tribune's* Bross, used the telegraph and "conversed familiarly for half an hour with a member of his family who was in the Chicago office fifteen hundred miles to the east!"

Reaching Virginia City, in Nevada's silver-mining region, Richardson exclaimed: "Here has sprung up like Jonah's gourd a city upon a hill, which cannot be hid; a city of costly churches, tasteful school-houses, and imposing hotels; many telegraph wires, many daily coaches, two theaters, three daily newspapers — one nearly as large as the eight-page journals of New York! But five years past, a desert — today, a metropolis! The fables of old Romance grow tame before these grand enchantments born in the nation's restless brain and wrought by its tireless arm."

After a stay in San Francisco, he explored the Northwest Coast, largely over rough roads and by river steamboat, but now and again on infant one- to 14-mile segments of railroad along the Willamette and Columbia rivers. Could it be true, he mused, that the first American settlers had reached Oregon only a quarter century ahead of his own arrival? "Our road," he wrote, "threads lovely valleys of tall timothy and golden wheat, among dazzling white farm-houses flanked by immense barns for the long winters."

Here, where Oregon City, the oldest incorporated American town west of the Missouri, was only 23 years old and Portland, the state's metropolis, only 20, Richardson observed: "It is full of suggestiveness to remember that a generation has matured on this far-off coast — to find leaders of public opinion born, reared and educated on the soil — to hear young men and women who have resided from infancy in what nine-tenths of our people regard as wilderness, discuss appreciatively and critically Emerson and Herbert Spencer, Thackeray and Tennyson." He also found significant the fact that the *Oregonian,* the state's oldest and most prestigious newspaper, was being edited by a graduate of the state's own university.

Leaving Oregon City, he traveled in September with the Central Pacific Railroad's president Leland Stanford — by rail, horseback and stagecoach — to a meeting in an inn at Donner Lake, near where the railroad's iron rails were soon to be laid over the backbone of the Sierra Nevada.

"There was a long earnest conference," he reported, "to determine upon the route near the summit. The carpet was covered with maps, profiles and diagrams, held down at the edges by candle-sticks to keep them from rolling up. On their knees were president, directors and surveyors, creeping from one map to another, and earnestly discussing the plans of their magnificent enterprise. Outside the night-wind moaned and shrieked, as if the Mountain Spirit resented this invasion of his ancient domain."

By this time Richardson had been in the West, on and off, for eight years. The long sojourn, and his far-ranging travels, had given him a unique perspective on the era and the place. He had seen most of the great West, from the Missouri to the Pacific, from El Paso to the Canadian border. He had watched it grow from an empty vastness to a fast-filling land, and he could take a proprietary pride in such developments as the new Agricultural College at Manhattan, Kansas — the town where Greeley had joined him on the stagecoach. Only seven years later, he was able to write, "Tuition is free; the college knows no distinction of race, color, or sex. Of the one hundred students, more than half are girls. They excel their masculine competitors even in composition, declamation and the higher mathematics. All honor to young Kansas, color-bearer in the great army of progress!"

Now and again as he patrolled his enormous beat, cataloging its richness and variety, Richardson would venture into the risky art of prophecy. Once that temptation came upon him in California where, like Greeley before him, he stood amazed at the state's agricultural bounty. After measuring a tomato 26 inches in circumference and hefting a 53-pound head of cabbage, he turned his attention to fruit and testified that the "enormous peaches, the rich pears, the strawberries and grapes, have a peculiarly rich and generous taste that lingers lovingly on the palate." Of all these, the grape was destined to become California's crown, he hazarded. "The grape crop never fails, and averages double the yield per acre of the vineyards of Ohio, France and Germany. The vineyards of the state cover upward of ten thousand acres. The wine product is between one and two millions of gallons annually. One day the wines of California will excel those of all other countries on the globe."

Then, having gone so far in prediction and praise, he hedged a little and confessed that the Californians of the 1860s really didn't much like their own wines, which were considered to be better after their arrival in New York because "the long sea voyage makes them smoother." California connoisseurs, their palates attuned to French and German vintages, were still finding the home product too "new, raw and 'heady.'" But, the reporter felt sure, these flaws would be remedied with time.

Early in 1867 Richardson left the West to work in the *Tribune*'s New York office and compile his newspaper correspondence into a book, *Beyond the Mississippi*. Along with the main currents of history, he packed it full of a good reporter's lode of oddities and fascinating, if not always scientifically correct, perceptions. In the silver-mining districts of Nevada, he said, he had discovered that the rarefied atmosphere at 6,000 feet made it difficult to keep false teeth firmly seated in the mouth. He learned to tell on which side of the Continental Divide he was by the color of the specks on a mountain trout's scales — red for the east, black for the west. In Oregon he determined that human fecundity increased in direct proportion with the need to fill up a new country; as evidence he cited one birth to a woman of 60 years and two within ten months to a younger woman.

He learned that the best way to carry eggs safely from the Missouri to the Colorado mines was to pack them in lard. In Marysville, Kansas, he was interested to observe that a dozen men indicted for betting on a horse race were to be tried by the same jurist who had judged the race. In San Francisco, invited to a dinner by the leading Chinese merchants of the city, he was impressed by the serving of 325 dishes, some 70 of which he was able to sample before he had to give up. In southern Colorado he learned that the soda-charged waters of the Fontaine qui Bouille were just the thing for mixing light, quick-rising bread dough without any other leavening agent; and he observed that most West Coast businessmen entrusted their mail to Wells, Fargo rather than to the government postal service because Wells, Fargo delivered it much faster.

Of such fine grist, as well as great events and foresights, was fashioned the career of this prototypical Western chronicler. In length of service and depth of view, Richardson ranked among the greatest. He did not long survive that distinguished service. In November 1869, shortly after visiting his old beat for the last time, he was shot and mortally wounded in the *Tribune*'s office by a man named McFarland, whose divorced wife Richardson was planning to marry. But his influence survived between the covers of his book.

In his preface, Richardson declared: "No other country on the globe equals ours beyond the Mississippi River. Its mines, forests and prairies await the capitalist. Its society welcomes the immigrant, offering high interest upon his investment of money, brains or skill; and if need be, generous obliviousness of errors past — a clean page to begin anew the record of his life." The many westering settlers who answered his call were his monument. As he prophesied, "We seem on the threshold of a destiny higher and better than any nation has yet fulfilled. And the great West is to rule us."

The demanding craft of illustrated journalism

When the Civil War ended, the editors of big Eastern periodicals turned to the Great American West for much of their news and excitement. The two leading magazines at that time were *Harper's Weekly,* with a circulation of 100,000, and the somewhat smaller *Frank Leslie's Illustrated Newspaper,* both of which practiced a form of pictorial journalism. Their prime agent was the roving artist-reporter, who sent back cover pictures and inside essays like those on the following 11 pages, depicting the struggles and triumphs of the venturesome men and women who set off into the immense land.

In a day when photographs could not be transferred to the printed page, these drawings, made on the spot and reproduced by means of woodcuts, had a powerful sense of immediacy, plus the appeal that came from their being recognizably the product of human hands —usually many hands. To make a woodcut the artist's original picture first had to be redrawn, in reverse, on the surface of a smooth block of boxwood. This time-consuming and highly skilled chore was usually performed back East at the journals' wood-engraving shops —though a few of the most versatile field artists sent in their work drawn right on the wood.

Ordinarily, when a drawing arrived it was sent to the art department where it was copied line for line, in reverse, on the wood. As in the shops of the Renaissance masters of painting, some artists drew foregrounds, some middle-distance figures and others concentrated on backgrounds. In the interest of speed, large illustrations were usually done not on a single block but on small ones tightly joined together by means of bolts set in recesses in their backs.

When the reversed drawing had been transferred to this smooth surface, the blocks were unbolted and distributed to wood engravers like the man shown at left. The engravers carefully cut away all the areas between the lines to create the forms and highlights and shadows of the scene. They cut their lines to within a hairsbreadth of the edges of their blocks. When the carving was completed, the blocks were bolted back together and the line ends were joined by a master carver.

So deft were these artist-engravers at matching their sections with the adjoining ones, pen stroke meeting identical pen stroke no matter how fine or how numerous the lines, that when the blocks were bolted together they usually printed a picture with seams that were virtually invisible. The resultant woodcuts remained as pillars of illustrated journalism right up until the mid-1880s, when the perfection of chemical halftone engraving allowed photographs to be mass-printed—and a new era of pictorial reporting began.

Working with a powerful lens and a steel cutting tool called a burin, an engraver painstakingly excises areas of a woodcut that will be white in the printed picture.

Across the continent in six days

Frank Leslie, editor of *Leslie's Illustrated,* was famous for his sense of what would fascinate—as well as inform—his readers. When the first transcontinental railroad was completed in May 1869, Leslie got the idea of sending one of his best field artists, 28-year-old Joseph Becker, to ride the line west. But Leslie cannily waited for five months so that some of the kinks could be ironed out of transcontinental rail travel, and a passenger could make the journey with style as well as speed.

By the time Becker boarded the train in New York City in mid-October, the Union Pacific and Central Pacific railroads had decided to run a train made up of gleaming new Pullman cars clear through to San Francisco. This gave passengers the luxury of opulently appointed dining cars and comfortable sleepers—as well as a trip uninterrupted by the inconvenience of changing trains at the lines' Utah junction.

True to Leslie's expectations, Becker sent back superbly detailed drawings of his posh train ride, highlighted by the glimpse at right into the dining car, evoking the elegance of the salon of a transatlantic steamer. And he also provided a panorama of wayside scenes such as the Colorado version of the Sermon on the Mount *(opposite),* in which a clergyman addressed a congregation of gold prospectors. These and other drawings also confirmed Leslie's uncanny judgment about reader reaction: during the seven months that Becker's drawings were printed, circulation of the *Illustrated* rose to 70,000.

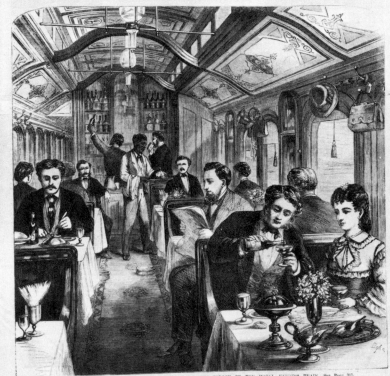

ACROSS THE CONTINENT, ON THE PACIFIC RAILROAD.—DINING SALOON OF THE HOTEL EXPRESS TRAIN. See Page 301.

SUNDAY IN THE ROCKY MOUNTAINS.—See Page 195.

1. Exterior of Hotel.   2. Proprietor.   3. Registering.   4. Bedroom.   5. Chambermaid.   6. Toilet.

ACROSS THE CONTINENT.—HOTEL LIFE ON THE PLAINS—ON THE LINE OF THE PACIFIC RAILROAD.—From a Sketch by Our Special Artist.

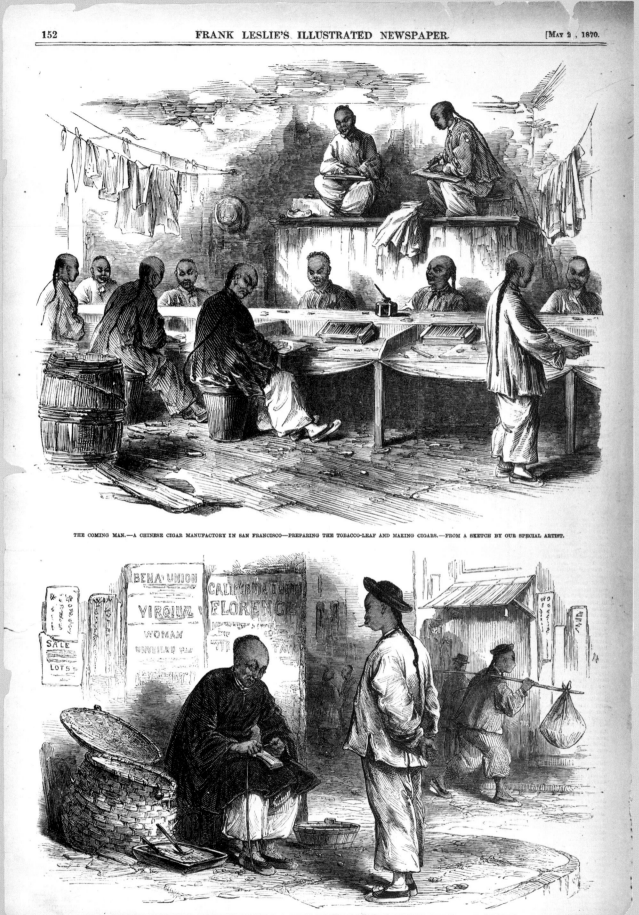

THE COMING MAN.—A CHINESE CIGAR MANUFACTORY IN SAN FRANCISCO—PREPARING THE TOBACCO-LEAF AND MAKING CIGARS.—FROM A SKETCH BY OUR SPECIAL ARTIST.

THE COMING MAN. — A STREET SCENE IN THE CHINESE QUARTER, SAN FRANCISCO—A COBBLER REPAIRING THE SHOES OF ONE OF HIS COUNTRYMEN.—FROM A SKETCH BY OUR SPECIAL ARTIST.

An unvarnished look at the rugged life of the West

In September 1873, the editors of *Harper's Weekly,* reacting to competition from *Frank Leslie's Illustrated,* decided to give their readers a fresh look at life in the West — through European eyes. The artist-journalists selected for this mission were a pair of well-known Frenchmen, Paul Frenzeny and Jules Tavernier. Both were accomplished horsemen, and the *Harper's* article announcing the expedition stated that the pair would "not restrict themselves to the ordinary routes of travel," but would "make long excursions on horseback into regions where railroads have not yet penetrated."

For a little less than a year the artists traveled the Great Plains, the Rockies and the Pacific Coast. Their material (at $150 a spread), which *Harper's* published over four years, added up to one of the best-detailed records made of the westward move.

As perceptive artists they could make an intriguing scene of an ordinary day in a Kansas land office *(right).* And as republican Frenchmen they had a special feeling for the humbler classes, particularly the emigrants. Rail cars carrying emigrating families were frequently attached to freight trains and were customarily "switched off" at way stations *(opposite page)* so that more freight could be taken on. In the case illustrated in the sympathetic drawing at far right, top, *Harper's* complained, "old people, delicate women, and children were compelled to remain all night exposed to a cold, drenching rain."

A KANSAS LAND-OFFICE.—[SEE PAGE 585.]

IN THE EMIGRANT TRAIN.

SWITCHED OFF.

BUILDING THE LOG-CABIN.

LAYING THE FENCES.

SCENES IN EMIGRANT LIFE.—[SEE PAGE 78.]

FIGHTING THE FIRE.—[DRAWN BY FRENZENY AND TAVERNIER.]

FIGHTING THE FIRE.

THE astonishing rapidity with which the prairie fire, driven by furious winds, sweeps on in its work of devastation is something beyond the power of description. Awakening terror under any circumstances, it is especially dreaded when it makes its way toward the settlements. In such an event the alarm is speedily given, and in the twinkling of an eye every man, woman, and child turns out to fight the foe. All sorts of expedients are used to stay the progress of the flames. Blankets, rags tied on ends of sticks, and every thing that can be used to beat down the fire, are brought into requisition. In the illustration on this page a scene of this description is given. "All men on fire-guard!" is the order, which is speedily obeyed, and not until the last spark has been quenched will the band cease the brave fight with the flames.

"BUSTED!"—A DESERTED RAILROAD TOWN IN KANSAS.—[SEE PAGE 195.]

SKETCHES IN THE FAR WEST—AN UNDER-GROUND VILLAGE.

SKETCHES IN THE FAR WEST.

OUR readers will remember the curious and interesting sketch of a deserted railroad village, or rather settlement, published a short time since in the *Weekly* ; in this number of our paper we give them, by way of contrast, a sketch of a village built on the under-ground plan, as if the hardy pioneers of civilization had taken a prairie-dog town as a model. Secure against the violent wind storms that sweep with irresistible fury over the plains, these "dug-outs" form an excellent shelter. The style of architecture is certainly not imposing, but as temporary shelters these under-ground habitations, constructed at little expense, serve their purpose well until substantial buildings can be erected. The settlers do a great deal of trading with the Indians and hunters, and a small guard of soldiers, under command of a sergeant, is generally posted at

SKETCHES IN THE FAR WEST—ARKANSAS PILGRIMS.

BRANDING.

RC

ON THE TRAIL.

HALTING-PLACE ON THE NINNESCAH RIVER.

THE TEXAS CATTLE TRADE.—D

TTLE.

SHIPPING FOR THE EASTERN MARKETS.

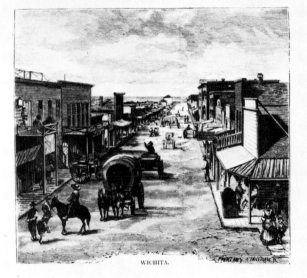

WICHITA.

AND TAVERNIER.—[SEE PAGE 385.]

HO, FOR TEXAS!

The staff and hangers-on cluster outside the Kingman, Kansas, *Mercury* in 1880. The town was so small the paper lasted only two years.

2 | Newspapers for every wide spot in the road

"American pioneers," a Nevada editor observed in 1867, "carry with them the press and the type, and wherever they pitch their tent, be it in the wilderness of the interior, among the snow covered peaks of the Sierra or on the sunny sea beach of the Pacific, there too must the newspaper appear." And indeed it was a rare town, even in the remotest reaches of the West, that did not boast at least one paper — often long before the place could claim a post office, school, church or even a jail.

In 1857, when the entire community of Emporia in Kansas Territory had only three buildings, one of them housed the *Kanzas News*. That journal's enterprising editor set the paper's type in a bedroom and printed it in a parlor. Denver's *Rocky Mountain News* had to settle for a saloon attic in 1859, but Oregon's *Harney Valley Item* claimed the most exotic quarters of all: a former house of ill repute.

In 1886, the proud editor *(left)* of the *Nebraska States-man* was so successful that despite competition from three other papers in the town of Broken Bow he was able to start a second journal in nearby Mason City. Like many Western editors the *Statesman*'s boss earned income by job printing, in this case cranking out fliers for a land office.

Editor George F. Canis of the Saratoga, Wyoming, *Sun* helped make ends meet in the 1890s by selling hay and grain, as well as doing job printing; he even rented space to a Chinese laundry. Canis had planned a daily, but after one issue concluded that there was barely news for a weekly.

The *Arizona Citizen* grew from a weekly to a daily after the Southern Pacific's tracks went through Tucson in 1880, bringing money and new readers. Editor John Clum, however, decided to move to the silver-mining boomtown of Tombstone, where he started the legendary *Epitaph*.

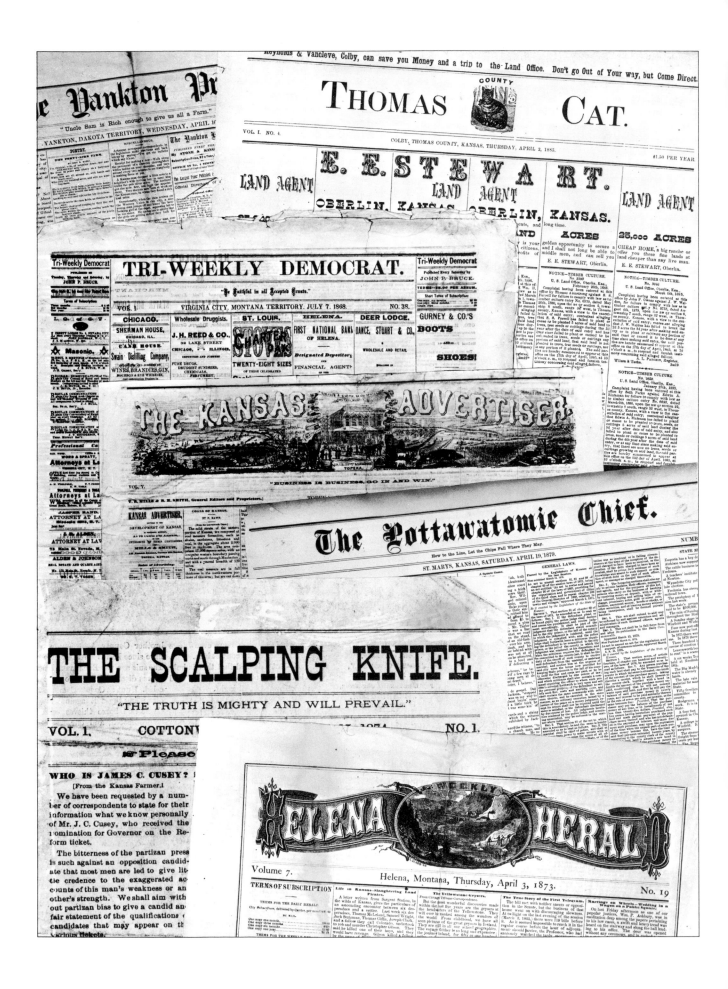

"Independence in All Things, Neutrality in Nothing"

One unlikely day in 1850, while being transported across the Isthmus of Panama en route to California, a Washington Hand Printing Press, Imperial Model No. 3, sank in the Chagres River when the Indian canoe carrying it capsized. After righting the canoe, the Indian paddlers tried but failed to recover the machine, which weighed 1,870 pounds. The story then goes that the distraught owner, a powerful man named Judge J. Judson Ames, dived into the crocodile-infested waters and, singlehanded, heaved the huge Washington back aboard. Improbable though the tale may seem, the fact remains that, one way or another, shortly after the mishap Judge Ames and his dampened but apparently undamaged machine pulled into Panama City. There the judge put his press to work, turning out a newspaper he briefly published called the *Panama Star.*

Thereafter the trusty Washington sailed for California, where it printed papers in San Diego and San Bernardino. Later it was carted over the Sierra to Aurora in the Nevada mining country and back again to turn out a weekly in Independence, California. At different times the press printed papers called the *Herald,* the *Patriot,* the *Star,* the *Union* and the *Independent.* With nonpartisan faith and facility, it served editors with abolitionist principles as well as editors who were rabid secessionists, and in an especially turbulent incarnation worked for a partnership composed of one hotheaded Republican and one quarrelsome Democrat.

The adventures and misadventures of this particular Washington Imperial No. 3 were typical in the work-ing life of a frontier printing press. In 1836, a press for the local paper in Harrisburg, Texas, was dumped into a bayou by the Mexican General Santa Anna because, among other irritants, he resented Publisher Gail Borden's use of the slogan "Remember the Alamo!" In 1859, in Genoa, Utah Territory, a Washington press suffered no physical damage but a measure of indignity when a suspected criminal was chained to one of its iron legs pending trial. In 1862, a hand press set up in Sioux Falls City, Dakota Territory, was pitched into the Big Sioux River by a war party of Santee Sioux; the raiders also carried away the type metal and melted it down to make decorative inlays on the red clay peace pipes they used as diplomatic devices when negotiating treaties with the white man.

In 1863, another press was severely damaged by fire when the Confederate guerrilla Quantrill sacked Lawrence, Kansas. In 1864, a brand-new press was swept away by a flash flood in Denver's Cherry Creek and was not seen again for 35 years, when parts of it were discovered buried in the sand downstream. Also in 1864, an overzealous politician in Ione, Nevada Territory, attempted to put an unfriendly editor's Washington Hand Press out of commission by making off with the main lever; he was thwarted when the editor whittled a new one out of a stout branch of mountain mahogany.

Just as the presses often had a hard time of it in recording the blustery days of the Old West, so did the long-suffering journalists who owned and operated those sturdy machines. Jesse Randall, publisher of the Georgetown, Colorado, *Courier* and a crusading Democrat, had to dodge cannon balls blasted through his front window by angry Republicans. William N. Byers, editor-publisher of the *Rocky Mountain News,* was kidnapped by a gang of outlaws who took exception to his editorial remarks about the saloon where they hung

---

Whimsical names and emblems and ringing mottoes distinguished many Western papers from their staid Eastern counterparts — and the news they printed was often as wild as the eccentrics who wrote it.

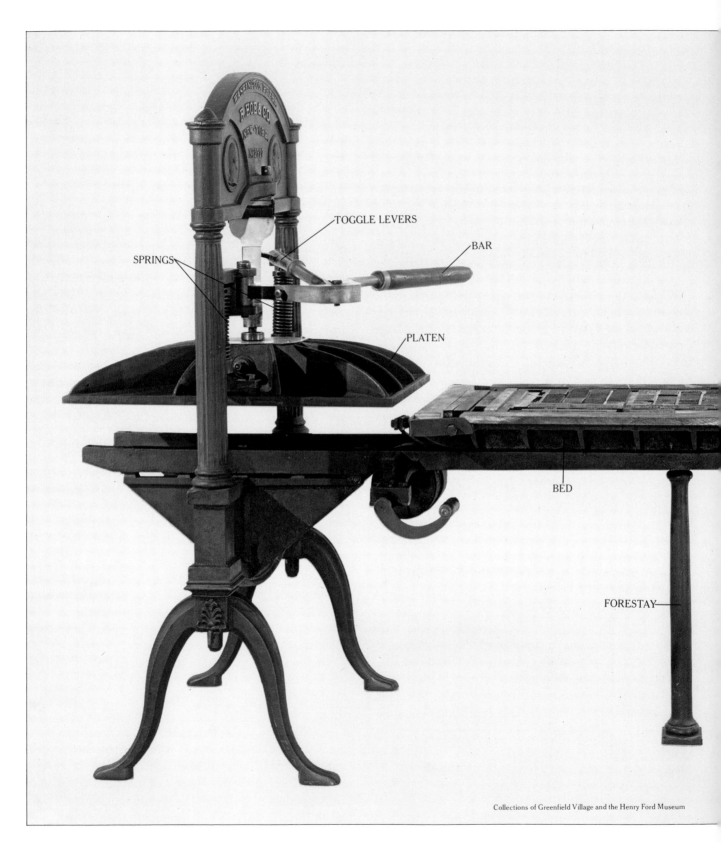

TOGGLE LEVERS

BAR

SPRINGS

PLATEN

BED

FORESTAY

Collections of Greenfield Village and the Henry Ford Museum

60

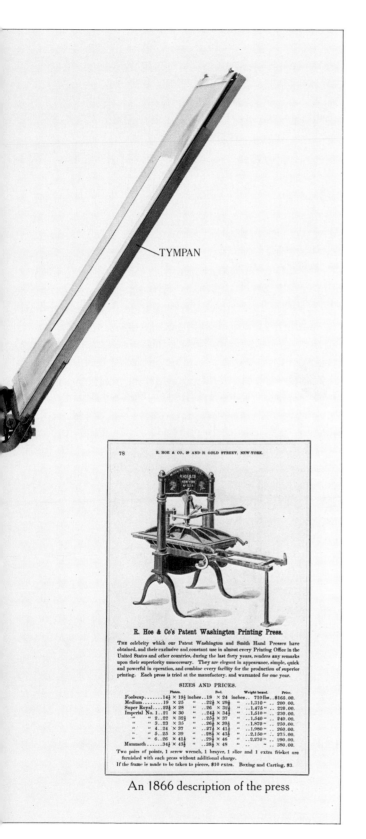

TYMPAN

R. Hoe & Co's Patent Washington Printing Press.

The celebrity which our Patent Washington and Smith Hand Presses have obtained, and their exclusive and constant use in almost every Printing Office in the United States and other countries, during the last forty years, renders any remarks upon their superiority unnecessary. They are elegant in appearance, simple, quick and powerful in operation, and combine every facility for the production of superior printing. Each press is tried at the manufactory, and warranted for one year.

SIZES AND PRICES.

	Platen.		Bed.		Weight boxed.	Price.
Foolscap	14½ × 19½ inches	.18 × 24 inches	..	710 lbs.	$165.00
Medium	19 × 25 "	.22½ × 29¼ "	..	1,310 "	200.00
Super Royal	22½ × 28 "	.26 × 32½ "	..	1,475 "	220.00
Imperial No. 1	21 × 30 "	.24½ × 34½ "	..	1,510 "	230.00
" 2	22 × 32½ "	.25½ × 37 "	..	1,540 "	240.00
" 3	23 × 35 "	.26½ × 39½ "	..	1,870 "	250.00
" 4	24 × 37 "	.27½ × 41½ "	..	1,980 "	260.00
" 5	25 × 39 "	.28½ × 43½ "	..	2,150 "	275.00
" 6	26 × 41½ "	.29½ × 46 "	..	2,270 "	290.00
Mammoth	34½ × 45½ "	.38½ × 48 "	..	"	380.00

Two pairs of points, 1 screw wrench, 1 brayer, 1 slice and 1 extra frisket are furnished with each press without additional charge.

If the frame is made to be taken to pieces, $10 extra. Boxing and Carting, $3.

An 1866 description of the press

out. Asa Shinn Mercer, publisher of the *Northwestern Live Stock Journal* in Cheyenne, Wyoming, was clapped into jail by cattle barons who disliked being called "the Banditti of the Plains." The unpopular publisher of the Ogden, Utah, *Morning Rustler* was tarred and feathered; in Medicine Lodge, Kansas, on the other hand, disgruntled subscribers to the *Barber County Mail,* when they discovered the town lacked tar and anyone willing to surrender a feather bed, ingeniously coated Editor M. J. Cochran with sorghum molasses and sandburs before riding him out of town on a rail.

Nature, too, took a hand in visiting its wrath against this hardy band of chroniclers. D. B. Louden, editor of the Delphos, Kansas, *Herald,* unluckily stood in the path of a tornado that smashed his printing plant, scattered his type and inflicted a variety of humiliations on his own unhappy hide. The editor of the Fort Union, Dakota Territory, *Frontier Scout,* an army journal, complained bitterly about the post's bedbugs, or "BBs," as he called them. "We have seen them in battalions, in divisions, in army corps, all sizes, regularly organized, thoroughly drilled. Not content with disturbing our sleep, they are on the paper when we sit down to write. If we have a game of cards, bed bugs form the hearts, spades, diamonds and clubs." And Joe Ellis Johnson of the Wood River *Huntsman's Echo,* in Nebraska Territory, whose print shop was set up near the open range, almost lost his one and only employee when grazing buffalo persisted in peeking into the office and scaring the daylights out of the printer.

Clearly, however, the most unfortunate of them all was young Horace W. Myers, editor of the Corinne, Utah, *Daily Reporter;* he suffered so much acute men-

THE PRIDE OF THE WESTERN PRESSROOM

The Washington Hand Press that spread the news across the West was a rugged and versatile version of the classic flat-bed press invented by Gutenberg in the 1400s. The printer applied ink with the roller to type locked in a form. Next, he placed a sheet of paper on the hinged wooden tympan, folded it over the type and then slid the bed bearing the form to a position beneath the cloth-covered platen. By pulling the bar, or lever, he caused the platen to press the paper against the type and produce an impression. A system of toggle levers kept the platen from twisting and smudging the impression when the bar's leverage forced it downward.

tal anguish trying to keep solvent that at last he ended it all by swallowing a lethal dose of laudanum.

Despite the hazards and the casualty rate among editors who exposed their lives and property, the Old West fairly teemed with local newspapers. One scholar has calculated that, in the last two thirds of the 19th Century, the truly staggering total of 10,000 weekly and daily journals was published in the 17 Western states. Between 1858 and 1899, Nevada alone saw the launching of 205—and the demise of all but 25 of them. Some of these newspapers were as fleeting as the *B-B-Blizzard,* printed at Kinsley, Kansas, late in January, 1886, to entertain 300 passengers of the Atchison, Topeka & Santa Fe railroad who had been stranded there by a raging snowstorm. Other journals, like the San Francisco *Chronicle,* Denver's *Rocky Mountain News* and Salt Lake City's *Deseret News,* were stout enough to survive for decades and become honored fixtures of life in the West.

The thousands of men—and some women—who put out these papers were as various, and sometimes as rugged and untamed, as the great sprawling country around them. Most had been something else before they became journalists: lawyers, preachers, politicians, teachers, postmasters, farmers, miners, land speculators and even one circus clown. By nature they were restless, spunky, outspoken. They practiced a highly personal brand of journalism, and in the heady atmosphere of the new territory were tempted into experiments that would have struck more settled publishers as downright lunacy. Take the case of one ambitious young Virginian, whose story might well stand as the quintessential saga of Western newspapering.

In 1865, a 22-year-old Confederate soldier named Legh Freeman was released from 13 months of misery in the North's prisoner-of-war camp at Rock Island, Illinois. The price of freedom was a distasteful oath of allegiance to the Union, but it restored Freeman's citizenship and enabled the former combat telegrapher

Moving his offices constantly to keep up with the Union Pacific's westering railhead, editor Legh Freeman often outraced his supplies. He was forced to print one issue of his *Frontier Index* on wrapping paper.

to land a job with the U.S. Army at Fort Kearney, in Nebraska Territory. There, in addition to sending and receiving military messages for his former enemies, Legh Freeman took over publication of the fort's newsletter, the *Kearney Herald.*

Soon Freeman sent for his older brother, Fred, also a former Confederate telegrapher, and together they turned the *Herald* into a genuine newspaper. Having access to the Army's telegraph wires, they enjoyed a built-in advantage over other journals in the region and promised national and international news "at least two days in advance of any other means of intelligence." Brother Legh also took on a stringer assignment for Horace Greeley's *New-York Tribune.*

The coming of the Union Pacific in 1866 brought Fort Kearney first a boom and then, when the railhead moved west, a disillusioning bust. But the Freeman brothers, exhilarated by their few profitable months amid thousands of free-spending tracklayers and their camp followers, hit on a stupendous idea. They would become editors as transient as the railhead itself; even better, they would get out ahead of the rails. Whenever the construction crews approached a new hamlet along the right of way and turned it into a roaring boomtown, the Freemans would be waiting and ready to reap a harvest.

They bought a new Washington Hand Press. They hired a train of heavy freight wagons, four yoke of oxen to the wagon, and loaded up press, type, imposing stones, ink and paper and set out for North Platte, a hundred miles to the west. Their new paper, the *Frontier Index,* was in business before the tracks came in sight. They quickly began to thrive as circulation and advertising boomed with the arrival of the crews. They opened a job shop and charged an outrageous 20 cents a word to uncomplaining merchants eager to unload their wares on the railroad crews.

The North Platte boom lasted six months. When it began to wane, the Freeman brothers packed up and rolled with the railroad. The *Frontier Index*'s progress

Shoestring journals dashed off by hand

Frontier editors were often so determined to have their say that they forged ahead with newspapers before they had presses to print them on. The result of such enterprise was a spate of handwritten "manuscript" papers, each edition consisting of as many copies as its creator had strength to write. The editorial tone of these shoestring journals usually was satirical. A case in point was *Flumgudgeon Gazette and Bumble Bee Budget,* which appeared twice weekly during the single summer of 1845 while the territorial legislature was in session, and devoted most of its space to poking fun at that august body.

The *Gazette's* irreverent editor was Virginia-born Charles Edward Pickett, whose nom de plume was Curtail Coon. Curtail appeared over the title in a cartoon assumed to be drawn by Pickett accompanied by the admonition: "Don't stroke us backwards! There's enough of *villainy* going on to raise our bristles without that." Pickett wrote his paper in a combination of English and nearly indecipherable Chinook Indian jargon, turning out 12 copies of each issue —his total circulation.

Other such handmade newspapers sprang up all over the West, as fancifully named and as ephemeral as the *Flumgudgeon Gazette.* Oregon also boasted the *Like It or Lump It,* Kansas had the *Redwing Carrier Pigeon* and Utah was home of the *Gold Canyon Switch.* Their editors skewered any target that hove into view: in the process they not only amused the sparse readership but left behind some memorable reflections of their times.

Volume 1, Number 8 of the *Flumgudgeon Gazette* takes a swipe at some windy legislators.

westward could be charted on the changing masthead: North Platte, Julesburg, Cheyenne, Laramie City, Fort Benton, Green River, Bear River City; according to one estimate, the newspaper was ultimately published in 25 different locations. At least once along the way, the brothers suffered delusions of permanence. In Laramie the future temporarily looked so promising that they commissioned a two-story log building to house their enterprise. But again the boom collapsed and they had to travel on.

Moving once in the dead of winter, Fred was knocked face down in a foot of snow by a fractious mule, and a wagon loaded with 6,700 pounds of printing equipment rolled across his shoulders. He was grievously hurt but the yielding snow saved him from death. Between Laramie and Fort Benton, the *Index* wagon caravan was attacked by a party of renegade whites got up as Indians; the raiders abandoned the wagons in disgust when they discovered that the *Index*'s properties included nothing to eat, wear, spend or get drunk on.

The nomadic *Index* came to an untimely end in November 1868, in Bear River City, Wyoming Territory. Until the rails came in, Bear River City had been a huddle of shacks at the mouth of a mountain ravine. Now, suddenly, it was a wild and wide-open town swarming with graders and tracklayers and the gamblers, grog sellers and prostitutes who lived off them. These temporary head-of-track metropolises had been growing progressively more lawless as the rails moved toward their meeting place at Promontory in Utah Territory, and Bear River City was proving to be perhaps the worst of the lot.

As editors, the Freemans wholeheartedly endorsed the vigilante committees that sporadically tried to enforce a degree of order. One day, when a group of graders, grown bellicose on popskull whiskey, staged a noisy riot, the vigilantes broke up the demonstration and jailed three of the miscreants. Brother Fred evidently was away at the time. Legh published a relatively mild—for him—editorial asserting that "Bear River City has stood enough of the rowdy criminal element." Incensed, the graders rioted again, broke open the jail to free their comrades, then got a rope and headed for the *Index,* which was housed in a tent. The story goes that a townsman named Topence, apprised

The day after fire had consumed Seattle's business district in 1889, the *Daily Press* stood ready to roll in makeshift quarters. During the blaze the staff had to move the equipment three times — but managed to publish on schedule.

of Legh's imminent peril, took a mule to the back of the tent, slit it open, helped Legh mount and wished him Godspeed in a dash for Fort Bridger 20 miles away.

Next day the editor hurried back from Fort Bridger with a troop of cavalry, and the riot was put down. But the *Index* was defunct; nothing remained but ashes of the tent, a jumble of type and a smashed Washington press. The Freemans never truly believed that the attack was only a simple expression of the mob's displeasure. They thought it was at least in part a put-up job, and lay a measure of blame on the Union Pacific, with which they had been feuding. The underlying source of contention, according to the Freemans, was a coal mine the brothers claimed to have staked out and opened in western Wyoming Territory. But the Union Pacific jumped the claim on grounds that the mine lay within the railroad's land grant. The Freemans had accused the railroad of illegal seizure — to no avail. They were convinced ever after that the Union Pacific had helped put them out of business to silence any campaign of protest by the *Index.*

With the *Index* dead — its entire career had spanned not much more than two years — Fred Freeman retired from publishing. But some years later, in 1875, Legh entered the field again, this time in the heart of Mormon country as editor of the *Ogden Freeman* in Utah Territory. His four years in that city consisted of a running battle with Mormonism, spiced by attacks on plural wives as "concubines" and on Salt Lake City as a fit place for the Sultan of Turkey.

In these circumstances, Legh did not enjoy any great editorial popularity among the Mormons. Mutual antipathy came to a climax when he was beaten up by a club-wielding Ogden postmaster whom he had caught deliberately consigning eastbound copies of the *Freeman* to a westbound freight. Later he published other newspapers in Montana and Washington, usually in an atmosphere of hostility to local authority. He died in 1915, unrepentant to the last, an enduring embodiment of his first masthead motto at Kearney: "Independence in All Things, Neutrality in Nothing."

In the emptiness of the newly opening territories, newsmen like Legh Freeman, cantankerous though they might be, supplied the only sustenance for the ravenous frontier appetite for real news — especially news of men and deeds beyond the local horizon. Before the telegraph began to spread its wire across the nation in the early 1860s, acquiring fresh news from outside was well-nigh impossible: by the time it reached the West, the so-called news more properly qualified as history. In February 1846, the Oregon City *Spectator* learned — via a letter written to one of its subscribers in August of the year before — that Texas had been annexed by the United States, and printed this antique intelligence as a local scoop. In June 1850, the *Deseret News* shocked Salt Lake City with the report that San Francisco had burned on Christmas Eve, 1849. In circumstances like these, men would cheerfully pay $1 and up for a months-stale Eastern paper, and any local editor lucky enough to find one would mine nuggets of news from it for weeks.

Supplying news of the editor's own town was usually a more expeditious undertaking. There was always the regular grist of marriages, births, deaths, Fourth of July celebrations and strawberry festivals. The Portland *Oregonian* of September 4, 1852, reported the marriage, three days earlier, of Mr. Simon B. Marye and Miss Sarah Eveline Chapman. "The lateness of the hour at which the above was received will prevent us from making 'only a few brief remarks' at this time," said the *Oregonian,* and then added a gooey benediction that was typical of the chatty, person-to-person editorial style of the Western press. "Our best wishes go with the happy couple through all the varied scenes of life — may peace and plenty attend their steps and *pledges* of undying affection rise up around their hearthstone, who shall call them 'blessed.'"

Prairie fires, lodge meetings, and the assay findings of gold and silver strikes also made good copy, but on the subject of local shootings, journalistic opinion was sharply divided. Some editors gave the last item short shrift or ignored the violence entirely, reacting to a generalized feeling that such tidings were inclined to give a town a bad name. In one 1866 issue, for example, the Sante Fe *Weekly Gazette* noted laconically: "One man was killed, and several wounded in a row which took place in this city at the southwest corner of the plaza on Monday night. We did not learn any of the particulars." Other editors, less fastidious, took a positive relish in lawlessness, some of them recording the outrageous doings of famous gunslingers with a delight

The newspaper that talked to Indians in their own tongue

To most 19th Century whites, Indians were the rudest of savages, barely able to communicate in grunts and jabbers. But that was a colossal misapprehension. Many tribes had traditions of elegant elocution, and had developed intricate pictographic writing forms as well. Indeed, one particularly sophisticated people, the Cherokees, not only boasted an 86-letter alphabet, but for many years published their own Indian-language newspaper.

The alphabet had been devised about 1820 by the tribe's renowned leader Sequoyah (in whose honor the giant redwood tree was later named), when the Cherokees were still living on their native ground of Georgia. There, too, they first published the weekly *Cherokee Phoenix* in 1828. The paper languished in 1830 when the United States Army uprooted the tribe and forced it to migrate westward to Oklahoma's Indian Territory.

In 1844 it was reborn as the *Cherokee Advocate.*

The *Advocate*'s founding and style-setting editor was William Potter Ross. The Princeton-educated son of a chief's sister and a Scottish trader, Ross was a sharp and crusading journalist. He made the paper bilingual, with some articles duplicated in English in the hopes of interesting whites in tribal affairs and points of view. He ripped into the U.S. government for its uncaring Indian policies—and frequently took his own tribe's ruling National Council to task for its failures. The *Advocate* printed the most important national and international news, and even made a brave stab at unraveling the mysteries of the white man's sports, such as prize fighting.

Alas, the *Advocate* never made money, but relied on a subsidy from the Cherokee National Council. Po-

Editor Ross in 1874 after his retirement

litical bickering and hard times forced the paper's suspension from 1851 until 1870. But after that, under a series of editors, the voice of the Cherokees appeared continuously until well past the turn of the century.

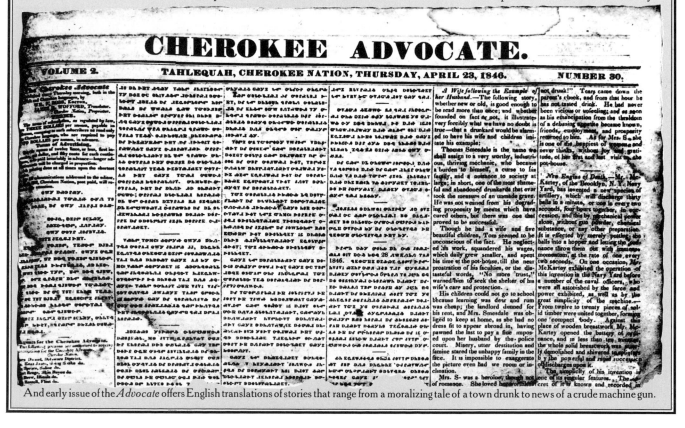

And early issue of the *Advocate* offers English translations of stories that range from a moralizing tale of a town drunk to news of a crude machine gun.

that now and then went far beyond the bounds of duty.

Once in a blue moon there was a genuine news break, sometimes of such enormous proportions that even the intrepid editors of the Old West were hard put to cope. When severe earth tremors split the floor of California's Owens River Valley one night in late March of 1872, typesetters at the Inyo *Independent* rummaged through cases of type scrambled by the quake, and managed to come up with a stirring series of headlines running halfway down page one: "HORRORS! APPALLING TIMES! EARTHQUAKES! AWFUL LOSS OF LIFE! 25 PERSONS KILLED! EARTH OPENS! HOUSES PROSTRATED! LONE PINE! ITS TERRIBLE CONDITION! MOST HEART-RENDING SCENES! MIRACULOUS ESCAPES! INDIVIDUAL HEROISM!" And with pardonable pride in its accomplishment, the *Independent* ended the series: "A DEMORALIZED PRINTING OFFICE!"

But often enough, in the sod and clapboard villages plunked down in the middle of nowhere, even the well of local events ran dry all too quickly. Editor John R. Curry, putting out the Silverton, Colorado, *La Plata Miner* in the 1880s, sourly complained at one point that his most determined efforts to scrounge some news items had been "as barren of results as the browsing of a calf on a sand bank." Yet the columns of blank space had to be filled, and that necessity mothered some marvelous stratagems. When there was not enough to say about their own localities, Western editors cheerfully appropriated stories verbatim from neighboring newspapers — or, if the mail was getting through, from eldering copies of big-city journals. The only rule of the "exchange," as the game was called, was an honor-system commitment to acknowledge the source of all borrowed items.

Another much-honored institution of Western journalism was the out-and-out hoax — some tall tale or mendacious thriller dreamed up by an imaginative editor with space to fill and a deadline staring him in the face. Readers usually knew that they were being lied to; but they enjoyed it, and the more outrageous the whopper the better. One of the most popular hoaxes, a sure-fire repeater that could be used in a new version every issue, was the creation of Editor Don Biggers of the Rotan, Texas, *Billy Goat*. Biggers invented a terrible monster, the Wampus Cat — "a ferocious beast, a cross between a wildcat, a badger and a lobo wolf" — and turned it loose to terrorize the countryside. Every week he solemnly reported a new effort by Rotan's courageous citizens to hunt down the predator. The Wampus Cat lived on and on, too mean and wily for even the fastest guns in Texas.

Displaying the ultimate in ingenuity, Sam Davis of the Carson City, Nevada, *Appeal* blended the hoax with the exchange and came up with a mythical newspaper known as the *Wabuska Mangler*. During the 1880s and early '90s the *Appeal* entertained its readers with a number of wild and wonderful items supposedly clipped from the *Mangler*. One printed in the May 2, 1890, *Appeal* told of the terrible destruction of the *Mangler*'s forms, just as the paper was preparing to go to press, by a charging Holstein bull that enemies of the journal had specially trained to attack printing presses. When Davis tired of his brain child, he killed off the *Mangler* by announcing that the editor had closed up shop and gone East — ostensibly because of poor health, wrote Davis, but more likely to avoid a grand jury indictment.

Disseminating the news — or a diverting facsimile thereof — was only one of the functions expected of Western editors. They served the special interests of their communities by agitating for territorial status, then for statehood, and even before these large prizes were won, they fought like Kilkenny cats over the location of a county seat. This last was of particular personal interest to the editor since it meant the income from official county printing and from private legal business as well. Furthermore, by printing state constitutions, county laws and town ordinances, editors acted as the young country's unofficial historians. The only existing record that Texas had ever had a provisional government after declaring its independence from Mexico is contained in a single copy of Gail Borden's *Telegraph and Texas Register* that somehow escaped General Santa Anna's wrath in 1836.

Western editors also campaigned for the building of railroads, demanded free coinage of silver, fought for the abolition of slavery or defended its continuance, argued against restrictions on the Texas cattle drives, or, alternatively, stood up for the dirt farmer whose livestock were being infected by disease-carrying longhorns. In the early days, they supported summary vigilante justice because no other kind was available; later they voiced dismay at its excesses. In both cases, by painful degree, they measurably helped gentle the bronco wildness of the West.

Here and there a Western editor puts his journal to the vociferous service of a personal crusade. In the 1880s and '90s, in Valley Falls and Topeka, Kansas, Moses Harman made his *Lucifer, the Light Bearer* the seductive voice of free love. In 1901, temperance agitator Carry Nation issued her *Smasher's Mail* in Topeka to trumpet her triumphs with a hatchet in Kansas saloons. The cause of feminism found early support in the *New Northwest,* a paper launched in 1871 by Abigail Scott Duniway, who was known as the Mother of Equal Suffrage in Oregon; and in 1897 the *Idaho Woman* came out under the credo of "Equality Before the Law."

However, woman's role in Western journalism was not confined to special pleading. While the great majority of frontier editors were men—largely because the first Western society was almost exclusively male —women began to participate in regional journalism as soon as editors began to acquire wives. Many women continued to publish family newspapers when they were widowed or, as sometimes happened, while their husbands were disabled by the wrath of an offended reader. An occasional bold spirit such as Caroline Romney of Durango, Colorado, undertook publishing on her own. Her Durango *Record* at one point announced: "The rumor that the editor of this paper is about to be married is without foundation. In fact, we can't afford to support a husband yet."

Other ladies came into journalism by way of the print shop, where their fingers were more dexterous and often soberer than those of male typesetters. Women reporters and so-called sob sisters made their appearance late in the century, not always to the approbation of male colleagues. "They killed it—they literally killed it, with their namby-pamby school-girl trash," complained a male editor of his female compatriots on the San Francisco *Golden Era* when that journal was forced to shut down in 1893.

Though Western editors as individuals frequently managed to make themselves *personae non gratae* in a given region, editors as a breed remained in lively demand. Prideful town promoters were eager to shanghai any practitioner who possessed the tools and talent to publicize their nascent metropolis. In 1864, James Reynolds, an ambitious young newspaperman from Maine, had nearly reached his intended destination in Idaho City with his press in a freight wagon when he was overtaken by a messenger on a fast horse. If Reynolds would turn his team around, the messenger said, a subsidy of $1,500 and a rent-free print shop awaited him in Boise, 50 miles away. The print shop turned out to be a log cabin with no door in the doorway, but the *Idaho Statesman* went to press anyhow. And with the passage of time it became an important voice in the affairs of a thriving young state capital, while Idaho City, nearly a century later, had a population consisting of only 188 souls.

Kansas and Nebraska in the late '50s and early '60s went through a flamboyant time of boom and boost when, as Horace Greeley wryly noted, "it takes three log houses to make a *city* in Kansas, but they begin *calling* it a city so soon as they have staked out the lots." In that era speculators picked out sites for and bestowed names on upward of 2,000 towns in Kansas alone. Most never came any closer to realization than a forlorn sod hut or two. But any cluster of buildings that stood even a remote chance of enduring had to have a newspaper.

In 1854 the New England Emigrant Aid Society hired George Brown of Conneautville, Pennsylvania, to launch the *Herald of Freedom* in the bleak plains of Kansas Territory. The promoters furnished him with a subscription list of several thousand people, all of whom lived somewhere in the East and were considered likely subjects for temptation to move to Kansas. Although the first issue of the paper was datelined Kansas Territory, it was actually printed in Brown's office in Pennsylvania. But by the time the second issue came out, Brown and his equipment had arrived in Lawrence. It was still so new that the editor had to unload on the open prairie. His first editorial act was to take his seven typographers out to cut trees to build a roof over their heads.

Looking back in amused wonder at those early days, J. Sterling Morton, who in his youth had been an editor press-agenting for the infant Nebraska City on the local *News,* marveled at the consummate bravado with which enterprising journalists had attempted to conjure

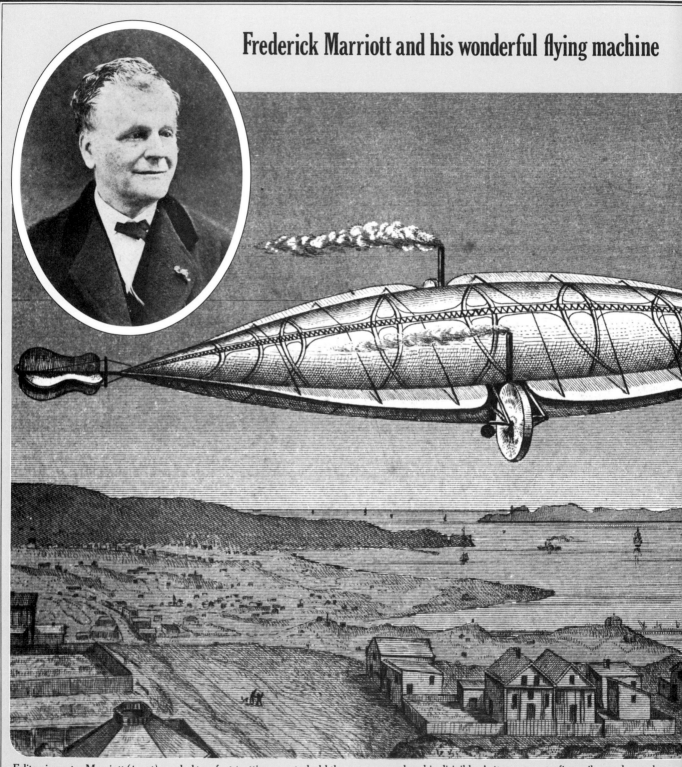

Frederick Marriott and his wonderful flying machine

Editor-inventor Marriott (*inset*) needed two fast-trotting men to hold the guy ropes when his dirigible *Avitor* got up to five miles an hour above a

n Francisco race track.

Most Western editors had their hands full just putting their journals to bed and keeping them solvent. Not so British expatriate Frederick Marriott, who flourished as both financier and editor, and also found time to invent a flying machine. Arriving in San Francisco in 1849, the hustling Marriott first started a loan company. When that prospered, he started the *San Francisco Newsletter,* a free-swinging weekly of gossip and satire. The terror of politicians and socialites, it featured Marriott's own enemies list in a column titled "Our Quacks," decorated with a skull and crossbones.

But even journalism took a back seat to Marriott's dream of devising a machine that could soar from coast to coast. Working by candlelight in the basement of his newspaper building, he spent more than 12 years on a 37-foot-long pilotless model of a lighter-than-air craft. At last his hydrogen-filled, steam-propelled *Avitor (left)* was successfully sent aloft. Onlookers "cheered loud and many fairly danced with delight," reported the *Newsletter.* But before Marriott could start on a full-scale 150-foot craft that would carry a pilot and four passengers, a carelessly tossed match set fire to *Avitor.* The hydrogen exploded, destroying the machine.

Refusing to quit, Marriott turned to developing a heavier-than-air steam powered "aeroplane" (a word he coined). He completed his design in 1881, but the Patent Office refused to patent it because "an apparatus for navigating the air which does not depend upon a gas field for the elevating means, is an impractical structure."

cities from empty space. "Young Chicagos, increscent New Yorks, precocious Philadelphias and infant Londons were duly staked out and lithographed, divided into shares and puffed with becoming unction and complaisance." The odd thing about this cheerful mendacity was that often enough it worked and created something substantial out of nothing. Partly through Morton's efforts, the new state of Nebraska grew important enough to send Morton himself to Washington in 1893 as Secretary of Agriculture during the Presidency of Grover Cleveland.

Even in areas already settled, the pioneer Western editor needed a reservoir of optimism almost as much as he needed a press, for he was getting into a venture with a risk factor close to the point of foolhardiness. In New Mexico any editor had to create a readership out of a scattered population that was largely illiterate or literate only in Spanish. And in the mining camps of Nevada, Montana and Idaho he scrabbled for subscribers and advertisers amongst a transient population sure to vanish overnight if the lode pinched out.

While newspapers everywhere found eager readers, and a copy often passed from hand to hand until it completely disintegrated, the popularity of his product often did little to line an editor's pockets. Money was in acute and chronic shortage all across the frontier, and editors had to resign themselves to taking out an often ruinous proportion of their bills in trade. A Wichita, Kansas, editor settled his advertising account with one merchant for a can of oysters and a barrel of apples. Another offered to accept any produce "except babies" from his subscribers.

In desperation, one editor resorted to blackmail, threatening to publish the name of a subscriber he had caught in the classic sin of kissing the hired girl unless the delinquent paid his back bill. The threat succeeded in bringing in the overdue payment. Reflecting on his career in the 1870s as city editor of the *Statesman* in Salem, Oregon, Colonel John Redington commented: "I used to rustle ads for a four-page paper, but it was worse than painful dentistry, and when I tried to collect bills I invited getting shot. So I joined the army and went scouting through three Indian wars, thus getting into the safety zone."

Except in thriving San Francisco, where newspaper circulations could run into five figures, an editor had to learn to get along with a minuscule subscription list. As late as 1873, the Los Angeles *Star* had a mere 500 paid-up subscribers, the Houston *Age* could count on only 325 and the Seattle *Dispatch* listed but 144 cash customers. That year's frontier champion was the Portland *Oregonian,* which boasted 1,960 paying readers; the 14-year-old *Rocky Mountain News* was runner-up with a roster of 1,475 subscribers in the environs of Denver.

Given only this meager nourishment with which to meet the rigorous challenge of the West, back-country papers suffered a calamitous mortality rate. Sadly shutting down the *Oasis* in Hawthorne, Nevada, in 1881, Editor Orlando Jones penned his valedictory: "It may be possible to publish a newspaper on one square meal a week, but to undertake to do so on one square a month, and hash only once in thirty-one days for the long months is a little more than human nature can stand." And in Laramie in 1877, the editor of the *Sentinel* saluted the demise of the rival *Wyoming Morning News* with an epitaph in verse:

> *Leaf by leaf the roses fall,*
> *Dime by dime, the purse runs dry;*
> *One by one, beyond recall,*
> *Mushroom papers droop and die.*

By the score, then the hundreds, finally the thousands, pioneer papers passed into oblivion, surviving only as crumbling files for antiquarians to ponder. Occasionally, back issues lingered on as wallpaper in some settler's shanty or, even more obscurely, as mattress padding or insulation under rugs; a few saw service as ladies' bustles. So many newspapers perished that any that endured for a dozen years were considered honorably ancient.

Even the venerable survivors had had to struggle through times of near-fatal adversity. The *Oregonian* was ten years old and nigh to its deathbed when, in 1860, President-elect Lincoln extended personal salvation to its editor-publisher, Thomas Dryer, by promising to appoint him United States Commissioner to the Sandwich (Hawaiian) Islands. Gratefully preparing to leave, Dryer presented the newspaper to a youthful reporter, Henry Pittock, in lieu of unpaid wages. Unlike Dryer, Pittock was a shrewd businessman who turned the paper from a weekly into a daily and hired

A printer's apprentice, clutching his ink roller, stands by the proof press of the *Delamar Lode* with his editor. The Nevada newspaper, which was begun in 1894 after a gold strike, perished when local mining came to a stop in 1906.

San Francisco *Bulletin* editor James King
of William tacked on his father's first name
to distinguish himself from several other
James Kings who were in his hometown.

a brilliant editor, Harvey Scott, whose force of character and immense learning earned him the title of Schoolmaster of the Press of Oregon. Under their twin leadership the newspaper became so firmly established that the people living in the Willamette Valley, it was said, "are raised on the *Oregonian* and the Bible."

Next to unquenchable optimism, what a pioneer editor needed most was the ability to perform an occasional small miracle. With newsprint supplies far to eastward, sometimes on the other side of Indian country and usually available only for cash on the bale, Western subscribers were neither surprised nor shocked when their favorite journals came out printed on brown wrapping paper. At least one California journal began its existence printed on large sheets of Mexican cigarette paper, and a Dakota editor resorted to white muslin cloth for several issues. Type, too, was a problem; it was expensive, and type foundries were as far away as the newsprint mills.

But a clever editor always found ways to make up for his font's deficiencies. An odd couple, a United States Navy chaplain named Walter Colton and a Kentucky backwoodsman named Robert Semple, decided to start a newspaper in Monterey when in 1846 they found an abandoned printing press in a Spanish monastery. In their broadside announcing publication of the *Californian,* Chaplain Colton included a mild apology: "OUR ALPHABET — Our type is a Spanish font picked up here in a cloister and has no VVs in it, as there are none in the Spanish alphabet. I have sent to the Sandvvich Island for this letter; in the meantime vve must use tvvo Vs. Our paper at present is that for vvrapping segars; in due time vve vvill have something better. Vvalter Colton." Sharp-eyed historians, however, discovered that the *Californian's* first issues did contain a sprinkling of Ws, and concluded that Colton's and Semple's font simply lacked enough of the troublesome letter. That introductory broadside seems to have been just another attention-getting hoax

—but a vvonderfully vvitty one.

George Curry, as he prepared to launch the Oregon City *Free Press* in 1848, suffered even more grievous handicaps: no printing press, and no funds with which to acquire one. The enterprising Curry designed his own model and hired a handyman to build it for him. While the builder toiled, Curry himself carved hardwood letters to fill out missing items in a font of old French Didot type he had obtained from some Catholic missionaries. In his first issue Curry described the origin of his press and commented: "Although it is made of wood, Mr. W., our builder, thinks it will be able to tell the truth quite as well as an iron one."

Besides this kind of straight-eyed perseverance a Western publisher needed both courage and a resilient physique — especially if he had the kind of abrasive temperament so typical of the breed. Colonel Daniel Read Anthony, Massachusetts-born and brother of suffragette Susan B., was full to the brim with all of the above qualities; a contemporary said of him that his blood "boiled on a minute's notice." Anthony was so ardent and outspoken an abolitionist that, even before he became a publisher to disseminate his views more widely, proslavery elements in Leavenworth, Kansas, began taking pot shots at him. Within six months after founding the *Conservative,* he took umbrage at remarks about him in the rival *Herald* and killed one of its publishers, R. C. Satterlee, in a shoot-out on a Leavenworth street. A few years later he got into a quarrel with a man named C. R. Jennison and exchanged pistol shots with him; Jennison was wounded in the leg. Later on, in a fit of editorial wrath, he took a cane to E. G. Ross, a former United States Senator and rival publisher. He was not always the victor in these meetings: in other encounters with offended readers and competitors he was spat upon, twice wounded by gunfire, beaten up with an umbrella and — at age 67 — horsewhipped.

Probably not even Anthony was surprised at the frequency and vehemence with which others took ex-

A "notorious" quintet of junketeering journalists

Local Reporters of the daily newspapers of Virginia and Gold Hill, Nevada. Dec. 16, 1865.

Wm. M. Gillespie, "Enterprise" Virginia. Chas. E. Parker, "Even'g News" Gold Hill. Dan. De Quille, "Enterprise" Virginia. Robt. E. Lowery, "Union" Virginia. Alf Doten, "Enterprise" Virginia.

Comstock country reporters Gillespie, Parker, De Quille, Lowery and Doten offer a sober front in this 1865 portrait.

The five men above might easily be taken for dignified—and abstemious—19th Century businessmen; in fact, they were journalists out on a spree in Nevada's Comstock mining country. Alf Doten, Dan De Quille and William Gillespie worked for Virginia City's *Territorial Enterprise,* Bob Lowery for the same town's *Daily Union,* and Charley Parker for the nearby Gold Hill *Daily News.* Doten and De Quille were big names in Western journalism; both knew Mark Twain well. In December 1865, the quintet—tipplers to a man—staggered over to the Sutterly Brothers' studio to have their picture taken. The Sutterlys produced a photograph that made their subjects look like teetotaling pillars of society.

One of the wags sent a copy to Twain, then San Francisco correspondent for the *Enterprise.* Twain replied in print. Playing dumb about his pals' identities, he called them "a pictured group of notorious convicts and the worst lot of human faces I have ever seen." After describing the reporters as "murderers" and "thugs," Twain wound up wickedly: "I have permitted the Chief of Police to take a copy, for obvious reasons."

Bob Lowery counterattacked in the *Union,* declaring Twain the real menace to society for the "crimes" he had committed on paper in Nevada. This infamous character, Lowery lamented, was "allowed to roam at large in San Francisco," where he was "keeping quiet, subsisting on free lunches and basking in the sunshine of a community that knew him not."

ception to his editorial style. Once, in a fit of pique at competing editors, he wrote that they were "three of the lowest, dirtiest, filthiest scoundrels that ever infested any place on earth." To this invective, one of the editors retorted that Colonel Anthony would be passed up even by "dogs writhing with agony in search of a cleaner post."

This kind of vitriolic exchange between competing publishers was not unusual in the West. An 1868 editorial in the Marysville, Kansas, *Enterprise* was addressed to Editor John Cone of the Seneca, Kansas, *Nemaha Courier* in this wise: "Cone—you idiot—you Jackass—red-headed, frizzle-headed, mush-headed, slab-sided, brainless deformity and counterfeit imitation of a diseased polecat."

In early San Francisco, where dueling was taken for granted as the correct way to settle disputes between gentlemen, a trigger-tempered editor was in real danger unless he had an accurate trigger finger as well. In 1852, Edward Gilbert wrote a scurrilous editorial in the *Alta California* castigating the melodramatic showmanship with which General James W. Denver had charged into the Sierra to rescue a party of snowbound migrants. It was, wrote Gilbert, more a case of exhi-

bitionism than mercy. Offended, Denver in turn wrote an intemperate letter to a Sacramento paper implying that Gilbert was a poltroon or worse.

Now that he considered *himself* insulted, Gilbert rashly challenged the soldier to a duel, although he must have known that the general was a far better marksman—indeed, a dead shot. The antagonists, accompanied by their seconds and physicians, came together one dawn and faced off with rifles at forty paces. When the signal was given, Gilbert fired and missed; the general had deliberately aimed his weapon to one side and his shot went wide of the mark. The general then declared himself satisfied but Gilbert insisted on a second shot, asserting that the general had once derided bloodless dueling as a farce. So the unwise and inept editor fired again and missed again; but the general, by now as angry as the editor, did not miss. Gilbert died shortly after Denver's bullet struck him in the body above the left hip.

Another San Francisco editor, the whimsically named James King of William of the *Bulletin,* one day took it into his head to print that a rival editor, James P. Casey of the *Sunday Times,* was an ex-convict who had served time in New York for robbing his mis-

The Kansas City, Kansas, *Times's* proudly named *Fast Newspaper Train* prepares for its daily 55-mile round trip to the state capital, Topeka.

76

tress. Naturally upset, Casey stalked into King of William's office where, according to still another paper, the following exchange took place:

Casey: What do you mean by such a statement?

King of William: Is it not the truth?

Casey: Yes, but I don't wish my past acts raked up, on that point I am sensitive. I was young and inexperienced when that happened.

King of William: I will publish what I see fit.

Casey: Then you must be prepared to defend yourself, for I intend to attack you on sight.

King of William: Leave my office at once. If you do not I shall kick you into the street.

Late that afternoon, James King of William left the *Bulletin* office on Merchant Street and walked toward Washington Street. As was his habit, he walked with his head down, paying little attention to his surroundings. James P. Casey was waiting at the corner of Washington. As King of William drew near, the *Times* editor yelled, "Draw and defend yourself!", threw aside his cape and fired before King of William even looked up. In spite of the bullet in his left breast, King of William lingered on for nearly a week, being treated, at different times, by a total of 20 doctors.

When he died, the vigilante committee assaulted the county jail, seized Editor Casey and hanged him in the street. Nine months later, in 1857, a jury investigating the shooting came to the decision that King of William had died, not from Casey's bullet, but from the ineptitude of the doctors who treated him.

While most of the pioneers of Western journalism died broke and unrenowned, a few managed by luck or talent or good humor—or, sometimes, a happy blend of all three—to win a lasting place in the history of the frontier. Dave Day, who pursued his career as an editor in the remote San Juan Mountains of Colorado, grew so famous for his bold outspokenness and stinging barbs that his papers were sold on newsstands as far away as London. Editor and publisher of, first, the Ouray, Colorado, *Solid Muldoon* (which he named after an Irish fight promoter whom he admired) and later of the Durango *Democrat,* Day by his own admission was inclined to be "candid and impetuous." At one point he had 42 libel suits pending against him simultaneously, on none of which the plaintiffs collected so much as a penny.

Clearly, one of Day's saving graces was his wit. Once when he was covering a visiting Congressman's

n 1876. The flier got the paper's morning edition to Topeka before breakfast and returned with news of the legislature for the next day's issue.

speech in Durango, he grew bored at the overlong oration and stretched out full-length on some chairs in the front row. When the speaker apologized and offered to wind up his remarks quickly, Day retorted, "Don't hurry, Jim, we can lie down here as long as you can lie up there." Day was still at the helm of the Durango *Democrat* when he died in his own bed, of natural causes, at 67; to the end, said the admiring *Rocky Mountain News,* "he spoke his mind as few newspaper men ever have dared do."

Even better known as a humorist was Edgar Wilson (Bill) Nye, who acquired international fame for the bon mots that he first wrote for his *Laramie Boomerang,* a newspaper he named after his pet mule. Nye also functioned as town postmaster, but had to relinquish that job when ill health threatened. Readers in Laramie—and eventually practically everywhere—relished the open letter of resignation he addressed "To the President of the United States," datelined "Postoffice Divan, Laramie City, Wyoming Territory, October 1, 1883."

"Sir," wrote Nye, "I beg leave at this time to officially tender my resignation as postmaster at this place, and in due form to deliver the great seal and the key to the front door of the office. The safe combination is set on the numbers 33, 66, and 99, though I do not remember at this moment which comes first or how many times you revolve the knob or which direction you should turn it in order to make it operate.

"You will find the postal cards that have not been used under the distributing table, and the coal down in the cellar. If the stove draws too hard, close the damper in the pipe and shut the general delivery window.

"If Deacon Hayford does not pay up his box-rent, you might as well put his mail in the general delivery, and when Bob Head gets drunk and insists on a letter from one of his wives every day in the week, you can salute him through the delivery window with an old Queen Anne tomahawk, which you will find near the Etruscan water-pail.

"Tears are unavailing. I once more become a private citizen, clothed only with the right to read such postal cards as may be addressed to me personally."

Yet another frontier editor secured his place in Western history with a single well-chosen word. "Every Tombstone needs an *Epitaph,*" declared John P.

Clum when he founded that estimable Arizona journal in 1880. The name alone, he thought, would be worth a million dollars in publicity. Clum insured his paper's lease on life with good, responsible editing that earned the town's respect and helped elect him mayor. His tenure coincided with the brief, gaudy period when the discovery of silver made Tombstone overnight one of the liveliest and toughest mining camps in the West. During the two years that Clum published, anything could and did happen in Tombstone, including the famous gunfight at the O.K. Corral.

The *Epitaph* faithfully recorded it all—not only dueling deaths and the cockfights and stagecoach robberies and night-riding posses, but also the Sunday school picnics, the Christmas visit of Santa Claus to Tombstone's 250 school children, and the formation of the Tombstone Literary and Debating Club. And though Clum sold out in 1882, to move on to other careers in the United States postal service and as a lecturer, he left behind a solid reputation as one of early Arizona's most vigorous and able public servants.

Perhaps the most successful of all the Old West's small town editors, in terms of lasting service and achievement within the area he covered, was Clement A. Lounsberry, an ex-Army officer and Minneapolis newspaperman who headed west in 1873 with a wagonful of printing equipment to publish his own weekly newspaper in a little Missouri River settlement in Dakota Territory.

Bismarck was then scarcely more than a collection of shacks and tents, and had yet to acquire a school, a bank, a church or even a road. But the Northern Pacific Railroad tracks were due to cross the Missouri River at Bismarck. Editor Lounsberry knew this, and established himself there accordingly. His gamble that the town had a promising future paid off handsomely: not only did it grow to be the capital of North Dakota, but Lounsberry's *Bismarck Tribune* survived to become the oldest continuously published chronicle in the state. Obviously the founding editor's judgment and professional skill had a lot to do with this; and the three-year-old *Tribune* received a substantial boost when Lounsberry landed the most sensational and enduring story to come out of the West in the latter half of the 19th Century. This was the awful account of General George Custer's dramatic defeat and death at

Wild Bill Hickok: they had him covered

In the flamboyant cast of characters who roamed the West, one of the sure-fire headline makers was James Butler Hickok, known to all as "Wild Bill." To hear some of the papers tell it, Hickok had, during his peregrinations as Army scout, lawman and gunslinging private citizen, killed no fewer than 200 men. Disinterested observers put the figure considerably lower, at perhaps only a score. Even so, Wild Bill had done away with enough miscreants and busted up enough saloons to make wonderful copy — and in the latter part of his career papers in Missouri, Kansas, Colorado and Dakota Territory followed his every move with avid interest.

It took an Easterner to discover Wild Bill. In 1867, Colonel George Ward Nichols wrote a lurid account for *Harper's* of "Wild Bill, the Scout of the Plains." A few Western editors, who had been reporting his doings haphazardly, felt obliged to correct elements of the story. Wrote the *Missouri Weekly Patriot:* "Hickok's extraordinary black mare Nell (which was in fact a black stallion blind in one eye), wouldn't 'fall as if struck by a cannon ball' when Hickok 'slowly waved his hand over her head with a circular motion' worth a cent. Nor did she (or he) ever jump upon the billiard table of the Lyon House at 'William's low whistle.' "

But the editors could see what they had been missing, and soon after the *Missouri Democrat* printed an account of how a party of Indians attacking a lone rider had fled when they saw that their intended victim was Hickok, "one of the most famous men on the prairie." A few months later, the Central City, Colorado, *Daily Register* reported that Hickok had rescued a party of ranchers who were surrounded by Indians by mounting "their fleetest horse" and

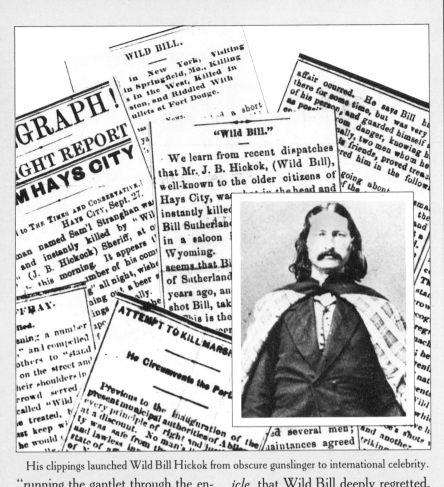

His clippings launched Wild Bill Hickok from obscure gunslinger to international celebrity.

"running the gantlet through the enemy's line, receiving only a slight wound in the foot."

Before long, the smallest incident was news, and Topeka's *Kansas Daily Commonwealth* advised one and all that their hero had been fined $5 "for striking out from the shoulder and consequently hitting a man." A little later Bill got into a quarrel with five soldiers at Hays City, and killed one and severely wounded another. Newspapers disagreed about whether or not the shooting had met popular approval or whether Hickok had been chased out of town. In any case, he moved away to become Abilene's city marshal, and in a few months had killed two more men, including a deputy who blundered into his line of fire, a mischance, reported the *Chron-*

icle, that Wild Bill deeply regretted.

In 1873, Wild Bill himself was reported slain twice in one week, in Galveston, according to the *Dickinson County Chronicle,* and in Fort Dodge, according to the Kansas City *News.* Hickok corrected both these errors in a letter to the *Missouri Democrat,* saying: "No Texan ever has, nor ever will 'corral William.' "

The Hickok saga finally came to its end in the August 17, 1876, issue of the Ellis County *Star:* "Mr. J. B. Hickok (Wild Bill) was shot and killed by a man named Bill Sutherland, while playing cards in Deadwood Gulch, Wyoming. This is the long looked for ending of one who deserved a better fate." Wild Bill also deserved a little better reporting: the name of his killer was Jack McCall.

The staff of the Topeka *Daily Capital* pounds out a fresh edition in a newsroom equipped with the very latest of patent typewriters. Founded in the corner of a print shop in 1879, the paper flourished with Topeka and by 1898 boasted a brisk circulation of 12,675 in a town of 31,000.

the Battle of the Little Bighorn on June 25, 1876.

In the late spring of '76, Lounsberry was acting as stringer for the New York *Herald,* and on behalf of both his own paper and the *Herald* he had dispatched a young *Tribune* reporter, Mark Kellogg, to cover the Army's expedition against the Sioux. Kellogg sent word to his editor on the eve of battle: "By the time this reaches you we will have met and fought the red devils, with what result remains to be seen. I go with Custer and will be at the death." His prophecy proved grimly accurate: Kellogg was slain when the Indians overwhelmed and killed Custer with 215 of his men.

After the battle subsided, the Army detachments that had fought in support of Custer on the fringes of the Little Bighorn gathered their wounded aboard the steamboat *Far West* and raced toward Bismarck. Unaware of what had happened, the town of Bismarck was dark and sleeping when the steamer docked at 11:00 p.m. on the night of July 5th. Routing Lounsberry from bed, members of the party gave him the news and handed him the scribbled notes that were found in Kellogg's pouch next to his body. With a telegrapher, John M. Carnahan, Lounsberry sprinted to the railroad station and dictated a bulletin back to New York, then handed Carnahan a copy of the New Testament and told him to start tapping to keep the telegraph line open, so that a follow-up could be filed with no delay or interruption.

In the meantime Lounsberry rushed off to interview those who had been near the scene of the battle. For 22 hours, editor and telegrapher gathered and transmitted the terrible news. (For his feat, Lounsberry received a bonus of $2,500 from the New York paper, plus $3,000 to cover the telegraph bill.) Blazoned forth in the *Herald,* this first full account of the massacre spread like a shock wave across the nation. Much of the story's power lay in the complete and unblinking detail with which Lounsberry set down the event, not flinching to describe even the Indians' stripping and mutilation of the dead. And Lounsberry noted a curious phenomenon. "The body of Kellogg alone remained unstripped of clothing, and was not mutilated," he wrote. "Perhaps as the Indians had learned to respect the Great Chief, Custer, and for that reason did not mutilate his remains, they had in like manner learned to respect this humble shover of the lead pencil."

One man's view of Socorro, New Mexico

Pack mules arrive at Joseph Smith's adobe studio with a delivery of firewood.

Some of the most keen-eyed pictorial documentation of the frontier was the work of local photographers. Making portraits and pictures of regional doings, they, like newspaper editors, were a fixture of almost every town.

In 1883 the Rio Grande community of Socorro, New Mexico Territory, found just such a historian in Joseph Edward Smith. A Bay State Yankee who had dropped out of the Massachusetts Institute of Technology for lack of funds, Smith briefly apprenticed himself to a Chicago photographer, then headed west. He took root in booming Socorro and used his savings from several short-lived jobs to buy out a photography business. Then he sent East for a new camera—and for a wife, a girl named Myscie Driver whom he had met in Wisconsin. When the camera and bride had arrived, Smith had a backlog of $100 in orders for photographs of his Socorro neighbors.

Joseph Smith put in time at cowpunching and mining before he turned to photography. Excelling at that, he later opened a drugstore he called "the best in the city."

With wife, Myscie, at the piano, Smith launches into song for the entertainment of her cousin Nellie and two children. The long-curled child is their son Marvel

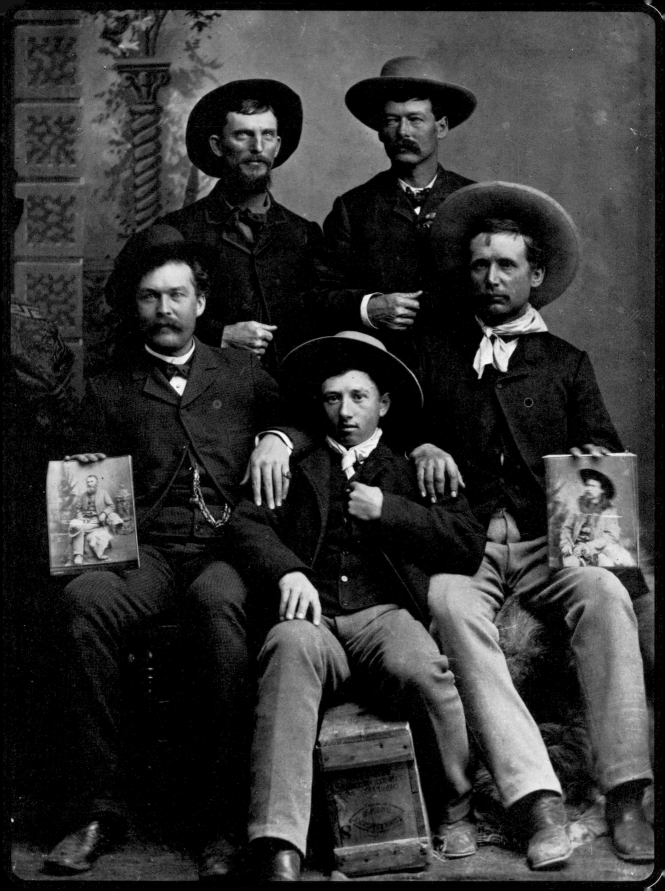

Smith could have recorded the faces of central New Mexico without stirring from his studio. Not only did Socorro's citizens beat a path to his door, so did people from the nearby towns of Kelly and Magdalena. Some frugal clients, like two of the gents on the far page, got extra value by including pictures of friends or relatives. But Smith also knew how to stretch his pennies: he made one setting do for such disparate subjects as three Chinese businessmen, a Mexican family and a pair of stylish aristocrats dressed for a *paseo* on the plaza.

A Mexican religious procession—with high-stepping youngsters tagging along—winds through the center of Socorro. The town received its name

in 1628 from Friar Alonso de Benavides, who built a Franciscan mission for local Pueblo Indians and dedicated it to Our Lady of Succor.

Husbands, wives, children, horses and assorted domestic animals gather for a portrait on a ranch near Socorro around 1890. Cattle-raising was one

of the economic mainstays of the region, although periodic droughts made it risky. Smith himself lost $4,000 on an investment in livestock.

Incredulous Socorrans, a few providentially equipped with skates, test the ice that covered the countryside when a flash flood was followed by an

early freeze. The Rio Grande inundated the town itself at times; Smith was once flooded out of his house and his gallery across the street.

A mourner makes a lonely pilgrimage to a fenced-in grave on the plain outside the town of Socorro. "In those times," Joseph Smith wrote in

ooking back on the dozen years that he spent as a photographer there, "life was full of dangers. New Mexico was sure FRONTIER country."

3 | Putting the West on canvas

"Go not abroad in search of material," the well-known Eastern artist and critic Asher B. Durand advised aspiring painters in an 1855 article for the influential art magazine, *The Crayon.* Asher urged young landscapists to concentrate instead on "the virgin charms of our native land." In its vast forests, mountains and prairies, he rhapsodized, the painter would find his eye captured by "forms of Nature yet spared from the pollutions of civilization."

Just so, and during the mid-19th Century artists ventured West to carry back images of the land beyond the Missouri. No school of Western art ever came out of this migration. The topic was too vast, and the men who recorded it too diverse. Their work ranged from the finely detailed animal studies of Titian Ramsay Peale *(pages 100-101)* to the romantic and often grandiose scenes of Albert Bierstadt *(pages 136-143).* Together, they gave Americans—and the world—a highly personalized view of the West that in some ways transcended the efforts of either the writers or the photographers.

Albert Bierstadt's companion Eadweard Muybridge made this photograph

94

the painter as he sketched Mariposa Indians on an 1872 journey to Yosemite. Above is the oil that resulted: *Indians in Council, California.*

CATLIN'S
INDIAN GALLERY:
In the Old Theatre,
On Louisiana Avenue, and near the City Post Office.

MR. CATLIN,

Who has been for seven years traversing the Prairies of the "Far West," and procuring the Portraits of the most distinguished Indians of those uncivilized regions, together with Paintings of their

VILLAGES, BUFFALO HUNTS, DANCES, LANDSCAPES OF THE COUNTRY &c. &c.

Will endeavor to entertain the Citizens of Washington, for a short time with an Exhibition of

THREE HUNDRED & THIRTY PORTRAITS & NUMEROUS OTHER PAINTINGS

Which he has collected from 58 different Tribes, speaking different languages, all of whom he has been among, and Painted his pictures from life.

Portraits of Black Hawk and nine of his Principal Warriors,

Are among the number, painted at Jefferson Barracks, while prisoners of war, in their war dress and war paint.

ALSO, FOUR PAINTINGS REPRESENTING THE

ANNUAL RELIGIOUS CEREMONY OF THE MANDANS,

Doing penance, by inflicting the most cruel tortures upon their own bodies—passing knives and splints through their flesh, and suspending their bodies by their wounds, &c.

A SERIES OF ONE HUNDRED LANDSCAPE VIEWS,

Descriptive of the picturesque *Prairie Scenes* of the Upper Missouri and other parts of the Western regions.

AND A SERIES OF TWELVE BUFFALO HUNTING SCENES,

Together with *SPLENDID SPECIMENS OF COSTUME*, will also be exhibited.

☞ The great interest of this collection consists in its being a representation of the *wildest tribes of Indians in America,* and *entirely* in their *Native Habits* and *Costumes:* consisting of *Sioux, Puncahs, Konzas, Shiennes, Crows, Ojibbeways, Assineboins, Mandans, Crees, Blackfeet, Snakes, Mahas, Ottoes, Ioways, Flatheads, Weahs, Peorias, Sacs, Foxes, Winnebagoes, Menomonies, Minatarrees, Rickarees, Osages, Camanches, Wicos, Pawnee-Picts, Kiowas, Seminoles, Euchees, and others.*

☞ In order to render the Exhibition more instructive than it could otherwise be, the Paintings will be exhibited one at a time, and such explanations of their Dress, Customs, Traditions, &c. given by Mr. Catlin, as will enable the public to form a just idea of the CUSTOMS, NUMBERS, and CONDITION of the Savages yet in a state of nature in North America.

The EXHIBITION, with EXPLANATIONS, will commence on Monday Evening, the 9th inst. in the old Theatre, and be repeated for several successive evenings, commencing at HALF PAST SEVEN O'CLOCK. Each COURSE will be limited to two evenings, Monday and Tuesday, Wednesday and Thursday, Friday and Saturday; and it his hoped that visiters will be in and seated as near the hour as possible, that they may see the whole collection. The portrait of OSEOLA will be shewn on each evening.

ADMITTANCE 50 CENTS.—CHILDREN HALF PRICE.

☞ These Lectures will be continued for *one week only.*

"Something burglars wouldn't have, moths eat or time blacken"

At 77, Charles Willson Peale still had dreams. But they were no longer for himself. A celebrated portraitist of Revolutionary heroes, Peale was also an enthusiastic naturalist who maintained in the Philosophical Hall in Philadelphia what amounted to the country's only natural history museum. He had been much stimulated by the discoveries of the Lewis and Clark expedition of 1804-1806, and now, in 1818, fresh excitement arose in his breast when he heard that Congress had appropriated funds to undertake a second expedition up the Missouri.

Since age prevented the grand old artist himself from venturing off, he was determined that the family should be represented by one of his sons. And there in his own museum, diligently making scale drawings of insects for a volume on entomology and feeding the museum's two live grizzly bears, was Titian Ramsay Peale. Titian was the third son in the second family of the oft-married Charles and a precocious stripling of 19 who was already a member of the Academy of Natural Sciences of Philadelphia.

Charles Peale hastened to the nation's capital to obtain the ear of Secretary of War John C. Calhoun, under whose auspices the expedition was to be made. Soon afterward young Titian received from Washington a letter appointing him assistant naturalist and painter to the 20-man group of explorers and scientists to be led by Major Stephen Harriman Long, a topographical engineer.

Extravagant preparations were made for the expedition. Special uniforms, bearing seven-pointed-star collar insignia, were designed for the members. Congress, in its enthusiastic wisdom, earmarked funds for the building of a shallow-draft, stern-wheel steamboat with several novel features which young Peale described: "She has a mast to ship and unship at pleasure. On the bow is carved the figure of a large serpent through the gaping mouth of which the waste steam issues. It will give, no doubt, to the Indians an idea that the boat is pulled along by this monster." Just in case the sea serpent did not sufficiently overawe any hostile savages the party might encounter, the steamboat was also equipped with four brass howitzers, a dozen muskets, six rifles, numerous pistols and fowling pieces and one compressed-air gun.

Boarding this unusual vessel, prosaically named *Western Engineer,* Titian carried with him his official instructions to examine, dissect and otherwise describe all the new flora and fauna the expedition was bound to come upon. He also bore with him the parting advice of an older half brother named Rembrandt: "I know how well you draw when you have the object placed quietly before you, but if you practice sketching from human figures as well as animals and trees, hills, cataracts, etc., you will be able to present us with many a curious representation. Make drawings of the Indians in their warrior dresses; these will be infinitely more interesting than if made from the dresses put on white men afterwards. Give us some accurate drawings of their habitations. I have never seen one that was decently finished." Titian took due note of his older brother's words.

Starting up the Missouri River on June 22, 1819, the members of the Long expedition made slow headway through the snags and sand bars of the capricious river. Their dragon-headed argosy earned them a critical reception from river Indians, who commented, according to the *St. Louis Enquirer,* "White man, bad

An 1838 show bill advertises the Washington, D.C., opening of artist George Catlin's traveling Indian Gallery, which offered the first authentic representations of the faces and the folkways of the Western tribes.

man, keep a great spirit chained and build fire under it to make it work a boat." The Indians, however, took no violent exception to this mistreatment of a serpent and were perhaps even frightened by it, since the cannon were not used except to salute forts and fur trading posts along the way.

Young Peale was kept occupied collecting and became the party's chief huntsman and, probably because of his skill at dissection, the camp's butcher. As the year progressed, small frustrations began to attend his scientific work: captured ground squirrels kept escaping from their cages; swans were too wary to be taken alive; and the only way—a most unsatisfactory one—he could acquire a new species of mouse was to blast it with a fowling piece.

More serious obstacles lay ahead. While Long's party was spending the winter and spring at a field station near the confluence of the Missouri and Platte rivers, the major himself journeyed to Washington and came back to the encampment bearing discouraging information. Congress had cut back the expedition's appropriation and had prohibited any further exploration of the Upper Missouri River. The dragon boat and its crew retreated downriver to St. Louis while the remainder of the party set out overland, with its charter foreshortened to the discovering of the headwaters of the Platte River and to tracing the course of the Red River to the Mississippi.

In spite of constant threat of Indian attack, searing summer temperatures that reached 100° F. and the rapid diminution of the party's inadequate stores, young Peale persevered with his scientific inquiry and his field sketches. To keep up his strength, he learned to eat, if not to relish, the flesh of famished horses. But in September came the final blow in the season's hardships and disappointment; the party discovered too late that it was going down the wrong river—the Canadian instead of the Red.

Discouraged, the men trekked out to the Mississippi River and headed for New Orleans, where the party broke up. Titian Peale boarded ship and sailed for Philadelphia to sort out his collection of sketches, which proved to be not only a naturalist's bonanza but also a pioneering picture catalogue of both the animal and human life of the Great Plains. Altogether he had turned out 122 careful studies of animals, birds, fish-es, reptiles and insects. And, remembering his half brother Rembrandt's advice, Peale also produced many "curious representations" of the hide-covered tipis, log forts and bare-back buffalo-hunting expeditions of the warrior tribes.

These early glimpses of the fauna and the people in a world as yet barely encroached upon by whites were instrumental in helping to open the world's eyes to the look of the American West. In so doing they established Titian Peale as one of the first of the frontier's pictorial chroniclers—a charter member of a fraternity of artists who traveled beyond the Mississippi to paint, sketch, engrave or sculpt what they saw.

These storytellers with sketchbooks were men of widely varied tastes, motives and backgrounds. Some had been hardened in the foot-slogging campaigns of the Civil War, some were nurtured in the effete salons of the Old World. Many visited the West only once and then went home to the East or Europe and painted from field sketches, photographs or memory; a number of dedicated souls traveled repeatedly beyond the Mississippi; a few made the vast land their home. But for all their differences they proved a remarkably adaptable lot. Not only did they picture the rugged hinterland for the rest of the nation, they participated in its life and action as well. They learned how to load a pack mule and browbeat it into action, to pole a keelboat upstream among the snags of the muddy Missouri River, to protect themselves against Indian attack, to rope a mustang, pan for gold, bulldog a steer, and accept with grace and tolerable appetite when offered a feast of stewed dog in the lodge of an Indian warrior. Some even learned how to relish a buffalo steak cooked over a fire of buffalo dung. "There is no better broiling fuel than a perfectly dry buffalo chip," testified *Harper's* illustrator Theodore Davis, who often doubled as camp cook for any party he joined.

Together these venturesome men created a mighty canvas on which they catalogued the West's creatures, celebrated its splendors and preserved its fast-fading aboriginal past with an impact impossible to achieve with words alone.

The first artists of any distinction to follow Peale focused their talents on the Indians. One of the most successful was a Philadelphia colleague of the Peales' by

Titian Ramsay Peale, resplendent in the uniform he wore on his Western expedition, is the image of the clear-eyed young naturalist-artist in this 1819 portrait by his famed father, Charles Willson Peale.

PEALE: THE ARTIST AS NATURALIST

"You must have long hearts to undertake such a journey with so weak a force," said a Pawnee chief who met a party of 20 men led by Major Stephen Long in the wilds of Nebraska territory in 1820. They did indeed. The Long Expedition, with Philadelphian Titian Ramsay Peale as naturalist, had set out from St. Louis some 350 miles east to explore the wilderness, traveling up the Missouri by boat, then trekking 1,200 miles by land to Pikes Peak and back to civilization, a trip taking some 15 months. Along the way Peale made his mark as an artist with more than 100 detailed studies of such little-known animals as buffalo, mountain sheep, coyote and wapiti.

This hasty sketch by Peale shows the expedition's steamboat *Western Engineer* off Long's winter camp near present-day Omaha. Normally Peale's renderings (*overleaf*) were more painstakingly authentic.

While he was hunting along a river in Nebraska, Peale not only helped shoot a dozen buffalo for provisions but also painted *Bulls,* the earliest known picture of these creatures grazing upon the Great Plains.

the name of George Catlin, who had begun his career as a lawyer but abandoned that profession in his middle twenties to teach himself to paint. He quietly showed enough promise to be adopted into Rembrandt Peale's circle of artistic friends, and was in a fair way to establishing himself as a portraitist in the Philadelphia area when, in 1824, something happened to change permanently the direction of his life: a delegation of Indian chiefs passed through Philadelphia while on a tour of the East.

Catlin was both fascinated by these "lords of the forest" and perceptive enough to know that they were fated to fall before the march of white civilization. He was also—instantly, it seems—smitten by the notion

that he must paint these "vanishing races" while there was still something to commit to canvas. To Catlin, the Indian was "man in the simplicity and loftiness of his nature"; and he made himself an extravagant promise: he would visit, get to know and paint the faces, the costumes, the arts and customs of every tribe in North America. "Nothing short of the loss of my life," he declared, "can prevent me from visiting their country and becoming their historian."

Catlin was delayed in starting his crusade by the simple necessity of making a living. But by 1830, with his work bringing increasing amounts of cash, Catlin was able to pay his way to St. Louis, which then lay on the fringe of Indian country. There he attached him-

self to General William Clark, once the partner of Meriwether Lewis and now Superintendent of Indian Affairs for the entire territory acquired in the Louisiana Purchase. For nearly two years, Catlin painted Indian delegations that came from the hinterland to treat with General Clark, and tribes that were camped within easy reach of the city. But he yearned to get away from civilization and meet unspoiled natives on their home ground. Finally, in 1832, he seized an opportunity to travel aboard the American Fur Company's new steamboat, *Yellowstone,* bound up the Missouri for trading posts in the heart of Indian country.

At every landing, Catlin sought out Indians with an almost obsessive energy. He had a passion for detail and accuracy, and the portraits that emerged were remarkable for the meticulous care with which he traced out the minutiae of each tribe's hair style, dress and decoration. The Indians themselves, while fascinated by Catlin's arcane doings, were never quite able to understand the distinction between the living model and the two-dimensional image. At Fort Pierre in the Dakota country, Catlin was working on a portrait of a warrior named Little Bear when a Hunkpapa chief known as The Dog, an ill-tempered leader of a rival band, happened to view the work in progress. Scowling, The Dog carefully inspected the flat surface of the painting, then turned to the sitter and derided him for being only half a man. Little Bear, in response, called The Dog a coward. Catlin's subject was slain in the bloody fight that followed, and the artist hastily packed up and departed with the portrait unfinished.

On this first painting expedition Catlin produced no fewer than 102 portraits and scenes of Indian life, sometimes whipping out as many as six finely detailed works in a single day. In the fall of 1832 he returned to St. Louis, and he spent the next year painting in the backgrounds and otherwise finishing his many canvases. Then, in the spring of 1834, he returned to Indian country, eager to expand his knowledge of tribal cultures. This time, at Fort Gibson on the Arkansas River, he joined a force of 500 Dragoons being dispatched to the Southwest to pacify the warlike Wichita and Comanche tribes.

The going was brutally hard on the almost treeless plains of the Southwest as the summer heat bore down. So many of the Dragoons fell out with fevers and exhaustion that the commander reduced his force to 250 able-bodied men, leaving the ailing to recuperate in camp. Catlin pushed on with the rest, riding one horse and leading another that carried his painting equipment in the packsaddles. They ran into enough reasonably peaceful tribesmen, including even a smattering of Comanches, to keep Catlin furiously occupied. But near the present site of Fort Sill, Oklahoma, he, too, fell ill. Nevertheless he continued to paint the Indian encampments and warriors until, dispatched back to Fort Gibson to recover, he sank into delirium and had to be carried for eight days in a baggage wagon.

While recuperating at Fort Gibson, he went doggedly back to his easel. Working from his field sketches, he completed a gallery of portraits of Comanche chiefs and tribal horsemen who, he commented, "in racing horses and in riding are not equalled by any other Indians on the continent."

He returned to the East, where the paintings from his first trip had already excited great interest and curiosity. In 1837, after two more visits to the West, he collected all of his works, some 600 of them, into a huge exhibit that he called his Indian Gallery. Opening in New York, the show drew such vast crowds that the gallery had to be moved to more spacious quarters. After his New York success, the show moved on to equally enthusiastic receptions in the cities of Washington, Philadelphia and Boston. Although a few crit-

ics complained that Catlin's mastery of anatomy left something to be desired, they were unanimous in their acclaim for his essential grasp of the facts of Indian life and his scrupulously accurate attention to detail.

The *United States Gazette* of Washington crowned its accolade for Catlin's work by observing that "perhaps no one since Hogarth has had, in so high a degree, the facility of seizing at the moment the true impression of a scene before his eyes, and transferring it to the canvas." And although Catlin never really came close to fulfilling his enormous ambition to paint all the tribes in North America, he did, in fact, paint 48 of them, including the Mandan, Sioux, Blackfoot, Osage, Crow, Comanche, Wichita, Piegan, Assiniboin, Cree, Delaware, Kansa, Oto, Ojibwa, Omaha, Sauk, Fox and Arikara tribes. It is well that he did. Within a few decades these tribes had virtually been wiped out by smallpox and warfare with the white man. They were on their way to obliteration, with Catlin's paintings the only permanent record of how they lived—or that they had ever lived at all.

While Catlin was primarily concerned with depicting Indians in their unique and natural splendor, a young contemporary named Alfred Jacob Miller showed them in a broader context. Schooled in Rome and at the Ecole des Beaux-Arts in Paris, Miller was eking out a slim living as a 27-year-old portrait painter in New Orleans in the spring of 1837 when a debonair British army officer appeared at his studio and asked to see his work. The visitor bought nothing, but a few days later he reappeared and asked Miller to join an expedition to the Rocky Mountains.

The stranger was Captain William Stewart, a veteran of the Battle of Waterloo under Wellington and later to become Sir William Drummond Stewart, master of Murthly Castle in Scotland. The aristocratic Stewart had been coming to the American West on hunting expeditions since 1833, and had become the familiar and friend of the mountain men. These traders and beaver trappers—legendary figures such as William Sublette, Joseph Reddeford Walker and Jim Bridger—were among the first whites to penetrate the corners of the deep West. Stewart had traveled with them for fun and adventure, bringing along such rare and welcome luxuries as good liquor and expensive cigars. ◉

A fanciful 1849 portrait done in London by English artist William Fisk depicted a well-scrubbed but buckskin-clad Catlin at work in the West with brush and palette.

CATLIN: "GREAT MEDICINE PAINTER"

Realizing early that Plains tribes were doomed, a young portraitist named George Catlin resolved to use his art "in rescuing from oblivion the looks and customs of the native man in America." He first went West from Albany, New York, in 1830, and in the next six years produced no fewer than 600 portraits and scenes encompassing 48 tribes. At times, he found it almost impossible to get his subjects to sit: the superstitious Indians believed that the "great medicine painter" was out to capture their soul, as well as their likeness.

In his pencil sketch of Mandan women bathing in the Missouri, Catlin wryly positions himself in the foreground, a decent distance away, but armed with a telescope.

Catlin's homeless gallery

When George Catlin put together his Indian Gallery of some 600 paintings and several thousand native artifacts in New York in 1837, he regarded it as more than a simple exhibit, to be sold piecemeal once the show was over. Catlin intended the fruits of his six years in the wilds to be a monument to a people vanishing from the American West, and he vowed to dispose of the collection as a whole or not at all.

The artist hoped Congress would buy the gallery as the cornerstone of a national museum. He had reason to think the legislators might be interested: during a tour of the Eastern seaboard, crowds clamored—at 50 cents a head —to view the collection. But Congress, resentful of Catlin's attacks on federal Indian policies, rebuffed him.

In 1839, Catlin sought a home for his work in Europe. For years, he dis-played his gallery to acclaim in Britain and France. Queen Victoria had part of the exhibit brought to Buckingham Palace for a private showing; France's King Louis Philippe commissioned —and never paid for—copies of some of the paintings. But nowhere did Catlin find a patron to pay the $35,000 he was asking for the collection.

He fell deep into debt, and the gallery was attached for nonpayment. In 1852, one of his creditors, a Philadelphian named Joseph Harrison, paid the principal debts, then shipped the exhibit back to America, where it moldered in a warehouse. Catlin did not return home until 1870, and he died two years later at the age of 77. Had he lived a little longer, he would have seen his ambition realized: in 1879, his gallery went to the Smithsonian Institution as a gift from Harrison's heirs.

Catlin sketched the French royal fam

Sweet-scented Grass, an Arikara girl

Cannot Be Thrown Down, a Kansa warrior

...nd their guests on a visit to his Indian Gallery in the Louvre in 1845. The artist's four children *(right)* were on hand for the occasion.

Mink, a Mandan girl

Buffalo Bull's Back Fat, a Blackfoot chief

In addition to being generous, Stewart was brave and a good companion; the trappers liked him. Now he wanted to return to the Rocky Mountains with an artist who could make on-the-spot sketches as a record of his travels and of his wilderness friends.

Miller eagerly accepted Stewart's offer. Before the end of spring their 10-man party joined forces with a large wagon train that was transporting a year's supplies to trappers in the mountains. The train was heading for the valley of the Green River, 1,000 miles from St. Louis on the far side of South Pass. The entire caravan, Stewart's group included, consisted of more than 100 men, 20 horse-drawn carts laden with the fur company's trade goods and provisions, and Stewart's two mule-drawn wagons packed with hunting equipment, Miller's art supplies and luxurious necessities for the junketing aristocrat.

Miller had no camp or trail duties save the care of his horse. He sketched in sepia ink and painted in watercolors as the caravan advanced. Once it had passed through Pawnee country and crossed to the north fork of the Platte, Miller was in a land totally new to white American artists. He became the first to see and paint the classic landmarks — Chimney Rock, Scott's Bluff and Independence Rock — along the route that, in four short years, would carry the vanguard of perhaps 100,000 wagons: the Oregon Trail.

In what would one day become Wyoming, Miller painted the palisaded and bastioned Fort William, built three years earlier by Sublette as the last permanent outpost on the fringes of fur country. There the party rested, regaled the isolated traders with the latest news, and then moved on. By mid-July, Stewart and his entourage had crossed the continental divide and reached the site of the fur rendezvous in the valley of the Green. There they met and exchanged uproarious greetings with several hundred white trappers who had spent the previous year in the wilderness, plus about 3,000 Shoshoni, Crow, Bannock, Nez Percé and Flathead Indians who had come to seek trade goods in exchange for their furs.

For the month that the rendezvous lasted, Miller sketched and painted the hard drinking, hard playing and hard bargaining of the trappers. He painted an Indian council and parade; and he recorded quieter and lonelier scenes of solitary hunters setting beaver traps

Kiowa Indians gather wild grapes in a painting Catlin included in

collection titled *Indian Cartoons*, which the aging and hard-pressed artist offered in New York in 1870 as a last-ditch attempt to pay his debts.

in the streams. He painted what may be his master-piece, a portrait of mountain man Joe Walker; and he painted what became his best-known picture, *The Trapper's Bride,* in which an Indian father gives his shy but comely daughter in marriage to a half-breed trapper—who, as Miller observed in his field notes, paid $600 in trade goods for the bride.

Alfred Jacob Miller made only that one brief journey to the West, but he went at just the right time, in the right company and under the right circumstances. By a quirk of fortune, besides becoming the pictorial trailblazer of the principal pioneer route to the West and portraying the life of the rough mountain men before their time passed away forever, he was able to observe and to reproduce one of the rarest scenes in the whole history of the American frontier: a meeting of white men and Indians as equals in a united undertaking, rather than as the imbalanced and implacable enemies they were to soon become.

The face of the West, and artists' conceptions of it, changed mightily in the decades after Peale and Catlin and Miller. But one aspect, in particular, remained essentially the same: the rugged splendor that all but overwhelmed explorers and artists alike. Of the many artists of the period who attempted to convey the majesty of the West, for a long time only two seemed equal to the undertaking. They were Albert Bierstadt, who reached the frontier in 1859, and Thomas Moran, who followed him in 1871.

Bierstadt, born in Germany, was brought to New England by immigrant parents as a child. When he reached his twenties, he returned to the land of his birth to study painting. After four years of training in Düsseldorf, interspersed with sketching trips to the Alps and Apennines, he came back to the United States and settled in New Bedford, Massachusetts. But he longed for broader vistas, and in the spring of 1859, at his own expense, he joined a United States government expedition that was led by a civil engineer named Frederick W. Lander, whose assignment was to improve the mountain portion of the Oregon Trail from Fort Kearney through South Pass and down to the border of California.

As he followed the same route traveled by Miller 22 years before him, Bierstadt was entranced by the

Miller did this self-portrait around 1837.

MILLER: CHRONICLER OF THE MOUNTAIN MEN

Alfred Jacob Miller made one trip West, in 1837, accompanying fur traders to a rendezvous with trappers in Wyoming territory. Yet this journey produced history's richest documentary of the mountain men—who instead of fighting the Indians joined them in a mutually profitable enterprise.

A mountain man relaxes in his buckskins.   A trapper takes a bride at the rendezvous.

Rocky mountain
Trapper

In Miller's watercolor, *Moonlight—Camp Scene,* painted near the continental divide during the trip to rendezvous, a grizzled trapper spins a tall tale by a campfire.

magnificent mountains. "Their jagged summits, covered with snow and mingling with the clouds, present a scene which every lover of landscape would gaze upon with unqualified delight," he rhapsodized. "The color of the mountains and of the plains, and indeed that of the entire country, reminds one of the color of Italy; in fact, we have here the Italy of America in primitive condition."

All that summer he made field sketches, in pencil and in color, and reinforced his store of images with stereopticon views he captured with primitive camera equipment. In the autumn he returned to his studio in New York, laden with sketches and photographs. And there the real Albert Bierstadt emerged. The artist's vi-

sion expanded as he worked and, if a mountain could have been painted full size, Bierstadt probably would have tried it. One of his early works, entitled *The Rocky Mountains,* was spread across 60 square feet of canvas. It depicted soaring misty peaks guarding a wooded mountain valley peopled by an encampment of Shoshoni Indians in the foreground.

The Eastern public thronged to see the painting when it was exhibited in New York in 1864. Bierstadt, to his pleasure and profit, soon found that huge peaks on huge canvases exactly suited the enormous appetites of wealthy patrons of the era. A London collector paid $25,000, reported to be the highest price ever for an American landscape up to that time, for his

painting of Lander's Peak in Wyoming. Others of his mammoth works found their way to the Hermitage in St. Petersburg, the Imperial Palace in Berlin and the Capitol in Washington.

Bierstadt continued to go back to the West for two decades, painting in the Rockies, along the Oregon Trail and in California's precipitous Yosemite Valley canyon, producing dozens of outsized landscapes. He became so closely identified with the Western mountains that one of the mightiest peaks in the Rockies, a 14,045-footer, was named Mount Bierstadt.

Toward the end of his career, tastes changed and critics took to complaining that he exaggerated beyond the limits of taste, that he lacked technical skill and that he flawed his gigantic canvases with too much distracting detail. No matter; he had given his adopted countrymen their most powerful visual impression of how it really felt to stand in the presence of the magnificent mountains of the West.

According to many of these same critics, Thomas Moran contributed more than Albert Bierstadt to the American people's perception and appreciation of the scenic marvels of the Western regions of the country. Unlike his well-schooled predecessor, Moran was largely self-taught. And his original introduction to the West was strictly secondhand.

In 1871, *Scribner's Monthly* of New York was preparing to publish an article called "The Wonders of

Indians and white trappers assemble in the verdant countryside at the foot of Wyoming's Wind River mountains for the 1837 rendezvous with fur traders. Miller spent a month painting the scene — and participating in the riotous revelry.

the Yellowstone" written by one N. P. Langford. But the magazine had no drawings to illustrate the piece except some crude pencil sketches by a soldier who had escorted the author. Richard Watson Gilder, a *Scribner's* editor, decided to improve them for publication. He hired his friend Thomas Moran, already one of *Scribner's* principal illustrators, to work from them and produce something more professional. Moran, fascinated by the spouting, steaming geysers he was asked to paint, longed to go West and see them for himself. Later that same year, he borrowed the necessary funds and wangled permission to tag along on a government expedition to Yellowstone under geologist Ferdinand Vandiveer Hayden.

Small and slender, Moran seemed to be the greenest sort of tenderfoot. He could not understand why stage drivers went armed against what they called road agents, since the name "agent" clearly indicated stagecoach personnel. He could not abide fried food, and on the trail Westerners ate almost nothing else. But if the West was a bit put off by Moran, the artist took to the West like an antelope.

His wiry slightness of stature proved an advantage when the party got into the mountains and had to work at high altitudes. "As light on his feet as a mountain goat," an admiring companion said of him. "He had no more conception of fear than if he were made of rubber, and the fall of a thousand feet was simply the question of how high he might rebound on striking the rocks below."

The renowned photographer, William Henry Jackson, was also a member of Ferdinand Hayden's entourage, and he and Moran soon formed a mutually admiring and enduring friendship. In those early years, a photographer's equipment was even more cumbersome than an artist's gear, and Moran was quick to lend Jackson a hand with it. The two of them were often ahead of the rest of the expedition, with Moran enthusiastically helping the photographer set up his tripod and unwieldy black boxes. Between times, the artist made his own detailed sketches and fed himself and Jackson bountifully on trout he skillfully snagged from mountain streams.

The wonders of the Yellowstone region filled Moran with an almost religious awe. He modestly told geologist Hayden, as they stood together amidst its hot

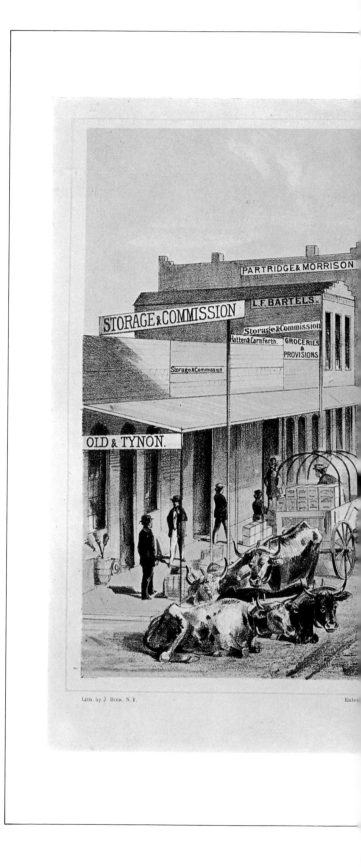

The hurly-burly of traffic on F Street, Denver, comes through in this scene by lithographer Alfred E. Mathews. Tradesmen grabbed up Mathews' sketches to promote their communities and wares; historians have found them even more valuable as a source of details on early Western towns.

F STREET, DENVER.

pools and the geysers and the crystalline formations, that "these beautiful tints are beyond the reach of human art." Moran quickly disproved his own assertion, however. His strong point as an artist was color—both watercolor and oil—and under the stimulus of his visit to Yellowstone, Moran's skills expanded at an exponential rate.

Back in the East that autumn, Moran the magazine illustrator established a studio in Newark, New Jersey, so that he could be near his market with New York editors. He turned out a series of Yellowstone drawings for *Scribner's* and produced voluminous quantities of watercolors and chromolithographs from his Yellowstone sketches. And then, following in Albert Bierstadt's broad trail, he began a mammoth seven-by-twelve-foot canvas of the Yellowstone canyon. "Watching the picture grow," commented his editor-friend Gilder, "was like keeping one's eyes open during the successive ages of world creation."

Meanwhile, in Washington, Ferdinand Hayden was busy lobbying for legislation to declare Yellowstone a national park—"as has been done," Hayden pointed out with perhaps a touch of bias, "with that far inferior wonder, the Yosemite Valley." His heaviest artillery in this endeavor were Jackson's photographs and Moran's sketches. In March 1872, Yellowstone became a national monument. So important was Moran's work as a factor in the passage of the national parks bill that the National Park Service later dubbed him "father of the park system." His own friends called him "Yellowstone" Moran.

Shortly after passage of the Yellowstone Park bill, Moran's spectacular panorama, *The Grand Canyon of the Yellowstone,* was hung in the nation's capital, first in the Smithsonian gallery and then in the office of the Speaker of the House. There it created such a sensation among Congressmen and their visiting constituents that Congress bought it from the artist Moran for $10,000, shipped it around the country for display in several major cities, and then, upon its return, hung it in the lobby of the Senate. It was the first landscape to be purchased by Congress and, according to art critic Clarence Cook, was "the only good picture to be found in the Capitol."

The press of his magazine commitments kept Moran occupied in his studio in Newark for more than a year. Then, in the summer of 1873, he joined Major John Wesley Powell on a surveying expedition through the Grand Canyon of the Colorado. Out of this venture he conceived a companion piece to his Yellowstone panorama, a seven-by-twelve-foot epic called *The Chasm of the Colorado,* which the U.S. Congress eventually purchased for another $10,000 to further grace the Senate lobby.

Late in the year of 1873, Thomas Moran was once again working by remote control, this time illustrating an article on the Rocky Mountains for *Picturesque America* from photographs taken by his friend Jackson. Of all the scenes that he had never seen, one fascinated him almost as much as had his beloved Yellowstone: this was the Mountain of the Holy Cross in Colorado, whose towering face was marked by a cross of snow. Once again he was overwhelmed by an obsession to gaze at the marvel with his own eyes. And so, in the summer of 1874, he persuaded James Stevenson of Hayden's staff to guide him to the miracle on the mountain.

Reaching a point from which the cross was visible proved to be, as Moran later wrote, "the toughest trial of strength I have ever experienced." It took two weeks of hard riding from Denver through the plains and mountains, across the Great Divide and up a neighboring peak before they achieved their goal. In the last few hours of climbing, their exhausted horses slipped repeatedly on rain-slick rocks and fallen timber. Moran and his party had wearily gained an elevation of 12,000 feet when the snowy cross—its shaft more than 1,100 feet long and the arms spanning 200 feet on either side—unfolded before them. Moran gazed at the sight for half an hour, and then turned back to camp with his guide.

The resulting painting was, in many ways, the triumph of his career as a painter of the West. Critics praised it lavishly, pronouncing it superior to either of his panoramas; and the *Aldine,* a New York monthly journal, described the canvas as "one of those exceptional professional leaps which bridge the chasm between reputation and immortality."

But for Moran the Yellowstone experience, which he transmitted so eloquently to his public, remained supreme. "I have wandered over a good part of the Territories and have seen much of the varied scenery of

BIERSTADT: GLORIFIER OF NATURE

"The Prince of Mountain Regions" was the title given to Albert Bierstadt by his admirers. A German-born New Englander with four years of formal art training, he went West for the first time at the age of 29 when he joined an expedition to Wyoming territory. In 10 years, his huge canvas monuments *(pages 136-143)* to what he called "the wildness and abandon of nature" were bringing up to $25,000, making him the highest-paid artist of the era.

Despite his quick fame, Bierstadt took himself lightly; here he poses for a satirical double exposure—taken by his brother—of one Albert Bierstadt pouring another a drink.

Surrounded by a gallery of curious Indians, the artist drafts one of hundreds of location sketches he made on his journeys through the Sierra Nevada in 1872 and 1873.

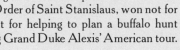

Among Bierstadt's trophies was the Russian Order of Saint Stanislaus, won not for art but for helping to plan a buffalo hunt during Grand Duke Alexis' American tour.

the Far West," he later wrote, "but that of the Yellowstone retains its hold upon my imagination with a vividness as of yesterday. The impression then made upon me by the stupendous and remarkable manifestations of nature's forces will remain with me as long as memory lasts."

Late in his career, to his considerable dismay, Moran learned of an ironic testament to the stature he had achieved as a Western artist. In his youth he had painted a darkly somber, impressionistic canvas and entitled it *Childe Roland to the Dark Tower Came.* Years later a New York art dealer, blessed with both an active imagination and a persuasive sales technique, dug the old canvas out of the gallery attic and sold it under the title *Lava Beds of Utah*—unabashedly assuring the buyer that Childe Roland was really a genuine, true-to-life Bannock Indian.

As memorable as the Western landscape to a very different school of artist was that other indomitable aspect of the frontier—the horseman. For two painters in particular, Frederic Sackrider Remington and Charles Marion Russell, the West became a stage on which their mounted heroes played out lives of exhilarating action, wild freedom, grace under hardship and masculine knight-errantry. Remington and Russell painted Indians and soldiers and cowboys, all in vigorous conflict with one another and with the harsh elements—and all of them hard-riding, fearless and enviable. Between them, these two celebrators of the cowboy put the Old West forever in the saddle, man and horse in a partnership undismayed by the devil himself. Somehow, out of their canvases the lowly cowpoke—in real life an overworked, underpaid, womanless, lonesome and usually unlettered laborer—emerged as the most heroic and exciting figure in the entire adventurous West. No matter that the legend was not quite the way things really were; it was enough to inspire generations with the belief that they had been and the wish that they could be again.

Frederic Remington was born in upstate New York in 1861, the son of a newspaper publisher turned Civil War cavalry colonel. Even as a young boy he exhibited a facility for sketching, scrawling crude but lively drawings of soldiers and horses in the margins of his school notebooks. By 17 he had grown into a burly, big-boned youth; sent to Yale, he succeeded mightily on the football field, but hardly at all in the newly established Yale Art School. The class he attended was made up of himself and one other student, a young man by the name of Poultney Bigelow; and Remington, although he became fast friends with "Big," found himself monumentally bored by the uninspiring, academic lectures that were delivered in the dingy, all but empty basement classroom.

He dropped out of college in 1880 when his father died and left him a modest inheritance. His mother, who had a low opinion of art, hounded him to get a real job and settle down. Over the next six months he took—and swiftly quit—several jobs, torn between doing what his mother expected of him and his desire to draw and paint. Then, in summer, he met a girl named Eva Caten whom he wooed assiduously—only to be turned away by her father as unlikely material for a husband. The sensible Mr. Caten was probably right, for when Remington did eventually marry he was often an absentee husband, and really felt so uneasy around women he once confided to a friend that he had "never drawn a woman—except once and then he had washed her out."

Nevertheless, Remington was sorely wounded and sought solace in a vagabonding trip to Montana. There, camping under the stars and sketching cowboys, he experienced his first taste of the wild, free life of the West. And those few months shaped him forever. In 1883, he invested his inheritance in a 160-acre sheep ranch near Kansas City.

Sheep-raising may have lacked the romance of cowpunching, but here at least was open land, where men broke broncos and lived and worked on horses. Remington reveled in his bachelor freedom, riding cross-country to visit yarn-spinning cronies, coursing jackrabbits at a dead run astride his golden-maned mare, Terra Cotta, drinking through the night with cowboys in the saloons of Kansas City, lassoing sunflowers for practice and the sheer joy of it. He minded his sheep, he sketched, and life was good but for a single flaw —the ranch was not making money.

After a year, Remington sold it and headed deep into the Southwest, wandering wherever his fancy took him and sketching as he went. He drew Cheyennes and Comanches in Indian Territory, hunted with

MORAN: EVANGELIST FOR YELLOWSTONE

Although Philadelphia-bred Thomas Moran had his problems in the West—he rode badly and detested the usual trail food—he emerged as one of its greatest landscape painters. Indeed, the numerous works that came from his five Western trips in the 1870s were so powerful, particularly his views of Yellowstone, that they played a major role in convincing Congress to establish a national park system.

Under the rapt gaze of his wife, Mary, Moran sits at the easel in his comfortable Newark, New Jersey, studio in the mid-1870s.

Moran displays a catch of trout, which he avidly sought for sport—and for an alternative to bacon, biscuits and canned food.

Moran's passion for Yellowstone inspired this monogram with which he signed many of his smaller works. He combined a stylized T and M in such a manner as to create a Y—for Yellowstone—in the center.

Moran finished the 7-by-12-foot *Grand Canyon of the Yellowstone* in two months after he returned from Wyoming. Bedazzled legislators, who had just made Yellowstone the first national park, appropriated $10,000 to buy the painting and later hung it in the Senate lobby.

More concerned than many Western landscapists with geological detail, Moran made
sketches like this to help him get the shapes
and colors just right in the final painting.

vaqueros in Mexico, sketched Apaches and cowhands
in Arizona, and came back to Kansas City after a few
months with a thick portfolio.

In the summer of 1884 he worked up his sketches
and at the same time tried his hand at saloon-keeping
with two friends in Kansas City. However what had
seemed at the time like a golden opportunity to earn income while painting turned into disaster. His partners
cheated him out of his one-third share, a predicament
that he was with some difficulty dissuaded from re-
solving with a gun.

His only success in this unhappy time was with
Eva. Returning to New York without friends or prospects, he managed to wear down her father's objections, married the girl and took her back to Kansas
City. But failure seemed to be Remington's lot. Although he doggedly kept sending his pictures to Eastern magazines, just one was accepted for publication.
Within a year he was forced to send Eva home to live

with her family and once again seek his fortune alone.

Somewhere during these trials he heard, as he later
wrote, of a "fabulously rich mine" which had been discovered "by a Negro named Seminole Bill, who had
disappeared." He set out with two acquaintances into
Arizona's Pinal Range to find the mine. It turned out
to be as elusive as Seminole Bill himself and Remington never found it. But his excursion happened to co-
incide with the United States Army's frustrating
pursuit of the renegade Apache, Geronimo, whose
swift and deadly raids were terrorizing settlers and prospectors in the territory.

"We were seated beside our little cooking fire about
9 o'clock in the evening," Remington wrote for Century Magazine a few years afterward, "engaged in
smoking and drowsily discussing the celerity of movement displayed by Geronimo. Conversation lapsed at
last and puffing our pipes and lying stretched on our
backs we looked up into the dark branches of the trees
above when I felt moved to sit up. To my unbounded
astonishment and consternation, there sat three Apaches on the opposite side of our fire, with their rifles
across their laps.

"'Heap hungry,' said one of the savage apparitions,
and again lapsed into silence.

"As we were not familiar with the personal appearance of Mr. Geronimo's countenance, we thought
we could see the old villain's features in our interloc-
utor's, and we began to get our artillery into shape
for use."

The visitors explained that they wanted food, not
fight, and departed peaceably when morning came.
That was as close as Remington ever got to Geronimo
—or, for that matter, the mine. But he did encounter
many more Apaches on his travels, and he spent considerable time in the company of government troops
pursuing Geronimo. All this, plus the workings of his
active imagination as he listened to campfire yarns of
desperate combat, was food for his sketchbook.

By the end of 1885 he was ready to try the New
York magazine market once again. Typically he arrived with barely $3.00 in his pocket. Eva journeyed
down to New York, and the two of them moved in
temporarily with Brooklyn friends.

His first small success came on January 9, 1886,
when one of the fruits of his Indian summer, a work

Moran climbed 12,000 feet to get this view of Colorado's Mountain of the Holy Cross—and for art's sake added a waterfall that could not be seen from his position.

called *Indian Scouts on Geronimo's Trail,* was used by *Harper's Weekly* as a full-page cover illustration. Soon thereafter he took an armload of unsold drawings into the offices of *Outing Magazine* and laid them on the desk of the art editor—none other than his old friend Poultney Bigelow.

"I was interrupted by a vast portfolio in the hands of some intruding one," Bigelow recalled later. "I did not even look up at the huge visitor but held out a hand for the drawings. He pushed one at me, and it was as though he had given me an electric shock. Here was the real thing, the unspoiled native genius dealing with Mexican ponies, cowboys, cactus, lariats and sombreros. These were the men of the real rodeo, parched in alkali dust, blinking out from barely opened eyes under the furious rays of the Arizona sun. I looked at the signature—Remington.

" 'It's an odd coincidence, I had a classmate at Yale,' I said to him. But before I could add another word, out he roared: 'Hell, Big, is that you?' And so it was. He had turned himself into a cowboy, and I had become a slave to a desk. Of course I bought all he had in his portfolio, and I loaded him with orders."

Suddenly Remington was on his way to becoming one of the era's best paid, most popular pictorial journalists and illustrators. His lusty horsemen began to crowd the pages of *Outing, Harper's Weekly, Youth's Companion* and even the scholarly *Century.* Very quickly, too, his work acquired the stature of real art; in 1887 his paintings were hung in exhibitions by the American Water Color Society and the National Academy of Design.

In spite of the critical acclaim—and the financial success that made it possible for him to build for his bride an imposing home in New Rochelle, New York —Remington continued to return to the West throughout the 1880s and into the 1890s. Gathering material for his paintings, he lived in cowcamps and Army barracks, absorbing the life of the plains, and listening to tales of the vanishing past. In December 1890, on assignment from *Harper's Weekly,* he was with General Nelson Miles in South Dakota and Montana to observe the Army's attempt to contain a ragtag band of renegade Sioux. He just missed the final agony at Wounded Knee—but painted the scene from descriptions supplied by surviving soldiers. The Wounded

Knee painting, a heroic and romantically inaccurate representation of two firing lines of soldiers and Indians trading volleys at close range, was one of the few departures from his almost unvarying theme—men and horses together, united in action.

It was a matter of pride with Remington that he was the first artist of any stature to portray accurately the action of a horse's legs in motion, particularly in the furious exertion of an all-out run or trying to throw an unwelcome rider. Critics scoffed when Remington depicted a horse running with all four feet off the ground at one time. Impossible, they said. But horses indeed ran that way, and it took Remington's keen eye to detect the fact.

His genius at portraying the horse became even more apparent around 1895 when he turned to sculpture. His interest in it was aroused by sculptor Frederick Ruckstull, who was then working on a life-sized equestrian statue near Remington's New Rochelle house. Ruckstull urged him to try the new medium, saying, "You will be able to draw on wax just as clearly as you do on paper."

Remington chose his own painting, *The Bronco Buster,* for a subject in his first attempt to work in wax and bronze. The resulting statue was an act of pure love, which few artists in history could have done so well, and none with such authority. "Only those who have ridden a bronco the first time it was saddled—or have lived through a railroad wreck—can form any conception of such an experience," he commented. When Remington had finished, and the figure was cast in some 50 pounds of bronze, he observed, "I wanted to do something which a burglar wouldn't have, moths eat, or time blacken. It is a great art and satisfying to me."

Bronze was probably the only medium with the tensile and twisting strength to support the wild action Remington portrayed in his sculpture. In *The Buffalo Horse,* only the two hind legs of a rearing buffalo support the bulk of the massive beast plus the weight of the Indian huntsman and horse impaled on his horns. In *Coming through the Rye,* showing four mounted cowpunchers on a spree, only 5 of 16 pounding hooves are in contact with the dirt.

In all, Remington turned out 25 bronzes, a small number in comparison with his enormous production of

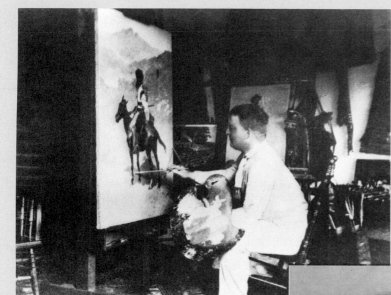

REMINGTON: "HE KNEW THE HORSE"

At 19, bored and unhappy in the East, Frederic Remington went West in 1881 seeking adventure and a fit subject for his talent. He found both in a wide-open world full of cowboys, soldiers, Indians—and particularly horses. He knew all types, from the husky cavalry mount to the tough little Comanche pony. He captured them perfectly in every position, standing or in a fury of bucking, legs curled under their bellies "like crabs." Remington suggested his epitaph should be: "He knew the horse."

Back in New York after a trip West, Remington works on a painting he had sketched earlier *(below)* as *The French Trapper.*

— *The French Trapper.* —

In the final painting, Remington turned his trapper into an Indian, wearing a blanket coat and carrying a brass-studded flintlock.

HARPER'S WEEKLY.

A JOURNAL OF CIVILIZATION.

VOL. XXX.—No. 1516.
Copyright, 1886, by HARPER & BROTHERS.

NEW YORK, SATURDAY, JANUARY 9, 1886.

TEN CENTS A COPY.
$4.00 PER YEAR, IN ADVANCE.

THE APACHE WAR—INDIAN SCOUTS ON GERONIMO'S TRAIL.—DRAWN BY FREDERIC REMINGTON.—[SEE PAGE 23.]

An Army patrol, led by scouts, pursues Geronimo along the Mexican border in Remington's first signed picture for *Harper's*.

more than 2,500 paintings and drawings. Most of this work was produced in an enormous, sunny studio in New Rochelle with a double door he designed wide enough to admit the live horse models he kept in a stable on his spacious grounds.

In the East he came to know Easterners who had fallen in love with the West — including Theodore Roosevelt and Owen Wister, the Philadelphia-born author of *The Virginian.* Frederic Remington, Roosevelt said, "is, of course, one of the most typical American artists we have ever had. The soldier, the cowboy and the rancher, the Indian, the horses and the cattle of the plains, will live in his pictures and bronzes, I verily believe, for all time."

Wister put it more succinctly: "Remington is a national treasure."

The same might well have been said of Remington's contemporary, Charles Russell. But Russell, who never really took himself seriously, was at least a dozen years behind Remington in winning his measure of fame and fortune. Born in St. Louis in 1864, young Charlie Russell hated school, hung around the Mississippi waterfront, and rode his pony with cavalier disregard for other people's lawns and flowers. The general impression he gave was of an uncombed and unwashed yet appealing ragamuffin, who was liked even by those who disapproved of him.

Oddly, this least arty of boys was a compulsive sculptor. When he was among a group of friends, he delighted in working away surreptitiously — on a piece of soap or a hunk of clay or a potato — and then suddenly producing a figure from his lap, like a magician triumphantly pulling a rabbit out of a hat. In March 1880, Charlie's parents despaired of ever civilizing him, and packed him off to work on the Montana sheep ranch of a friend. He did not last long. What the 16-year-old stripling wanted was to be a cowhand; he quit the job just ahead of being fired.

At this point Russell was broke, foodless and without possessions except for the decrepit clothes on his back and two horses — a black mare and a pinto named Monte who became his closest companion of the next 25 years. He might have actually starved had it not been for a grizzled hunter and prospector named Jake Hoover who found him riding aimlessly down a trail and took him along to the trapping grounds on the

METHOD OF SKETCHING AT SAN CARLOS.

south fork of the Judith River. Russell stayed with Hoover for two years, learning the mountains and the creatures thereof. He helped Hoover peddle elk meat to settlers and townsmen, but refused to slay any animal himself.

At last, in 1882, the long-awaited opportunity to become a cowhand occurred when he was offered a job as a night-hawk, or night-herder, for a cattle drive in central Montana. As it turned out, his love of the trade was not matched by aptitude. His clumsiness moved a crony to recall that "Kid Russell was no roughrider; he was always afoot in the saddle." But he was willing and hard working, and he cheerfully endured the hardships, including the blizzards of the Montana winter. And he was a great hand when it came to time off. The other cowpokes fondly remembered that "nobody could beat the Kid to the front door of the hottest place in town."

Although he still had no ambitions as an artist, he made little sketches of cowboy life to amuse himself. And on his nights off in the saloons, he entertained the

In his masterfully detailed oil painting *Cavalry Charge on the Southern Plains*, Frederic Remington shows well-disciplined United State

avalry troopers maintaining their cocked pistols at the prescribed ready position and keeping their mounts at a correctly controlled gallop.

other barflies by manipulating wax or clay out of sight while his companions placed bets on the outcome. Once a fellow drinker, much taken by the figurine emerging from Charlie's fingers, offered to buy it from him and asked how much. "Ten dollars," Russell said. "I'll give you five dollars," the buyer countered. Russell mashed the statuette, split the ball of wax in two and, in minutes, produced a half-sized duplicate. "Sold!" he said, and bought a round of drinks with the proceeds.

In the winter of 1888, on impulse, Charlie Russell saddled Monte and rode north into Canada, where for six months he lived with a band of Blackfeet. He became as Indian as he could, letting his hair grow and discarding his store clothes for buckskin. He learned how to use Indian signs and speak the Blackfoot tongue, became the bosom friend of a chief called Sleeping Thunder, and fell half in love with a maiden called Kee-Oh-Mee. He may even have considered marriage to her. He later took to writing range tales; in one of them he commented, in the semiliterate backcountry style he affected: "Most folks don't bank much on squaw-men. But I've seen some mighty good ones doubled up with she Injuns. Men's got finicky about matin'. I guess if I'd come to the country earlier, squaws would'a looked good enough."

During his Indian sojourn he sketched and painted as much as limited materials permitted. On one of his few canvases he painted a scene entitled *Canadian Mounted Police with Indian Prisoners,* using no more than five colors and employing crude brushes that he improvised himself, possibly by chewing the ends of matchsticks or green twigs. When he ran out of scraps of canvas and paper he took to producing the scenes around him—Indians in their villages, buffalo hunts, encounters between Indians and white men—on tanned buckskin, wood and tin.

Russell admired Indians and mourned the indignities to which white men had subjected them. "Unkle Sam tells him to play Injun once a year and he dances under the flag that made a farmer out of him," he wrote. "Once nature gave him everything he wanted, now the agent gives him bib overalls, hookes his hands around plow handles and tell him its a good thing push it along maby it is but their having a hell of a time prooving it."

In the spring of the next year Charlie Russell went back to being a roving cowboy, living the life which

When 16-year-old Charles Marion Russell set out for Montana from St. Louis in 1880, he took with him the American boy's fantasy of being a cowpoke. For fun, he also brought along a few pencils and brushes. Despite long practice under the eyes of real live ranch hands, The Kid, as he was dubbed, never became any great shakes as a rider or roper. But at the easel, where he was strictly self-taught, he became one of the West's most renowned painters. In his 40-year career, he poured a zealot's excitement—and a fine representationalist's authenticity—into thousands of sketches, watercolors, paintings and sculptures of cowboy exploits.

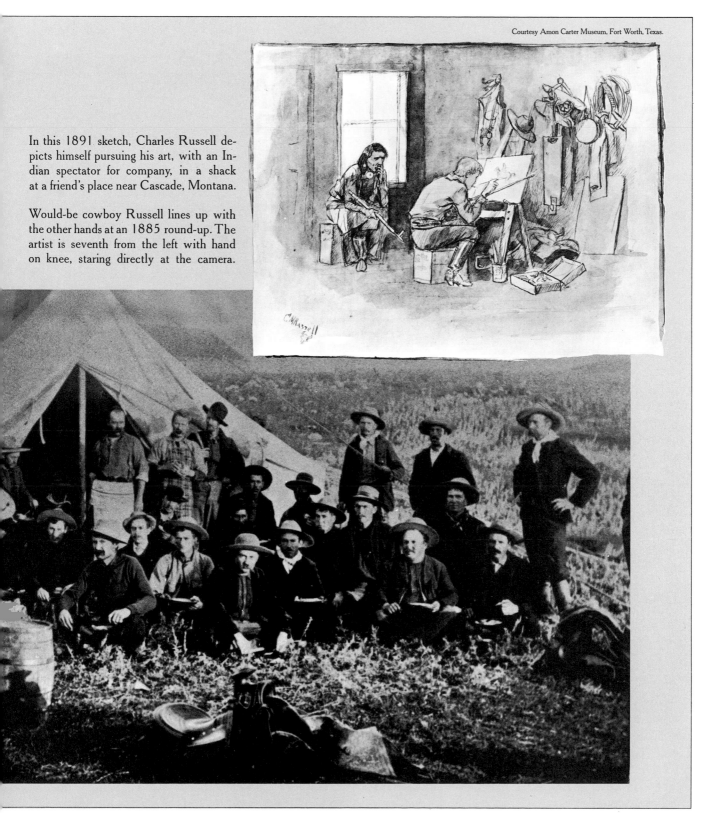

In this 1891 sketch, Charles Russell depicts himself pursuing his art, with an Indian spectator for company, in a shack at a friend's place near Cascade, Montana.

Would-be cowboy Russell lines up with the other hands at an 1885 round-up. The artist is seventh from the left with hand on knee, staring directly at the camera.

131

would always remain close to his heart. His operating base was the Judith Basin in Montana, which he had adopted as his home and which, in turn, had adopted him. With some pride, the local newspaper in Lewistown referred to him as "the cowboy artist." For during his wanderings he had acquired a modest local reputation for his impromptu sketches, paintings and statuettes of range life. In 1890 he went so far as to produce a portfolio of cowboy and Indian scenes under the title of *Studies of Western Life.* But Charlie Russell never tried very hard to make money out of art; generally, he gave away — or simply threw away — his earnings as well as his work.

In spite of Russell's own disregard, more and more people in the range country began to notice and covet his work. To his great astonishment in 1891 a Lewistown banker paid him $25 to paint the figure of a cowboy on the door of the bank vault. The $25 vanished the same night, spent on convivial companions in the nearest saloon.

Later in that same year he received a totally unexpected invitation to come to Great Falls in central Montana and take on a steady job painting. The offer came from the bartender at the Brunswick Saloon. "I received a letter from Charlie Green, better known as 'Pretty Charlie,'" Charlie Russell wrote long afterward, "saying that if I would come to that camp I would make $75 a month and grub. It looked good, so I saddled my gray and packed Monte and pulled my freight for that berg."

On arrival in Great Falls he learned that what Pretty Charlie had in mind was an artistic sweatshop. The enterprising bartender expected Charlie Russell to paint pictures for 12 hours a day for a year and turn the product over for Green to sell as his own property. Russell, understandably, lost interest in Pretty Charlie's offer. "I argued there was some difference in painting and sawing wood, so we split up and I went to work for myself."

Russell and a coterie of friends, including a cook, several wintering cowpokes and "a prizefighter out of work," set up housekeeping in a shack on the edge of town. Russell painted while his housemates acted as his agents, trading the paintings for past-due bar bills mostly, but now and then for necessities such as groceries. The good life came to its inevitable end — and

Russell's *The Herd Quitter,* painted in 1897 and based on the artist's firsthand experience, shows cowhands wielding lariats to haul in a wayward steer, a Longhorn-Durham crossbreed of a kind that roamed the range at that time.

success began to set its brand on Charlie Russell — in 1895 when he met in the home of a friend a spunky 16-year-old girl from Kentucky named Nancy Cooper. They were married in 1896, and when they had settled down in the town of Great Falls, Nancy set about the challenging task of reforming her 32-year-old husband. She never fully succeeded, but she did tame him enough to keep him at work in his studio (which turned out to be not all that difficult) and enough to prevent him from giving away his art (which proved to be exceedingly difficult).

Under Nancy's firm hand Russell worked diligently on a series of paintings and drawings for *Field and Stream,* including *Lewis and Clark Meeting with Mandans* and *Before the White Man Came.* He did pen sketches, and small wax figures of buffaloes and Indians, such as *Old-Man Indian, The Buffalo Hunt* and *Counting Coup,* which he cast into bronze. There were a few hard years, in spite of the fact that his work came into increasingly greater demand.

But times improved dramatically for the Russells after Nancy realized that she could sell his work for vastly higher prices than Charlie had been accustomed to getting. In 1898 modest, head-scratching, homespun Charlie Russell was completely dumfounded when Nancy received $6,000 from a New York gallery for a painting called *Whose Meat?* showing a mountain man protecting his kill from a hungry bear. And he was just plumb ashamed when she had the nerve to ask $15,000 for another of his paintings. "It's too much, too much," he muttered, and slunk away from the bargaining session with his disreputable hat pulled down low over his head.

Yet it was not too much to pay for a work that would keep alive in perpetuity the look of the Old West. For by this time, the real face of the Old West was living only in the images that men such as Charlie Russell, Frederic Remington and the other roving artists had formed.

All of them knew it, and each felt, in his own way, both a nostalgic sorrow at the loss of the reality and a pride in having preserved its reflections. Remington, musing once beside a Montana campfire, summed up eloquently: "I knew the wild riders and the vacant land were about to vanish forever, and the more I considered the subject, the bigger the Forever loomed."

After settling down in Great Falls, Montana, in 1897, Russell built himself this cluttered studio cabin where he loved to roll a cigarette and reminisce over a glass of whiskey with visiting cronies from his earlier days as a cowhand.

Extravagant panoramas of the wilderness

Of all the artists who went West in the 19th Century Albert Bierstadt, the German-born landscapist, most embodied the Victorian Romanticism of the day. The scenes he painted were outsized, dramatic, grander than nature. In his vast canvases, maelstroms of clouds swirled around mountains that glowed so brilliantly in the sun that the light seemed to come from inside the earth. Trees and crags grew to heroic size, while the men and animals in his pictures were reduced to Lilliputian scale, thus enhancing everything else.

Bierstadt's popularity lasted barely two decades. In the 1880s critics attacked his exaggerations and called his work "sensational and meretricious"; his commissions declined, and while he never lacked for money—he later married the widow of a millionaire—the art world rendered him the ultimate insult in 1889 when a Paris gallery refused to exhibit even one of his landscapes.

Towering cliffs dwarf riders in *Platte River, Nebraska*, 1863.

Clouds swathe a Matterhorn-like *Mount Whitney,* c. 1874.

Sunlight glows from *The Rocky Mountains, Long's Peak*, 1877.

Yosemite was never so lovely as in *Sierra Nevada Morning*. 1870.

4 | Visitors from abroad

If the confrontation of untamed West and civilized East fascinated Americans, it was drama of an almost cosmic order to Europeans. When the earl of Dunraven, touring Montana Territory in 1874, came across an Indian recoiling in disgust from an Eastern dude (*right*), he was moved to flights of prose that made James Fenimore Cooper seem downright dour: "Smooth and easy as a hawk's flight, the young warrior sweeps along, sitting on his foam-flecked mustang with the yielding gracefulness of a willow bending to the breeze, an embodiment of savage life, full of wild beauty and bright colour; glancing with supreme and undisguised contempt upon the plug-hat, black store coat and pants of some newly-arrived representative of civilization."

Almost as soon as Americans became aware of the lands beyond the Mississippi, Europeans like Dunraven arrived to describe the wilderness and its development to people back home. Not all of them had kind words to say: "Cowboys," wrote one traveler, "impressed me as brutal and cowardly," while another found the Indians "horrible looking, dirty and miserable." But mostly they were enthralled. The Polish journalist Henry Sienkiewicz gushed that "the soul soon ceases to be a thing apart, having been absorbed by the powerful presence of the prairie like a drop of water in the sea."

Other foreign visitors found remembrances of Europe in the new land. Sir Richard Burton, after viewing the Salt Lake valley, commented that "Switzerland and Italy lay side by side." And mining engineer Louis Laurent Simonin practically reclaimed the West for France. "The country is full of French names conferred on it by our former trappers," he wrote, citing places from Prairie du Chien to Des Moines. In fact, said Simonin "the very word 'prairie' was borrowed from our language."

Chancing on a scene in Virginia City that symbolized the changing West, Dunraven ordered his

personal artist, Valentine Bromley, to record it. Bromley made dozens of drawings and paintings of the earl's trip to the Yellowstone area.

The Wasp

SAN FRANCISCO, SATURDAY, JANUARY 31, 1885.

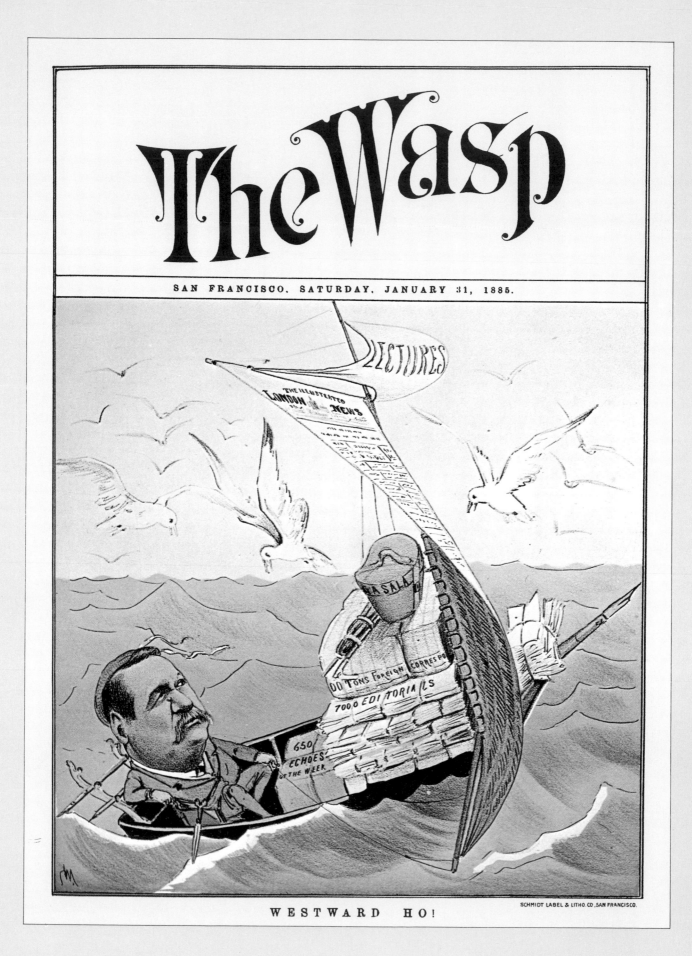

WESTWARD HO!

Old World perspectives on "Uncle Samuel's" West

Windham Thomas Wyndham-Quin, the fourth Earl of Dunraven and Mountearl, had no intention of becoming a Western chronicler when he arrived in Colorado in the summer of 1874. The 34-year-old nobleman, master of 30,000 lush acres back in Ireland and Wales, had come on a mundane errand—to check on some tracts of ranchland he had bought as an investment after two previous Western visits. But Dunraven was an insatiable adventurer and, after putting his affairs in order, he set off on a wilderness excursion. As his lordship phrased it, "Having two or three months of spare time, I determined to pay a visit to the far-famed region of the Upper Yellowstone, and to judge for myself whether the thermal springs and geysers there situated were deserving of the superiority claimed for them." He also planned to do some hunting, since "the pursuit of large game is to me a great delight." Greater delights than that awaited him: his side trip would so please Dunraven that he would be unable to resist sharing it with the world.

To travel in his accustomed style, the tall, handsome earl assembled a considerable body of retainers. They included his local guide, rancher Fred Boteler; his consultant on all things Western, noted frontiersman Texas Jack Omohundro; his own English artist, whom he employed as a supplement to his newfangled camera; his personal physician; his Scottish gunbearer; his all-purpose servant; and his collie, Tweed.

By American standards, it was a grossly oversized party to tend to the needs and whims of a single traveler. But compared to the entourages that several other European aristocrats brought with them to the West, Dunraven's group was modest to the point of deprivation. Two decades earlier, for example, Sir George Gore, a stupendously wealthy friend of his uncle's, had maintained adequate standards of comfort on a three-year-long hunting expedition by taking along 40 employees, plus 112 horses, three milk cows and enough champagne to float a small boat.

Dunraven spent several glorious weeks sightseeing and hunting in Yellowstone, which had been established as a national park just two years before. Late one afternoon as the party made its way toward the northern border of Yellowstone, the earl ordered a halt at the foot of Mount Washburn, a 10,243-foot peak that promised an easy climb and admirable vistas. Ominous rain clouds were scudding toward the travelers, but Dunraven was so eager to see the view from the top of the mountain that he refused to postpone the ascent until morning.

Before long he and his guide reached Mount Washburn's granite summit, at the very crest of the continental divide, and there they were greeted by a panorama far exceeding Dunraven's expectations. His eye encompassed hundreds of square miles of forest and upland prairie, lakes and mountains. Many small streams far below him flowed off in various directions to join larger streams, and these, he knew, alternately fed the Missouri, the Colorado, the Green, the Snake and other powerful Western rivers.

Awestruck by the spectacle, Dunraven sat down on a rock, gazed far and wide and thought poetic thoughts. More than anything else, it was this view—the perfect climax to his splendid excursion—that impelled him to write a fine volume of travel reminiscences, *The Great Divide*. In the book, he said of Mount Washburn: "Stretching out its arms between the streams, it seems

The Wasp, a San Francisco magazine, lampoons the arrival in 1885 of lecturer and *Illustrated London News* contributor George Augustus Sala, one of many illustrious Britons who reported on the American West. Sala's unhedged opinion: "a wonderful country and wonderful people."

Standing on a Wyoming ridge, the earl of Dunraven shares binoculars with his physician. When viewing such scenes, he said, "the senses are hushed, the nerves soothed, the soul steeped in the infinite beauty."

Standing on a Wyoming ridge, the earl of Dunraven shares binoculars with his physician. When viewing such scenes, he said, "the senses are hushed, the nerves soothed, the soul steeped in the infinite beauty."

to say to one, 'Run in this direction,' and to another, 'Flow in that.' From it has been traced out the geography of the country. The main divisions, the great centres of trade, together with the natural features that sway the fates of men and nations, radiate thence." He concluded that Mount Washburn should be "sacred ground" for every citizen of the United States.

Dunraven sat meditating atop his mountain until Boteler informed him that it was getting dangerously dark and that—"unless I had concluded to take root there"—they had better climb down posthaste. They did not reach camp until long after nightfall, but the descent was rainless and—to the earl—disappointingly uneventful. As he lamented in his book, "I never have an adventure worth a cent; nobody ever scalps me; I don't get 'jumped' by highwaymen. It never occurs to a bear to hug me, and my very appearance inspires feelings of dismay or disgust in the breast of the puma or mountain lion. It is true that I have often been horribly frightened, but generally without any adequate cause."

Dunraven's wit and modesty helped to popularize his book in England. Characteristically, he made light of its success. "Some clergy," he said, "bought *The Great Divide* supposing it to be a theological work expounding the separation of the sheep and the goats." After his dalliance with authorship, he resumed his usual round of aristocratic diversions, which included yacht-racing, fox hunting, government service, lovely women and bright coversation. But he returned occasionally to the West, and in 1877 he financed the building of a large English-style hotel near Longs Peak in Colorado. For decades the establishment, aptly but unimaginatively named the English Hotel, was considered the best in the region.

Fortunately for the unveiling and growth of the American West, Dunraven's enthusiasm for travel was the ruling passion of a whole species of 19th Century Eu-

ropeans. Like him, they were members of the well-off, well-educated upper classes, and they avidly cultivated innumerable hobbies, pastimes, skills and studies. They would dash about the globe to hunt challenging game, to collect rare plants and examine rock formations, or simply to enjoy the excitement of visiting faraway lands and seeing exotic peoples. Venturing abroad in ever-increasing numbers, these tireless enthusiasts made the United States their favorite faraway land, and they had only to trek beyond the Missouri River to view their favorite exotic peoples: Westerners and Indians. The American frontier offered so many thrilling sights and experiences that an English traveler wrote in 1860: "A tour through the domains of Uncle Samuel without visiting the wide regions of the Far West, would be like seeing 'Hamlet' with the part of the Prince of Denmark omitted."

To heighten the pleasures of a Western journey, many of the foreign visitors wrote lively accounts of everything they did and saw. En route, they kept journals and set down their impressions in letters to friends back home; and on their return, they published articles and books for the enlightenment of their less fortunate countrymen. Nothing Western was too diffuse or trivial to escape their detailed discussion and candid judgment—the weather (unpredictable), the natural resources (unlimited), the food and lodging (atrocious), the clothing (picturesque but malodorous), the political institutions (makeshift and baffling), chewing tobacco (unspeakable). Of the Westerner's universal addiction to chewing, one British visitor asked peevishly, "Why does the Westerner spit? It can't amuse him, and it doesn't interest his neighbours." Another Englishman admired the chewers' accurate volleys of tobacco juice but admitted that "when you are surrounded with shooters you feel nervous."

Though the European chroniclers wrote almost exclusively for readers in their own country, their West-

Near the northern entrance to Yellowstone, the approach of Sioux warriors gives Dunraven (*center*) and his party a suspenseful moment. "Man," he noted, "is the most dangerous beast that roams the forest."

ern commentaries inadvertently proved helpful to the Americans. Some of the earliest scientific studies of the West were made by pioneering German naturalists such as the redoubtable Prince Maximilian and Duke Paul Wilhelm of Württemberg. Paul Wilhelm made no less than eight surveys of Western flora and fauna between 1823 and 1851 (*pages 152-155*). In later years, when much of the West was secured for civilization by multiplying settlements and improving transportation, elegant foreign visitors kept an eye peeled for investment opportunities, and the glowing accounts they sent home brought the West a liberal transfusion of capital and sturdy immigrants.

In fact, the Europeans served a function no Americans could fill. For one thing, their Old World manners and attitudes broadened the outlook—and sometimes tickled the ribs—of the isolated Westerners whom they met in their travels. More important, the Europeans came at a time when most Westerners were too busy building their new society to step back and appraise it; foreign visitors had both the leisure and the detachment to do just that. Perceptive and worldly, they served as interpreters of the West and the Western character, and in that role they did much to remind frontiersmen of both their shortcomings and their undervalued achievements.

By the time Dunraven's book appeared, virtually every country in Europe was sending travelers to the trans-Mississippi realm. Some of these visitors made the trip mainly to see kinsmen who had settled there —Germans in Texas, Scandinavians in Nebraska and some eastern Europeans in Kansas and California. In addition, a smattering of well-to-do Frenchmen and Italians were traveling about to inspect the storied curiosities of the West. But the English, grown rich on the proceeds of their empire and not confronted with a language barrier, were the most numerous and most wide-ranging of the travelers—just as they had been the first

Huddled under an elk-hide shelter during a downpour, Dunraven's group lingers over afternoon tea. "If a man wishes to be comfortable in camp," commented the Earl, "he will find himself continually disappointed."

national group to visit the American frontier in force.

The first tantalizing reports on the West from British chroniclers had commenced wafting homeward as early as the 1820s, when merchants for the Crown-chartered Hudson's Bay Company sent back encouraging descriptions of the Oregon country from their fur-trading posts there. Then came big-game hunters who rhapsodized about the West chiefly by word of mouth; probably the first British Nimrod was Sir William Drummond Stewart, who in the 1830s traveled as far as the Rocky Mountains to match his marksmanship against the ponderous buffalo, the noble elk and the agile mountain sheep, not to mention assorted bears and antelopes. In 1849, hundreds of British fortune seekers joined the gold rush to California and wrote home of the glories of the Sierra Nevada country, whether or not they struck it rich there.

However, even in the 1850s, information remained spotty, and popular English notions of the West were based largely — and unreliably — on the romantic novels of James Fenimore Cooper, a New York gentleman-farmer who had never ventured farther west than Detroit. What would-be British travelers needed most was a comprehensive report, written from their own point of view and offering them enough hard detail and practical advice to permit sensible planning for journeys in the wilderness.

No one did more to satisfy these needs, or to interest Englishmen in the West, than Sir Richard Burton, who set out to tour the wilds in 1860. Sir Richard's derring-do had already made him a celebrity. At the age of 39, he had fought in the Crimean War and in India; had explored Africa with an expedition that found the principal source of the Nile; and, disguised as an Arab, had slipped into the Moslems' forbidden holy city of Mecca. Burton was not the first infidel to invade Mecca, but his description of the city was by far the most detailed and accurate. ◉

The scientific treasures of a German naturalist

One of the earliest foreign visitors to the West was an earnest young German nobleman by the name of Duke Paul Wilhelm of Württemberg. Arriving in 1823, the 25-year-old Duke came not to paint, nor primarily to write, nor even to savor an adventure. He regarded himself as a natural scientist, and he possessed a single-minded determination to catalogue the flora and fauna of this strange New World.

So little did the Duke care about the amenities of rank and wealth that he traveled incognito, with only a single servant. Indeed when the man took ill as they voyaged up the Missouri River aboard a fur-company keelboat, Duke Paul left him with some friendly Omaha Indians and pressed on alone.

During his three-month exploration of the upper Missouri Valley, he fought a grizzly bear, faced down a mutinous boat crew and participated in a shooting contest in which "my exceptionally good gun won for me the best prizes." But his attention to science never wavered for long. During the expedition, he found and classified several thousand plants, birds, insects and animals, and he also gathered a priceless trove of Indian artifacts.

Over the next 35 years, Paul returned to the West seven more times, and the treasures he carried home — including those shown here and on the following pages — grew into the world's largest private collection of Western natural history. But the Duke was more than just a gleaner and classifier: he was also an astute observer of the Indians he encountered. He was struck, for example, by the fact that Indians thought it laudable to steal horses or women, but that none would raid an enemy's unguarded garden of corn or pumpkins. A Pawnee medicine man explained to the scholarly visitor that he and the tribal elders performed rites to guard ripening vegetables from theft. When Paul asked whether the Indians really believed such taboos, the medicine man replied with a straight face, "Great father, if the enemies did not believe, old men would starve and priests perish."

BURROWING OWL

BLACK HAWK

STELLER'S JAY

CHEROKEE HUNTING BAG

CROW MOCCASINS

PASSENGER PIGEON

RED FOX

OTO QUIVER

SIOUX TOBACCO POUCH

BIGHORN SHEEP

POTAWATOMI HEADDRESS

BLACKFOOT SCALPING
KNIFE AND SHEATH

In his role as a man of letters, Sir Richard wrote books and articles on almost every conceivable subject, from falconry to military tactics to the folkways of African tribes. These outpourings were a perfect reflection of his character: pompous and intolerant, but also shrewd, vigorous and filled with a Rabelaisian gusto for life. Finding himself at loose ends after returning from an African trip in 1859, Burton decided to bring his literary talents to bear on the American West; and he knew full well that his many English admirers stood ready and eager to buy his book.

The starting point for Burton's tour was the railhead of St. Joseph, Missouri. There Sir Richard laid in supplies, logging them for the benefit of those with the gumption to follow him. His list included a pocket sextant and two compasses for navigation, a thermometer for air temperature, and—in preparation for the stage trip—"cigars in extraordinary quantities, as the driver either receives or takes the lion's share." For comfort, "there is nothing better than the old English tweed shooting-jacket," and, he added, "Let no false shame cause you to forget your hat-box and your umbrella."

Weapons, of course, were indispensable. Burton's arsenal consisted of two rifles and two revolvers. He discoursed on the optimum uses of these and other weapons, and offered instructions on the art of Western gunslinging: "The revolver should be carried with its butt to the fore, and when drawn it should not be levelled as in target practice, but directed towards the object, by means of the right fore-finger laid flat along the cylinder whilst the medius draws the trigger. The instinctive consent between eye and hand, combined with a little practice, will soon enable the beginner to shoot correctly from the hip; all he has to do, is to think that he is pointing at the mark, and pull."

Sir Richard's lethal hardware was not intended merely for hunting game; he cheerfully confessed to "the mundane desire of enjoying a little skirmishing with the savages." To this end, he had acquired letters of introduction to the commanders of several military districts, incorrectly assuming that these officers were under constant siege by one or another Indian tribe and that they would be profusely grateful for the formidable help of a genuine British soldier.

By the time all of his gear was assembled, Burton had found the local mint juleps so delicious that he was reluctant to leave St. Joseph. But he finally wrested himself away, boarded a westbound stagecoach, and made acquaintance with "a traditionally familiar feature" of this mode of conveyance—the chuckholes "which render travelling over the prairies at times a sore task." Sir Richard nonetheless took all the jolting and tossing in high spirits and labored with almost monkish dedication in his self-appointed role as British literary guide to the West. For potential immigrants, he carefully worked up a mile-by-mile, day-by-day itinerary from St. Joseph to Salt Lake City. He interrogated fellow wayfarers and calculated that a wagon party of six would require, among other things, two yoke of oxen, a milk cow, 24 pounds of raisins and a bushel of dried beans. The cost of their basic outfitting, he continued, would come to exactly $490.98.

Burton's stagecoach traveled along the Platte River, which happened to be one of several routes then under consideration by the U.S. Congress for a transcontinental railroad. Since Sir Richard was aware that British capitalists were interested in investing in the railroad, he pointed out that the valley of the Platte "offers a route scarcely to be surpassed for natural gradients, requiring little beyond the superstructure for light trains; and by following up its tributary—the Sweetwater—the engineer finds a line laid down by nature to the foot of the South Pass of the Rocky Mountains." For the benefit of prospective settlers as well as railroad investors, Burton added that, even in arid stretches, the river route offered "never-failing supplies of water, and, in places, fuel. Its banks will shortly supply coal to take the place of the timber that has thinned out." Sir Richard's appraisal of the route was right on the mark, of course. Though his recommendations had no effect on the decision, Congress authorized the building of the transcontinental railroad along the Platte River valley just two years after his trip.

At length Sir Richard reached Salt Lake City and quickly discovered that the town was seriously lacking in several respects. His hotel was short on servants and boot polish; and since the Mormons insisted on public temperance, he found no saloons and no mint juleps: "Bottles and decanters," he noted with aggrieved surprise, "were not forthcoming." He also concluded that the Mormon practice of polygamy was far from being as interesting as it had been advertised. "I looked

The lederhosen tales of Heinrich Möllhausen

To his doting fans he was known as the "James Fenimore Cooper of Germany"—yet even the prolific Cooper would have had difficulty keeping up with Heinrich Balduin Möllhausen. Over the course of a long career, the Potsdam novelist helped shape his country's view of the West by churning out more than a hundred volumes of frontier adventure.

High output was not the only similarity between Möllhausen and Cooper. Many of his stories were plainly modeled on the American writer's *Leatherstocking Tales.* In *The Half-breed,* for example, Möllhausen created a crafty frontier character named Lefèvre who bore an uncanny resemblance to Cooper's Natty Bumppo. In both *Savage Blood* and *The Mercenary,* he portrayed a noble Indian who was the sole survivor of his tribe—the Last Mohican reincarnated.

Still, Möllhausen had more going for him than a cast of Cooper-like heroes. Unlike most foreign novels about the American frontier, his stories were laden with authentic detail. In 1849 he had embarked on a three-year journey through the West that involved him in all sorts of high drama: at one point he was rescued from almost certain death in a Nebraska blizzard by a band of Oto tribesmen and spent the next month living with and observing his saviors.

After a quick trip home in 1853, he returned to the West for a yearlong stint as the topographer on a government survey of a possible transcontinental railway route. In Oklahoma, he witnessed prairie fires and buffalo stampedes; in New Mexico, he was introduced to the Zuñi and Pueblo civilizations; in Arizona, he stood in awe before the Petrified Forest and Painted Desert.

When Möllhausen finally settled down in Potsdam, his Western ex-

On his second trip to the West in 1854, Möllhausen shows off his frontier duds.

periences all came into vivid focus. "The mind's eye, searching the past, sees and comprehends more sharply than the body's eye once did," he said, and over the years his mind's eye dimmed not a whit. In 1904, a year before his death at the age of 80, he could still say of himself that "memories of the West made his blood race with excitement, taking him back to the days when he recognized no master other·than the one who created and bejeweled the prairie; days when he fearlessly met the numbing snowstorm, the raging sea of fire and the cunning Indian foe."

in vain," he said, "for the outhouse-harems, in which certain romancers had informed me that wives are kept, like any other stock."

Sir Richard spent three weeks in Salt Lake City and environs and reached some weighty conclusions about the Mormons. Because most Mormons were of working-class English stock, Sir Richard called their religion "the faith of the poor," and accused its ambitious adherents of "a materialism so levelling that even the materialist must reject it." But like virtually everyone else who had visited the place, he was forced to acknowledge that Mormon diligence had made Utah an outstanding success, and furthermore that "in point of mere morality, the Mormon community is perhaps purer than any other of equal numbers."

Having delivered himself of these social judgments, Sir Richard left Salt Lake City and went on to matters at which he was better qualified. Though he never got a chance to fight Indians, he was a quick study and presented creditable assessments of the tribes' martial skills and the U.S. government's muddled Indian policy. He described the great Sioux nation as "one of the most warlike and numerous in the U.S. territory," unsurpassed in single combat on horseback. "They are not, however, formidable warriors; want of discipline and of confidence in one another render them below their mark. Like the Moroccans in their last war with Spain, they never attack when they should, and invariably attack when they should not."

In spite of his general scorn of non-English methods of warfare, Burton was fascinated by scalping, which he called a "solemn rite." After questioning various soldiers and settlers about the practice, he gave his readers a lurid description of the operation, complete with sound effects: "When the Indian sees his enemy fall he draws his scalp-knife, and twisting the scalp-lock — which is left long for that purpose, and boastfully braided or decorated with some gaudy ribbon or with the war-eagle's plume — round his left hand, makes with the right two semicircular incisions about the part to be removed. The skin is next loosened with the knife point, if there be time to spare and if there be much scalp to be taken. The operator then sits on the ground, places his feet against the subject's shoulders by way of leverage, and holding the scalp-lock with both hands he applies a strain which soon brings off the spoils with

a sound which, I am told, is not unlike 'flop.' "

Sir Richard could not resist some passing remarks on the quality of Western justice. As the Westerners themselves admitted, their jerry-built version of law and order left something to be desired; and Burton unsympathetically cited a certain murder case as if to suggest that its miscarriage of justice was fairly typical. A Westerner in an unidentified town had shot an enemy to death in the midst of several bystanders, and they testified in court that the accused had first warned them with a shouted order that Burton expurgated thusly: "Stoop down while I shoot the son of a dog (female)." The prosecution cited that command as clear evidence of premeditated murder, but the accused argued that his intended victim had been a real female dog, not the deceased. The jury acquitted the culprit, who happened to be popular in town, and the judge approved of the verdict.

With his curiosity satisfied, Sir Richard returned to England in December 1860. There his book was published in 1861 under the title *The City of the Saints and Across the Rocky Mountains to California.* Unfortunately for its sales as a travel guide, the Americans were fighting their Civil War, and the widespread unpleasantries blocked easy access to the West until 1865. Meanwhile, Burton married and settled down to a career in the consular service. He never returned to the West but retained for it feelings of affection and optimism. The region's drawbacks, such as Indian attacks, were grandly dismissed by Sir Richard as only temporary obstacles in "the great current of mankind, which, ceaseless as the Gulf Stream, ever courses from east to west." And before long, Sir Richard's book was swelling the current of westbound Englishmen.

In May of 1869, the long-awaited transcontinental railroad was completed, ushering in the age of Western tourism. With overland travel now reasonably swift, the prosperous British responded in droves, streaming into the great Western interior. They generally agreed that the new sleeping cars were superior to the railroad coaches at home, though Lady Duffus Hardy complained of the overheated stoves: "The Americans, I think, as a race will stand more *baking* in their travels than any other civilized people." Without exception, however, they shuddered at the accommodations in the

new Western towns. Sportsman Charles Messiter complained that his hotel in Cheyenne "contained only one room for men, in which there were 27 beds, each meant for two. You never knew who you were going to have as a companion—very frequently a half-drunken waggon-driver, who before he got into bed deposited a loaded revolver under the pillow."

But then the British discovered Colorado—and started colonizing America all over again. In the last three decades of the century, so many Britons arrived in Colorado as settlers and investors—not to mention those who came as hunters and tourists—that the state was sometimes called "England beyond the Missouri."

The most obvious of Colorado's appeals to the English was its splendid climate. Its Rocky Mountain air, declared the noted British travel writer William Baillie-Grohman, was "dry and sparkling as perhaps none other on the globe. It seems to be composed not of one-fifth, but of five-fifths of oxygen. You feel that it is air which has never before been breathed." This champagne atmosphere attracted many English sufferers from lung ailments—and cured more than a few. In fact the mortality rate was so low that Englishman Charles Russell facetiously asked a Coloradan whether anyone died thereabouts. "Very few," was the reply. "They had to shoot a man a little further west, to give their cemetery a start."

Colorado Springs—described by an Englishman as "a charming big village, like the well-laid-out suburb of some large eastern city"—was the favorite resort of tubercular Britons on the mend. The town, dubbed "Li'l Lunnon," even had its own English mag-

159

Sir Richard Burton, English adventurer-writer, models the garb he wore to enter the sanctum of Mecca. His interest in arcane religions made the Mormon kingdom a prime stop on his 1860 Western tour.

azine, *Out West,* edited by a Britisher, J. E. Liller.

Another Colorado attraction was the cattle business. To many a Briton, the economics of cattle-raising was irresistible: the herds could graze at no cost on public lands that were rich in nutritious bunch grass. "A herd of 5,000 head," wrote T. S. Hudson, author of *A Scamper Through America or, Fifteen Thousand Miles of Ocean and Continent in Sixty Days,* "will feed the year round and grow fat on a stretch of arid-looking table-land, where an English farmer, if he saw it in the autumn, would vow there was not sufficient grazing for his children's donkey."

As this kind of news reached Britain, it pricked up the ears of small farmers as well as the lords of great es-

tates. The farmers were attracted by reports that a single cowboy could handle a thousand head of steers all by himself. The big stock raisers, already alarmed by the influx of cheap American beef, decided that it was wiser to join the Westerners than to compete with them; they dispatched their sons to the High Plains and backed them with a wide-open pocketbook. So many young Englishmen took up ranching in Colorado during the 1870s that, according to a British visitor named Samuel Townshend, they accounted for almost one cattle spread out of every three.

When the typical class-conscious English gentleman settled down to ranching, he was immediately given a stern lesson in the etiquette of Western democracy.

Cowboys, he learned, were rugged individualists who considered no man their master. Frederick Trench Townshend (who was not related to Samuel) observed in *Ten Thousand Miles of Travel, Sport, and Adventure:* "The assumption of the slightest tone of superiority or command is immediately resented by a display of obstinacy, sulkiness, or insolence." And travel writer Baillie-Grohman added that even the poorest cowboy "will assert his right of perfect equality with the best of the land, betraying a stubbornness it is vain and unwise to combat."

English cattlemen were quick to give their ranchhands the respect they demanded. Indeed it was hard to begrudge them sincere admiration; as visitor John Baumann said of the cowboy in England's *Fortnightly Review,* "He is in the main a loyal, long-enduring, hard-working fellow, grit to the backbone, and tough as whipcord." However, American egalitarianism posed one problem that struck closer to home — right into kitchens and dining rooms, in fact.

Isabelle Randall, who arrived in the West as the bride of a British cattleman and who wrote of her two-year stay in *A Lady's Ranch Life in Montana,* was initially democratic enough to invite her American neighbors to her social functions. But she came to regret this generous gesture, for her guests displayed the alarming habit of fraternizing with the household help. In her chatty book, Mrs. Randall complained, "How can anyone keep servants in their place when the people, whom we associate with, invite them to their houses as *equals?*"

Most wealthy Englishwomen who settled in the West shared the sentiments of the very conventional Isabelle Randall, although they eventually became Americanized. But in September of 1873, England sent the West another Isabelle — more precisely Isabella — who was so unconventional as to seem downright un-English. She was Isabella Bird, the 42-year-old spinster daughter of an Anglican clergyman. And she was many different people all wrapped up in one untidy bundle: a tomboy, a Samaritan, a social critic, a mystic, an enchanted child and the author of *A Lady's Life in the Rocky Mountains.*

Isabella arrived in San Francisco from the Hawaiian Islands on the homebound half of an 18-month trip around the world; she remained in the West for less

British traveler Isabella Bird crammed years of adventure, including a grand romance, into a three-and-a-half month Western trip in 1873. Here she wears a Manchu gown after a trek through China 25 years later.

than four months but made it seem like years. Wearing Turkish trousers under her ankle-length skirt, she rode far and wide through the mountains of Colorado and California. When she wasn't roaming the wilderness, she lived alone near Estes Park, Colorado, in a rude log cabin with a brood of skunks under her floor. She brightened the cheerless lives of a neighboring pioneer woman and her slatternly daughter by teaching them how to knit — the therapy she used herself in times of stress. She worked as an unpaid housemaid for a helpless London physician who had come to Colorado to recuperate from a lung ailment. She nursed a woman suffering from cholera; and, after searching in vain for a baby bottle to feed the patient's starving in-

1. The Commercial Traveller makes himself agreeable
   to the Passengers
2. Another gentleman of pleasing manner
3. Hands up, or die!
4. The old Broker swears most horribly
5. He objects to "Shell out"
6. Shoot away!
7. Stop that Engine or down you go
8. The robbers stand on the line till the train disappears

fant, she saved the child with a milk-filled sponge.

Exposure to such hardships convinced Isabella that the frontier was an ugly world, and she said so without mincing words. The new towns repelled her. Cheyenne was "this detestable place, utterly slovenly-looking and unornamental," and Denver was that "braggart city," so full of sufferers from respiratory ailments "as to warrant holding an asthmatic convention"; she said she "should hate even to spend a week there." The settler's life appalled her. "It is," she wrote savagely, "a moral, hard, unloving, unlovely, unrelieved, unbeautified, grinding life." It caused "the extinction of childhood" and, with greed, godlessness and profanity, it turned children into "debased imitations of men and women."

Yet the mountain country delighted her; "This scenery satisfies my soul," she exclaimed. One of Colorado's many peaks staked a special claim on her. When she first saw it from about 50 miles away, she succumbed to its raw majesty: "heaven-piercing, pure in its pearly luster, as glorious a mountain as the sun tinges red in either hemisphere—the splintered, pinnacled, lonely, ghastly, imposing double-peaked summit of Longs Peak, the Mont Blanc of Northern Colorado."

Later she climbed Longs Peak, guided by Mountain Jim Nugent, a mysterious misanthrope who lived in a crude cabin close by. The ascent was a day-long haul, exhausting, exhilarating, terrifying at times. Her strength nearly abandoned her in the last 500 feet up "a smooth, cracked face or wall of pink granite, as nearly perpendicular as anything could well be up which it was possible to climb." She was roped to Jim, al-

---

BRITISH SCENARIO FOR A TRAIN ROBBERY

The peril of travel in the West was a source of endless fascination to Europeans—particularly since so many were coming to see the incredible land. In 1891, the London *Graphic* published this guide to how Western train robbers went about their "very lucrative and daring work."

"At a certain moment," said the magazine, "two men, who have become the friends of all the passengers, station themselves one at each end of the day-car" and level revolvers at the company with the words, "Hands up, or die!" After pockets and purses have been rifled, one gang member goes to the locomotive and orders the engineer to halt the train. In the typical denouement, concluded the *Graphic*, "the train gradually slows up, the robbers alight, and soon the engine is again set in motion, widening every minute the distance between the robbers and the robbed."

ternately standing on his shoulders to scale boulders and being dragged upward "like a bale of goods."

Reaching the top, 14,255 feet up, Isabella had to struggle to breathe. But, she declared, "it was something at last to stand upon the storm-rent crown of this lonely sentinel of the Rocky Range, on one of the mightiest of the vertebrae of the backbone of the North American continent." Ever after, she loved Longs Peak as the Earl of Dunraven loved Mount Washburn—and she also loved Mountain Jim.

In their times together after the climb, Isabella made a fond but cautious study of Jim. He seemed two very different men, and the weird thing about it was that he actually had two faces. One side of his face was eyeless, scarred and misshapen—the result, he said, of an encounter with a grizzly. The other side was so handsome it might have been "modeled in marble."

Jim was educated—"a man of culture," she said—and would recite poetry to her by the hour. He was courteous and gentle; and when they camped out together on cold nights he would thoughtfully order his dog Ring to sleep beside her to keep her warm.

But Jim was also what she called a "desperado," and he told her once—in a long, tortured confession—of a vaguely lurid past. At 18, he had run away from home in Montreal, where his Irish father was stationed with the British Army, because his mother opposed his love affair with a teen-age girl. He worked briefly in Canada for the Hudson's Bay Company, then drifted south to the United States. For nearly two decades, he led a violent life as an Army scout, a wagon-train guard and a pre-Civil War border raider. Said Isabella, "The fame of many daring exploits is sullied by crimes which are not easily forgotten."

Worst of all, Isabella learned that Jim would get drunk periodically, and grow distressingly morose—at which times he "goes to Denver, and spends large sums in the maddest dissipation, making himself a terror, and going beyond even such desperadoes as 'Texas Jack' and 'Wild Bill.'" And then, his passions spent, he "returns to his mountain den, full of hatred and self-scorn, till the next time." Naturally Isabella tried to save Jim from himself. "I urged him to give up the whisky which at present is his ruin, and his answer had the ring of a sad truth in it: 'I cannot, it binds me hand and foot—I cannot give up the only pleasure I have.'" ◉

Sarah and Joe share front-cover billing.

Luke and Joe speed to an expiring Sarah.

When Sarah "dies," Luke rends his shirt.

"Stand aside, boys, if yew don't want yewr ribs tickled"

In Victorian England, almost everyone loved a long melodramatic novel set in strange, exciting places. And when that place was the West, so much the better. In 1891, "The Illustrated London News" devoted an entire issue to Henry Herman's "Eagle Joe: A Wild-West Romance."

Eagle Joe is a crusty old mountaineer who wants to marry the lovely Sarah. She rejects him for Luke, a brawny trapper. Joe's quest to regain her supplies the story's suspense. The

old man fails, of course, but not before some breathtaking developments: Sarah "dies" but is revived by an Indian potion; Luke strikes gold and sweeps her off to a life of luxury in Europe; Eagle Joe, using occult powers acquired from a circus hypnotist, bewitches Sarah. These and other improbable events were illustrated by noted artist Richard Caton Woodville. Excerpts from one lusty scene:

The clatter of a horse's hoofs was heard, and Eagle Joe dashed down the

street, and swung from the saddle. He went straight up to Luke. "I want to say a word or tew to yew, Luke."

The young man rose quietly. "I guessed it," he answered. "I guessed as yew'd come after us."

"Whar's Sarah?" hissed Eagle Joe between his teeth.

The little crowd saw what was coming. They knew both the men and their feud. They saw Eagle Joe with his hand upon his knife. Half a dozen of them moved around to prevent, if possible,

At a circus, Joe learns how to cast spells.

Gold-rich Coloradans go on a Paris outing.

Luke escorts Sarah at the Emperor's ball.

Joe holds Sarah after she returns to life.

Joe shoots a horse injured during a chase.

Mexicans parade in finery at a trading post.

the bloodshed. Joe waved them off.

"Yew jest stand aside boys," he said, "if yew don't want yewr ribs tickled. Luke and I's got to square this out between ourselves. Whar is Sarah?" he reiterated.

Luke's knife was in his belt. But he made no attempt to get his weapon.

"To-morrow'll be heap time, Joe," he replied, and turned away.

Joe gripped him by the collar of his shirt. The knife was in his hand.

"Whar is Sarah, you son of a hound?" he yelled.

The glittering knife was lifted high. Luke turned towards him quietly. "Sar-

ah's my wife," he replied. "What has it got to do with yew?"

The knife flashed in the moonlight, and cutting through Luke's cheek, buried itself in the side of his neck. The young frontiersman reeled under the blow. Joe's arm was lifted high to strike once more, when Luke, blood streaming over his face and shoulder, threw himself upon his intending murderer.

Once more the weapon struck, cutting through bone and sinew; but Luke wrenched it from his opponent's hand and threw it into the road. Then clutching Joe by the throat with a grip of iron he flung him fully six paces away. With

a savage yell Eagle Joe raised himself and darted for his knife. Again he rushed at Luke. Again the arm was raised. Luke, smothered with blood, was endeavoring to stanch its flow with his handkerchief. For a second he shrank back from the uplifted blade.

A flash from behind. The sharp crack of a rifle reft the air, and Joe staggered, reeled and dropped the knife. Then, waving his arms wildly, he fell forward with his face to the ground.

Luke, turning round, saw, standing in the door of the hut in back of him, like a white figure of Judgment, Sarah, with the smoking rifle in her hand.

Hypnotized, Sarah flirts with a nobleman.

Joe hastens to prevent Sarah's suicide.

Joe works a spell, then goes to his lookout.

In the end, the two-faced desperado was too much for the multifaceted clergyman's daughter. In December of 1873, Isabella departed for England praying that "Our Father which is in heaven yet show mercy to His outcast child!"

Her prayers were in vain. A few months later, Isabella heard from friends that Mountain Jim had been killed in a gunfight. For the next three decades, she continued her world travels and her humanitarian endeavors, founding several mission hospitals in the Orient. But she never returned to the American West.

In spite of Isabella Bird's grim view of Western life, and in spite of the petty complaints of inconvenienced British travelers, England's general attitude toward the West remained highly romantic. And the same attitude — if anything, more intense — held sway across the English Channel. The French had simply fallen in love with the American West, and especially with the Indians. They bought full-color posters showing Indians in war regalia and joyfully read gaudy newspaper accounts of raids by the Peaux Rouges — Red Skins — on wagon trains and frontier settlements. In the Frenchmen's popular imagination, the West was a glamorous stage for theatrical violence, and Westerners kept so busy performing heroics that they scarcely had time to repair a barn or earn a living.

Nevertheless, a goodly number of French travelers presented balanced pictures of Western life; and at least one, Louis Laurent Simonin, returned to the West often enough to keep abreast of its explosive growth, and to draw shrewd conclusions about its people.

Simonin, a widely traveled mining engineer from Marseilles, made five business-and-pleasure trips to the United States between 1859 and 1875 and covered the whole period with a steady stream of articles, books and letters to friends. He was fascinated by everything Western, from the popularity of bourbon whiskey ("What a treacherous liquor is the 'Old Kentuck!' ") to the public toothbrushes he found hanging on strings in stagecoach relay stations. He approved of almost everything he saw, and even admired the tough troublemakers who loitered about the railhead towns: "What virile characters, proud, fearless! What dignity, what patience!"

Possessing a normal Frenchman's interest in good food, Simonin passed many a judgment on the meals and foodstuffs offered by the West. He decided that vegetables grown in Colorado and California were tastier than the ones sold in Paris markets; and, in a vision that perhaps only a mining engineer could conjure up, he prophesied that one day underground tubes would be built through which Western legumes would be sucked pneumatically to France, much to the benefit of French cuisine.

Predictably, however, Simonin concluded that "there are no cooks in this country," and the only Western meals he found truly enjoyable were prepared by transplanted Frenchmen. He praised the Denver restaurant of countryman Frederick Charpiot, and he took it as a hopeful sign that "Americans are well acquainted with the path to his place." But Simonin ate his most memorable Western repast in the tent of one Guerut, a French fur trader doing business at Fort Laramie, Wyoming. The main course was roast dog, and unlike most American travelers who had experience of such fare, Simonin found it a gourmet's dream. "We have to say it without mincing words," he wrote to a friend in Paris. "We ate a young dog, fattened and killed for our benefit. The flesh of the finest sheep could not compare with it."

Simonin's most revealing Western visit, his second one, came in 1867 at the invitation of businessman J. P. Whitney; they had met while Whitney, the official representative of Colorado Territory at the Paris Exposition, was soliciting foreign investments in Colorado mines. By happy coincidence, Simonin reached the West in time to observe and comment on the rapid construction of the transcontinental railroad.

From the first, Simonin sensed that a distinctively American outlook — a certain bold originality that the Europeans lacked or had lost — was the driving force behind the colossal construction project. "While we build a railroad only toward populous locations," he wrote, "here the Americans in inverse fashion throw a railroad across the prairie desert in order to attract the settler as soon as possible."

What is more, the plan was stunningly successful. When the Union Pacific track-laying crews worked their way westward into Julesburg, Colorado, there was not a single town directly ahead of them all the way to Salt Lake City, more than 500 miles distant. Yet businessmen and settlers, learning that the next railhead

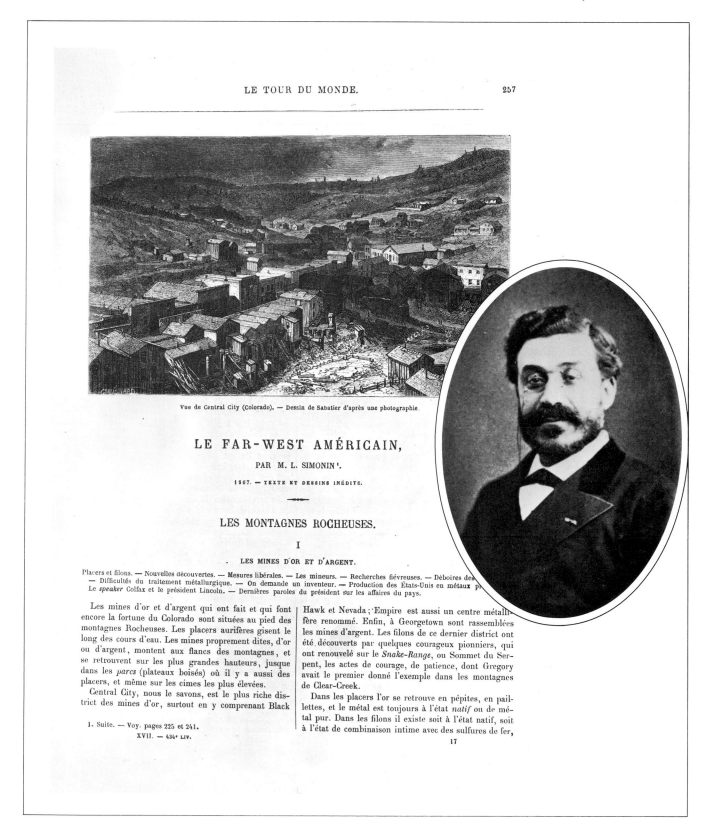

Vue de Central City (Colorado). — Dessin de Sabatier d'après une photographie.

LE FAR-WEST AMÉRICAIN,

PAR M. L. SIMONIN[1].

1867. — TEXTE ET DESSINS INÉDITS.

LES MONTAGNES ROCHEUSES.

I

LES MINES D'OR ET D'ARGENT.

Placers et filons. — Nouvelles découvertes. — Mesures libérales. — Les mineurs. — Recherches fiévreuses. — Déboires des
— Difficultés du traitement métallurgique. — On demande un inventeur. — Production des États-Unis en métaux pr
Le *speaker* Colfax et le président Lincoln. — Dernières paroles du président sur les affaires du pays.

Les mines d'or et d'argent qui ont fait et qui font
encore la fortune du Colorado sont situées au pied des
montagnes Rocheuses. Les placers aurifères gisent le
long des cours d'eau. Les mines proprement dites, d'or
ou d'argent, montent aux flancs des montagnes, et
se retrouvent sur les plus grandes hauteurs, jusque
dans les *parcs* (plateaux boisés) où il y a aussi des
placers, et même sur les cimes les plus élevées.

Central City, nous le savons, est le plus riche district des mines d'or, surtout en y comprenant Black

Hawk et Nevada ; Empire est aussi un centre métalli-
fère renommé. Enfin, à Georgetown sont rassemblées
les mines d'argent. Les filons de ce dernier district ont
été découverts par quelques courageux pionniers, qui
ont renouvelé sur le *Snake-Range*, ou Sommet du Serpent, les actes de courage, de patience, dont Gregory
avait le premier donné l'exemple dans les montagnes
de Clear-Creek.

Dans les placers l'or se retrouve en pépites, en pail-
lettes, et le métal est toujours à l'état *natif* ou de métal pur. Dans les filons il existe soit à l'état natif, soit
à l'état de combinaison intime avec des sulfures de fer,

1. Suite. — Voy. pages 225 et 241.
    XVII. — 434e LIV.

17

Chef Crow (Corbeau)

Le Scalpe

Chefs Chayennes

Chef Sioux

Indien Naya

Chef Yute

Acteurs de la danse des Bisons

Chef Paunie

Indiens Mandans

Danse des Esprits

Sur le sentier de la guerre

Danse de guerre des Sioux

Guerrier Apache

Le Calumet —— Comanches au Conseil

Guerrier Apache

168

Of all things Western, Indians fascinated the French most. In the 1890s, this mass-produced lithograph of assorted tribesmen and their customs was sold by Paris street vendors for the equivalent of 30 cents.

was to be located in Dakota Territory about 140 miles west of Julesburg, converged on the empty site and—eureka!—the town of Cheyenne was born overnight. During Cheyenne's four-month wait for the tracks, the town attracted some 3,000 inhabitants, prompting Simonin to revise an earlier comment: "Only recently it was the railroad which advanced where there were no cities; now the cities precede the iron path, establishing themselves in the midst of the desert and saying to the railroad, 'Come to us!' "

Soon after the rails reached Cheyenne, flatcars rolled into town with another novel product of American enterprise: prefabricated dwellings, which settlers had ordered by mail from catalogues. "Houses," Simonin wrote to his friend in Paris, "arrive by the hundreds already made, in the style, dimensions, and arrangements you might wish." Then, as if to reassure his friend and himself that he was seeing aright, Simonin added, "Houses are made to order in Chicago, as in Paris clothes are made to order at the Belle Jardinière."

However, the most astonishing thing—perhaps the most American thing—about Cheyenne was its self-confident political aspirations. The townspeople, feeling neglected by their Dakota capital, then 500 miles away at Yankton, demanded more responsive government; and it was rumored that, to mollify them, Cheyenne might be awarded to Colorado, which was at least closer. But, Simonin observed admiringly, "This little city does not want to be annexed to Colorado, it wants to annex Colorado. It does not even wish to be a part of Dakota. It dreams of detaching a fragment from this territory and from Colorado and Utah, which it will call Wyoming, and of which it will be the center. So is local patriotism born."

Finally, Simonin found that American creativity drew additional strength from the West's rich mixture of European immigrants. Writing of the miners he met in the Colorado Rockies, he praised the collective productivity of "the Spaniard Dominguez, married to a Frenchwoman; the mine captains from English Cornwall; the prospectors, the exploiters of lodes, Irish, Germans, Italians, Canadians, French—each with the distinctive characteristics of his race, and all with the common traits of persistence, energy, coolness." These thoughts led him to pay his host country what was —for a Frenchman—perhaps the ultimate compliment.

In a book of letters, he urged his French readers: "Let us try to imitate the American people who form today, as it were, a synthesis of all other peoples."

In 1876, just after Simonin's last Western visit, a journalist from far-off Poland set out for the West on a quixotic mission. The newsman was 30-year-old Henryk Sienkiewicz, and he was destined first for a rude awakening and later for a distinguished literary career, capped by a Nobel Prize for his novel *Quo Vadis?* In between, Sienkiewicz also served as Poland's trailblazing chronicler of the West, sending home lively reports that did as much to popularize the West in Poland as Sir Richard Burton's book had done in England.

Sienkiewicz learned of his mission on a bitter winter night in Warsaw in 1875. The journalist, who wrote a column for the newspaper *Gazeta Polska,* was invited, along with other young intellectuals, to spend an evening in the home of Helena Modjeska, the premier actress of Poland and her wealthy husband, Count Charles Chlapowski. The friends began discussing a subject dear to the hearts of 19th Century idealists: a utopian community, where everyone shared in the work and the benefits of the society, and where poverty and unhappiness no longer existed. In particular, the friends discussed one such experiment in group living—Brook Farm, established in Massachusetts in 1841. Then someone mentioned the American West as the sort of environment where a utopia might flourish.

On this point, the friends deferred to Sienkiewicz, who had become their Western expert by reading French or German translations of the novels of James Fenimore Cooper and the stories of a later American, Bret Harte. The journalist waxed so eloquent about the West that the academic discussion turned into an enthusiastic talkfest about starting a real utopia there, preferably in California, whose praises were so temptingly sung by Bret Harte. The count then made a splendid proposal: if they agreed to set up a utopia in the West, he would capitalize the venture.

The count's motion was adopted by acclaim, and Sienkiewicz was appointed to precede the main party and to select the perfect site for their perfect community. When the journalist informed his editor of his mission, he was retained by the *Gazeta Polska* to send back a regular series of *Letters from America.* ◉

The Czarevitch's shooting spree

One foreign visitor who never lifted a pen to recount his Western experiences was Grand Duke Alexis of Russia, yet no outlander's journey into the wilderness was more thoroughly recorded. Alexis, son of the Czar, had come to the U.S. in 1871 for a goodwill tour that received lavish newspaper coverage. The best copy of all seemed in the offing when the Czarevitch ventured to Nebraska for a taste of buffalo hunting.

It was heady stuff, all right. By the time the Grand Duke's private train reached "Camp Alexis," a hastily built tent-city outside North Platte, his hunting party numbered more than 500, and included four companies of U.S. Army soldiers and a regimental band. To set an authentic tone for the event, Buffalo Bill Cody staged a Wild West Show featuring Chief Spotted Tail and a thousand Sioux. And no less a personage than General Philip Sheridan organized the first hunt, with Lieutenant Colonel George Armstrong Custer performing as grand marshal.

Alexis started out well enough. "The Grand Duke has killed the first horned monster," a reporter wrote, "and reached the apex of American excitement." Altogether, however, he and the other hunters killed only 56 buffaloes—a lackluster tally that drew ridicule from one weekly newspaper (*opposite*) and left Alexis himself dissatisfied. After a brief appearance in Denver, he went out to shoot again in Colorado, with Sheridan and Custer still his mentors. This time, a single day's kill totaled 200 animals, and the Grand Duke personally claimed 12.

Pleased at last with his prowess, Alexis treated himself to a vacation of a few weeks at the Louisville home of his new-found friend Custer. Then he dutifully wound up his official tour with a visit to New Orleans' Mardi Gras before boarding a Russian warship for the voyage back to plains of his own.

The Union Pacific issued this souvenir packet to the hunters.

Grand Duke Alexis (*right*) and Custer display buffalo tails taken in the chase.

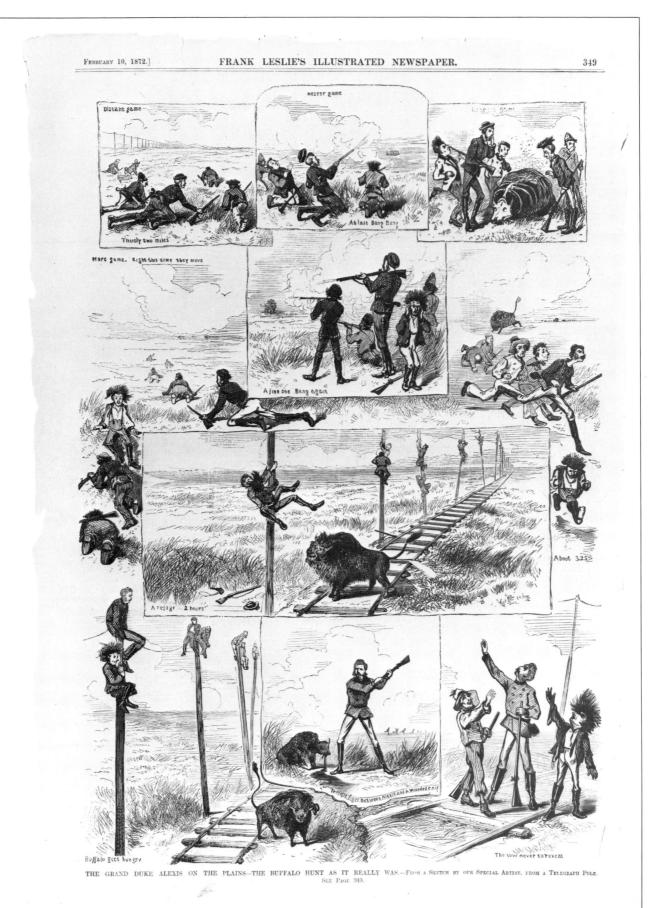

THE GRAND DUKE ALEXIS ON THE PLAINS—THE BUFFALO HUNT AS IT REALLY WAS.—FROM A SKETCH BY OUR SPECIAL ARTIST, FROM A TELEGRAPH POLE.
SEE PAGE 343.

Frank Leslie's Illustrated Newspaper aimed at the Grand Duke's first abortive hunt with less-than-respectful cartoons.

Sienkiewicz embarked for the United States as soon as possible, in February 1876. His expectations were only slightly less naïve than those that Modjeska confided to her diary: "Oh, but to cook under the sapphire-blue sky in the land of freedom! What joy! And listening to our songs would be charming Indian maidens, our neighbors, making wreaths of luxuriant wild flowers for us! And oh, we should be so far away from every-day gossip and malice."

Sienkiewicz carried out his mission intelligently, selecting as the site for the Polish Eden a sunny tract of farmland and fruit trees near Anaheim, California, and close to a settlement of Germans, whose language all of the prospective utopians spoke.

The utopians, less than a dozen in number, arrived in California in the autumn of 1876. But as pioneer farmers, the soft-handed intellectuals were dismal failures. To begin with, not a man or woman among them knew anything about how to plant a radish, milk a cow or harness a mule. Later, their self-taught lessons came to naught as their neighbors' cattle grazed on their crops and the neighbors themselves stole fruit from their trees. After a few months, with a great deal of money going out and no money coming in, the count went broke. The colony collapsed and its denizens scattered. So much for Utopia.

Modjeska, intent on repairing the family fortunes, proceeded to San Francisco and began studying English so that she might resume her theatrical career. In the meantime, Sienkiewicz had decided that he was in love with Helena. He trotted after her and besieged her with puppy-dog attentions, scandalizing the count. So much for her hopes of escaping "every-day gossip and malice."

But the debacle worked out for the best. Modjeska went off on tour, specializing in the Shakespearean roles of Juliet, Ophelia and Lady Macbeth; she soon became the toast of the American stage. Sienkiewicz, freed from farm chores and his misguided passions, spent two years at large in America, studying the West and informing his readers all about it in the pages of *Gazeta Polska.*

At the outset, the Polish journalist was revolted by Western society, its frontier roughness, its disregard for formality, its casual violence and ruthless competitiveness. But in time, he gradually grew tolerant, then open-

ly admiring. Finally he became a Western booster.

Sienkiewicz traveled about more or less at random. He talked with big ranchers and small farmers, mountain men and squatters, storekeepers and beekeepers, old pioneers and new immigrants—everyone who had time to spare and a story to tell. For variety's sake and the broader knowledge of his readers back home, he would spend periods living and learning in the wilderness. He built his own cabin, hunted and butchered his own game, gentled a mustang and made a pet of a young badger, who earned his keep as a rattlesnake slayer. Now and then he would emerge from the wilderness to sample the life of some cities. It was the most pleasant of regimens.

Sienkiewicz gave good reports on the fast-growing Western cities. But he was vitriolic about their women, especially the well-to-do California women. "They dress as in Paris, indeed, even better," he reported to his *Gazeta* readers. "They are so given to conspicuous extravagance that even in this California climate, be it summer or winter, they wear fur coats and fur neck pieces for the sole purpose of showing off. All day long they sit in their rocking chairs exposing their legs, grinning, prattling, giggling and coquetting in a naïve manner, but doing no work at all." The journalist could never quite fathom the American man's supine attitude toward these witless creatures: "He respects womankind as the highest gift of God" and "allows a woman to lead him by the nose," behaving all the while "like an enamored lion" and taking no pride whatsoever in his own demeanor or attire.

Still, Sienkiewicz was wary about judging any Westerner, male or female, by appearances alone. The need for caution was brought home to him forcefully during a visit to a silver mine in Virginia City, Nevada. A guide took him down the mine shaft to a depth of 900 feet, where the journalist observed that "Everything I was touching, gazing at, and standing upon was silver." Upon returning to the surface, he noticed that his guide was "a ragged and dirty individual dressed in a flannel shirt, a battered hat, and torn rubber boots." Sienkiewicz was tempted to offer the poor fellow $1 as a charitable tip. But, he reasoned, "Perhaps he'll be offended."

So Sienkiewicz resisted the impulse—and soon was thankful for it. That evening, the journalist was a guest in "a beautiful marble mansion" with a parlor "furnished in true oriental luxury, full of bronze statues, paintings, mirrors, velvets"—all of it presided over by a "beautiful blonde dressed in a silken gown and wearing a golden necklace." Then he was introduced to his host, a certain Mr. James Little, who, "with his face washed and his hair combed, had the appearance if not of a prince, at least of a banker." The host—a major shareholder in the mine—was, of course, his ragtag guide of the morning.

Remarkably, many plain Westerners turned out to be as successful as his host, and Sienkiewicz underscored the phenomenon for his readers. "A Yankee, however rich he may be, works all the time and in all capacities. If he is a merchant, he takes care of his store. If he is a farmer, he himself sows, plows, and harrows; in short, he works side by side with his hired hands and eats at the same table with them. It seems almost incredible to the European visitor that such is the case, but I assure you it is true."

Though the journalist himself had no democratic desire for menial labor, he fully realized that "respect and unprecedented passion for work—this is the invincible power of the Yankees, this will assure them a brilliant future and world leadership." And for the benefit of discontented farmers and workers back home in Poland, he commended the warm welcome that Americans gave to European immigrants of whatever class. "A Pole in France remains always an immigrant," he wrote, "while this vast land recognizes him immediately as her own. After five years he has the right to vote, to become a congressman, a senator, a cabinet minister; in short, he possesses the same rights and privileges as all other American citizens."

Sienkiewicz's message struck a responsive chord in his countrymen. Between 1825 and 1875, only 12,000 Poles had emigrated to the United States. But in the quarter century after Sienkiewicz's *Letters from America,* some 153,000 Poles arrived, settling mostly in Eastern and Midwestern cities, but more and more in the booming West.

Immigrants—people of all classes from every country in Europe—were the greatest gift that the foreign visitors gave to the West. After 1880, the immigrants themselves began to assume a proselytizing role in their letters home, and the contributions of come-and-go foreign travelers henceforth took the form of social interpretations rather than anecdotal, descriptive travel reports. These serious critics came to study the whole society of the West as intensely as the early botanist examined a prairie flower, and they tried to understand the frontier experience before it faded into history.

They often dished up food for thought that Westerners found especially hard to swallow. For example, James Bryce, a gifted British lawyer and politician who made three Western tours in the 1880s, said that he saw in the West too many signs of reckless, heedless enterprise: wild speculation in real estate, carelessly built and poorly run towns, irresponsible tolerance of lawlessness and "some refinements of political roguery which it is strange to find amid the simple life of forests and prairies."

All this, Bryce wrote in 1888 in his brilliant study *The American Commonwealth,* was a direct result of the Westerners' intemperate ambitions, their headlong determination to conquer the wilderness in one fell swoop and to wring from it the wealth and success for which they had dared to come West in the first place. Bryce deplored "the air of ceaseless haste and stress which pervades the West," and from time to time in his travels he was tempted to stop passing Westerners and to ask of them, "Gentlemen, why in heaven's name this haste? You have time enough. Why sacrifice the present to the future, fancying that you will be happier when your fields teem with wealth and your cities with people? In Europe we have cities wealthier and more populous than yours, and we are not happy."

But Bryce saw more clearly than any American chronicler up until then the true importance of the frontier. "The West," he wrote, "is the most American part of America"; thus an understanding of it was indispensable to an understanding of the nation as a whole; and the development of the West, whatever the faults of its developers, was a phenomenon "absolutely without precedent in history, and which cannot recur elsewhere." These compliments were sobering to Westerners who were both proud of their achievements and dismayed to see their work diminish and disfigure their magnificent wilderness. Already they agreed with Bryce's earnest prophecy: "Your posterity will look back to yours as the golden age, and envy those who first burst into this silent splendid nature."

A Swiss artist's love affair with the Indians

For a Paris-trained Swiss artist whose ambition was to rival Raphael, Rudolph Friederich Kurz found himself executing some curious commissions at Fort Union on the Yellowstone River in 1851. The American Fur Company boss at the post, having learned that Kurz was a painter, put him to work whitewashing the main building and its picket fence, and then promoted him to painting gaudy flags, which he traded to the Indians for 20 buffalo hides each.

Indians were the whole reason Kurz had come to America five years before. "From my earliest youth," he wrote in his journal, "Indians had an indescribable charm for me." Landing in New

Orleans he made his way to St. Joseph, Missouri, where he stayed for three years drawing the local tribes. Across the river was a camp of Iowas, whose "proud, easy bearing" filled him with delight — and also with feelings of another sort, which Kurz responded to by marrying a comely 17-year-old girl named Witthae. Unfortunately, when her tribe departed for distant hunting grounds, Witthae went with them.

Kurz then traveled 1,200 miles farther up the Missouri River, taking a job as clerk at the Fort Berthold trading post in Mandan and Hidatsa territory. George Catlin had painted these Indians two decades earlier, shortly before the tribes were decimated by smallpox. Now cholera broke out, and the Indians blamed Kurz for bringing bad medicine with his pen. To save his neck, he fled to Fort Union, where the head trader put him to practical painting. In his off hours, however, he had opportunities to draw the tribes thereabouts: the Assiniboin, Crow and Cree.

Kurz returned home in 1852, resolved to transform his sketches into paintings. Ill health and worse finances kept him from his task, but when he died in 1871, he left behind hundreds of deft drawings that constituted a brilliant record of life on the Upper Missouri River in the mid-19th Century.

While living along the lower Missouri, Kurz made this composite sketch of Omahas brandishing their quirts during a horse race, preparing for a ring-and-spear game, and playing out the game *(at bottom)*.

Indian women share a respite from domestic duties in a sketch Kurz made en route to Fort Berthold. He noted that their recreation involved "looking after their children, visiting, chatting and affairs of love."

176

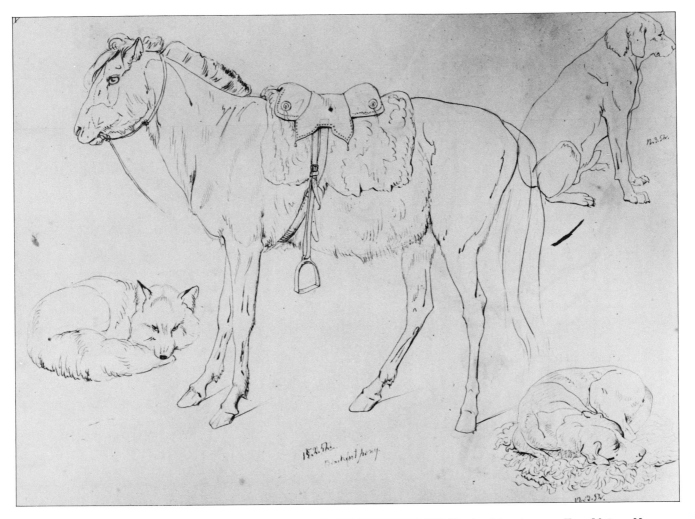

During his winter at Fort Union, Kurz drew this shaggy, heavy-headed Blackfoot pony, then managed to squeeze sketches of two breeds of dog and a captive fox into the unused corners of his sheet of paper.

Trappers and traders on the Upper Missouri often used dogs to carry their belongings. Kurz depicted one dog hauling a travois—a primitive sled made with two poles—and another bearing balanced skin packs.

In a random assortment of subjects using virtually every square inch of a precious sketch-pad sheet, Kurz portrayed American Fur Company officials, the Assiniboin chief *Ours Fou* (Crazy Bear), a French-Indian trapper family named La Bombarde, and a cariole, or one-seated, dog-drawn sled.

5 | A pride of literary lions

Ralph Waldo Emerson called her "the greatest American woman poet," but there was nothing the least bit poetic about Helen Hunt Jackson's first major literary venture into America's West. In a 342-page polemic entitled *A Century of Dishonor,* the celebrated writer from Massachusetts turned her pen into a crusader's lance, ripping ferociously into the government for its callous treatment of the Indian. After her litany of broken treaties and bloody massacres was published in 1881, she sent copies to every member of Congress. Yet Washington failed to reform, and so she tried again with a novel called *Ramona* —a piteous tale of a half-Indian maiden's doomed love for an Indian youth, and their degradation by the whites *(pages 194-195).* At least partly because of the book's emotional impact, Congress passed the Dawes Act in 1887, giving every Indian family 160 acres of farmland.

During the 19th Century, many other distinguished men and women of letters turned their talents westward, each adding a chapter to the chronicles of the unfolding frontier. They approached the subject from every imaginable angle. Francis Parkman wrote as a historian, Mark Twain as a humorist, Robert Louis Stevenson as a perceptive but irascible traveler (a man on the prairies, he said, "may walk five miles and see nothing, ten, and it is as though he had not moved").

A few of them saw the West as an almost mythic battleground of good and evil. William Sydney Porter, a sometime Texan who wrote under the name of O. Henry, mined this vein in nearly 40 stories, creating such unforgettable characters as the Cisco Kid. And yet his fiction often served the truth almost as well as that of Helen Hunt Jackson: the quick-on-the-trigger Cisco Kid was patterned after the Texas gunslinger John Wesley Hardin, who shot down no fewer than 44 victims in 10 years.

Helen Hunt Jackson was in her early fifties when she wrote *Century of Dishonor,* crying out for Indian rights. Her next novel, *Ramona,* she said, "sugared my pill."

In *A Tour on the Prairies,* fabulist Washington Irving delighted in Indian legends about animal spirits, haunted places and magically protected warriors.

In *The Amateur Emigrant,* Robert Louis Stevenson wrote that the West was painted with "eternal sage brush," and he characterized pioneers as "a race of gipsies."

Francis Parkman claimed that "war is the breath of their nostrils" after he spent three weeks with the Sioux when researching his tome, *The Oregon Trail.*

Bret Harte, author of heart-rending tales set in mining camps, confessed of a lachrymose passage that he himself had "wept when I wrote it."

Mark Twain treated the West's vistas with a rare irreverence in *Roughing It,* noting "nothing helps scenery like ham and eggs."

O. Henry used the term snappers for endings to stories like *The Caballero's Way,* in which a ranger is tricked into shooting his sweetheart.

Owen Wister eulogized the cowboy in *The Virginian* as a "hero without wings" who "whatever he did, he did it with his might."

It was early in October 1832. that I arrived at Fort Gibson, a frontier post of the Far West, situated on the Neosho, or Grand River, near its confluence with the Arkansas. I had ~~been~~ ~~travelling just~~ been travelling for a month past, with a small party, from S.t Louis, up the banks of the Missouri, and along the frontier line of Agencies and Missions, that extends from the Missouri to the Arkansas. One party was headed by one of the commissioners appointed by the Govern = ment ~~to stop~~ of the United States to superintend the ~~~~ settlement of the Indian tribes migrating from the East to the West of the Mississippi. In the discharge of his duties he was thus visiting the various outposts of ~~civili~~ ~~solem~~ civilization.

The enchanted land of the "scribblers"

During the last two thirds of the 19th Century a procession of talented writers set about accumulating that extraordinary and inexhaustible treasure trove, the literary heritage of the American West. Most embarked on their westerly quests as innocent as any Columbus of the high mission before them. Perhaps they did not even guess that they were simultaneously discovering and exploring what amounted to two distinct countries: the actual land in all its variety and infinite possibility, and the personal inner terrain where a great writer could forge observation and feeling into words that could change the lives of others.

Each of these "scribblers" — as they often referred to themselves — drew heavily on real events and true experience, yet the books they wrote emerged as something deeper and wider than fact alone. In their hands the West became a vicarious adventure ground of wonder, sentiment, laughter, escape. It expanded into a country of the imagination where the constricted soul could wander free.

Of these alchemists, the pathbreaker was Washington Irving, a man who was almost a stranger to his own country at the time he made acquaintance with the West. In 1832, Irving arrived home in New York after 17 years in the capitals of Europe. He had served as Secretary of the American Legation in London, had frequented the elegant salons of Paris, had dwelt graciously in the Alhambra in Granada. Yet he had begun to miss his country sorely, and he was deeply touched when a committee of New Yorkers headed by Philip Hone, the city's former mayor, welcomed the prodigal

son with a lavish dinner. The source of their pride was simple: during his long absence Irving had made his country respectable in the world of letters.

At home, to be sure, he had early established his credentials as a writer of uncommon talent, especially with his charming burlesque account of the old Dutch days in Manhattan, *A History of New York by Diedrich Knickerbocker,* published in 1809. Though its initial fame had been largely local, it came to be regarded as the first great book of comic literature by an American.

A decade later in England, the quondam amateur had settled down to writing in earnest. He published *The Sketch Book of Geoffrey Crayon, Gent.* — a collection of pieces like those an artist might bring home in his portfolio after a stimulating tour. In it he introduced Ichabod Crane of "The Legend of Sleepy Hollow" and the immortal Rip Van Winkle, who took a 20-year catnap; he also included essays on such hallowed English shrines as Westminster Abbey and Stratford-on-Avon, musings on the arts of angling and bookmaking, accounts of Christmas customs in rural England, and even two pieces on American Indians.

Issued in the United States in 1819 and in England a year later, the *Sketch Book* enjoyed an instant success and made its 36-year-old author an international eminence. The British, who had hitherto felt, as one put it, that every American writer was "a kind of demi-savage, with a feather in his hand instead of on his head," now found themselves reading an author with a graceful and cultivated style. A chorus of praise came from such literary luminaries as Sir Walter Scott and Lord Byron (the latter claimed he knew the book by heart), and each word was a soothing balm of Gilead to Americans who had long felt a raw inferiority complex in the matter of culture.

Irving followed the *Sketch Book* with another success, *Bracebridge Hall,* a delightful portrayal of coun-

A manuscript page from Washington Irving's *A Tour on the Prairies* recounts his trip to the West in 1832. Leaving nothing to memory, he took copious notes along the way that he later shaped — "filligree work" he termed it — into the finished book.

185

try life on an English manor. In Spain he increased his international following with his painstaking *History of the Life and Voyages of Christopher Columbus,* and *A Chronicle of the Conquest of Granada.*

By the time of Irving's homecoming in his 50th year, he was as famous a figure to Americans as John C. Calhoun or Henry Clay—so much so that many a hall of learning displayed a plaster bust of his image. Nevertheless, the writer's joy at the warmth of his reception was mixed with uneasiness. During his long absence a few mean-minded people had impugned his patriotism, muttering that he was more devoted to foreign scenes and peoples than his own land. Unjust as such an accusation might be, Irving keenly felt a need to re-Americanize himself, to experience all that he could of his rapidly changing nation—especially its frontier—and to write once more on American themes.

He was thus in no mood to resist when Henry Leavitt Ellsworth, a newly appointed peace commissioner to the Western Indians, impulsively invited him to tag along in the autumn of 1832 on an expedition into the region that later became Oklahoma. Out of that month-long ramble across nearly pristine wilderness emerged *A Tour on the Prairies,* one of three books Washington Irving would devote to the American frontier.

At first glance, the middle-aged Irving, soft from indulgent living, seemed ill-suited for a horseback sortie into rough country. But he accepted the discomforts with good spirits—and even a measure of relish. By choice he bivouacked in the open air. "A bear-skin spread at the foot of a tree was my bed, with a pair of saddlebags for a pillow. Wrapping myself in blankets, I stretched myself on this hunter's couch, and soon fell into a sound and sweet sleep." Uncomplainingly he forded streams on horseback, and once bobbled across the Arkansas River on a "cockle-shell bark" of buffalo hide. He washed his clothes in a creek, helped find and chop down bee trees for honey, made abortive efforts at rounding up wild horses and at length shot a bull buffalo. "Man is naturally an animal of prey," he wrote with some surprise, "and, however changed by civilization, will readily relapse into his instinct for destruction. I found my ravenous and sanguinary propensities daily growing stronger upon the prairies."

Everything interested him. He inspected a prairie-dog village of 30 acres and poked his rifle barrel down its holes to flush out the rattlesnakes and owls said to cohabit with the rodents. He observed how the juicy hump of the buffalo was considered the choicest cut by "epicures of the prairies"—and how they made do with skunk when nobler game grew scarce.

In this rediscovery of his native land, Irving was naturally most curious about the generation of young Americans that had grown to manhood during his sojourn in Europe. He had a lively sampling before him in the Volunteer Rangers, numbering more than a hundred, who served as military escort to the Ellsworth party and hailed mostly from Arkansas. "The troop was evidently a raw, undisciplined band, levied among the wild youngsters of the frontier, who had enlisted, some for the sake of roving adventure, and some for the purpose of getting a knowledge of the country. Many were the neighbors of their officers, and regarded them with the familiarity of equals and companions."

High-spirited and prankish, given to "loud ribald jokes" and "uncouth exclamations," the Rangers worked off their boisterousness with wrestling, horseplay and impromptu target-shooting. Impressed with their vigor, Irving made a judgment that was almost an act of disloyalty to his own past. "I can conceive nothing more likely to set the youthful blood into a flow, than a wild wood life, and the range of a magnificent wilderness, abounding with game, and fruitful of adventure. We send our youth abroad to grow luxurious and effeminate in Europe; it appears to me, that a previous tour on the prairies would be more likely to produce that manliness, simplicity, and self-dependence, most in union with our political institutions."

With his fondness for folk legends and yarns of the supernatural, Irving listened closely to the wondrous tales spun around the campfire. Some concerned the magic spirits that the Indians associated with such phenomena as thunder and lightning. One story told the fate of a warrior who saw an extinguished thunderbolt lying on the ground with a beautifully beaded new moccasin on each side of it. When he donned the moccasins they instantly sped him to the land of spirits, from whose precincts he never returned.

Another version of this tale told of a warrior who was struck senseless by lightning on the prairies near the Missouri. When the warrior recovered his wits, he saw the lightning bolt on the ground with a fine prancing horse beside it. Thanking the spirits for this piece of luck, he seized the bolt, thinking to take it home and forge arrowheads from it. "He sprang upon the horse," recounted Irving, "but found, too late, that he was astride of the lightning. In an instant he was whisked away over prairies and forests, and streams and desert, until he was flung senseless at the foot of the Rocky Mountains; whence, on recovering, it took him several months to return to his own people."

Still another story dwelt on the strange nature of albino deer and the power of medicine men to subdue them. This Irving heard from a French-Canadian frontiersman named Tonish, who served the expedition as groom, cook and hunter. Tonish, a braggart, had suffered several weeks of humiliation by missing every time he shot at a buffalo. At last, when he made a kill, he excused his earlier bad luck on grounds that he had been under an evil spell. It had happened before, he said, and related the marvelous circumstances.

While hunting when he was about 14, Tonish told Irving, he was astonished to see a beautiful white deer. Stalking the animal, he saw six more, all white as new snow. When in range, he fired. Nothing happened. He fired again and again, apparently missing every time. "He returned home despairing of his skill as a marksman," Irving related, but was consoled by an old Osage hunter who explained that white deer have a charmed life and could be killed only by special bullets.

"The old Indian cast several balls for Tonish, but would not suffer him to be present on the occasion, nor inform him of the ingredients and mystic ceremonials." Armed with the magic pellets, the youth again tracked the white herd and found them. He fired. A fine buck fell dead. The other six simply vanished and were never again seen by mortal man.

Irving returned to New York via New Orleans to transform his notes into *A Tour on the Prairies.* He sprinkled it with the fables he had heard, knowing that they could enrich the image of the land beyond the Mississippi as surely as Rip Van Winkle enriched the lore of the Hudson Valley. Though a slim volume, the book was written with such good humor and so observant an eye for detail that his American readers loved it, claiming him again as truly their own.

Even before finishing *Tour,* Irving had contracted with John Jacob Astor to write *Astoria,* an account of the fur magnate's attempt, 20 years earlier, to extend his empire by founding a trading post at the mouth of the Columbia River. More than the record of a commercial enterprise, *Astoria* had the sweep of an epic, embracing an ill-fated voyage around the Horn, an overland journey through unknown regions of the West and, finally, the conflicts that erupted in the War of 1812. Irving followed this with *The Adventures of Captain Bonneville, U.S.A.,* a kind of sequel to *Astoria* and like it a factual account—this time of the colorful young Army officer, fur trader and explorer who helped open up the Rocky Mountain country and led the first wagon train across South Pass in 1832.

Both books were instantly and deservedly popular. Not only did they reveal fascinating episodes in the development of the West but they did so with a clarity and elegance that marked a master stylist.

Irving had no monopoly on vivid historical chronicles of the frontier; indeed, he gave a personal boost to a man whose reputation in the field would someday surpass his own. In 1847, now the august elder statesman of American letters, he had occasion to comment favorably on some travel sketches in the *Knickerbocker Magazine.* Their author was 22-year-old Francis Parkman, destined to be ranked among the foremost in literary skill of the great historians. The *Knickerbocker* pieces, serialized under the title of "A Summer's Journey Out of Bounds," appeared in book form two years later as *The Oregon Trail.*

Parkman's interest in the West was almost as oddly motivated as Irving's. He was an impeccably proper Bostonian, the scion of an old New England family notable for both learned divines and wealthy merchants. A few months after receiving his degree from Harvard in 1846, he headed West with a singular purpose in mind: he was intent on gathering research for a history of the 1689-1763 French and Indian Wars. To set the stage for the conflict, he meant to trace the Indians back many centuries, but he could find no worthy source of information about the indigenous Northeastern tribes before the white man's arrival. It seemed to him that he might make up the deficit by studying the relatively untainted tribes of the Western plains.

Railroads, steamboats and stagecoaches took him as far as Kansas City. He then struck out on horseback

Hubert Howe Bancroft and his history factory

There never was any doubt that Hubert Howe Bancroft would amount to something. As an infant in Ohio, he had astounded his elders by learning to read the Bible before he was three. In 1852, when he was barely 20, he emigrated to California, tried various kinds of merchandising, then opened a bookstore in San Francisco that soon became the biggest publishing venture west of Chicago. Yet Bancroft yearned to create books as well as sell them, and he hit upon a truly grand design: he would assemble and publish the first comprehensive history of western North America, from Panama clear to Alaska.

What ensued was one of the most prodigious efforts in the annals of publishing. Starting in 1859, Bancroft spent 10 years scouring the United States, Europe and Mexico for source material. When he had accumulated 40,000 books, he wrote: "He who shall come after me will scarcely be able to undermine my work by laying another or a deeper foundation." The question was how to translate research into readable history.

After calculating that it would take him 400 years just to read the research, Bancroft hired a corps of assistants. All told, 600 people were in his employ during the project, as many as 50 at a time, never fewer than six. His headquarters on Market Street became known as the History Factory. At one end of a huge book-lined room was a unique filing system consisting of hundreds of note-filled paper bags hanging on clotheslines. Aides sat at small writing tables and, in the middle, behind a tall desk, stood Ban-

In an 1885 cartoon, the disembodied arms of Bancroft's assistants do his work for him.

croft with a revolving worktable at his elbow, like some Renaissance master directing students in his atelier.

The first five books, collectively titled *The Native Races of the Pacific States of North America* (or "savages" as Bancroft was wont to call them), appeared in 1875. Other volumes followed at more or less regular intervals — six on Mexico, seven on California, one on British Columbia — until 1890, when the series was complete at 39 volumes. The 39th book was Bancroft's autobiography.

Over the 30-year span, Bancroft had spent $500,000 on his monumental work. But he sold 6,000 complete sets and made a handsome 100 per cent profit. Although critics carped that he hogged all the credit (at one point he issued the series as *The Works of Hubert Howe Bancroft*), there was no denying either his leadership or scholarship. In later years, his vast reference library, grown to 60,000 volumes, formed the cornerstone for continuing research on the West at the University of California.

along the favored path of Oregon-bound emigrants, fording the South Fork of the Platte, pushing along the river's North Fork, crossing what is now the boundary between Nebraska and Wyoming, and finally, after three months en route, fetching up at Fort Laramie.

There Parkman learned that a group of Oglala Sioux were gathering in the vicinity to plot a major summer war upon the Snakes. "I was greatly rejoiced to hear of it," he wrote. It was Parkman's firm belief that the Indian's psychology was rooted in bellicosity, and he avidly sought news of the proceedings at the war council.

Only slowly — for it ran counter to all his preconceptions — did he begin to understand that, far from being ready to take the warpath on a moment's notice, Indians could be as hesitant and tamely practical as white men. With scorn, Parkman listened to reports of the backing and filling of the Sioux assembly's leader, a chief named Whirlwind. It was clear to Parkman that Whirlwind was well named for talk but less so for action. After hours of fierce argument and abortive war dances, Whirlwind and his lukewarm legion decided to forego battle for the season. Instead they proposed to foray into the Black Hills to kill buffalo for new lodge coverings and the winter's meat.

From the outset Parkman had felt that for his purposes it was absolutely necessary to live intimately with the Indians and "become, as it were, one of them." Fortunately for the project, his fur-trapper guide was married to a daughter of an Oglala chief and managed to persuade the tribesmen to take Parkman on their expedition. With considerable satisfaction, the Bostonian moved into the tipi of a warrior called Big Crow. He found life under a skin roof reasonably comfortable, except for children who insisted on crawling under the buffalo robes with him — he poked them away with a stick — and the host's habit of waking at midnight to chant songs of propitiation to his personal deities.

Big Crow, whose Indian name was Kongra-Tonga, was "one of the most noted warriors in the village. He had slain, he boasted to me, fourteen men and though, like other Indians, he was a braggart and a liar, yet in this statement common report bore him out." With curiosity but no particular sense of revulsion, Parkman heard Big Crow give the details of one of his killings. The victim was a Snake. Overpowering the man, Big Crow first scalped him alive, then slashed the tendons of his wrists and ankles and threw him into a campfire.

It was hard, Parkman acknowledged, to reconcile such cruelty with other traits of Indian character. At home his host was notably indulgent. "Both Kongra-Tonga and his squaw, like most other Indians, were very fond of their children, whom they indulged to excess and never punished except in extreme cases, when they would throw a bowl of cold water over them." It was equally difficult for him to understand that men so savage in battle could be so generous at other times. "The Indians will sometimes, when in mourning or on other solemn occasions, give away the whole of their possessions," Parkman wrote, concluding that the Sioux, "though often rapacious, are devoid of avarice."

The least hospitable of the camp's inhabitants were the dogs, which persistently yapped at Parkman's heels. He found one big white animal particularly obnoxious and decided to end the matter. "I intended that day to give the Indians a feast, by way of conveying a favorable impression of my character and dignity," he wrote. "And a white dog is the dish which customs prescribe for all occasions of formality and importance." He bought the dog for a gaudy handkerchief, a bit of vermilion dye and some glass beads, then hired two women to dispatch the beast and cook it for his guests. His gesture was well received; old Mene-Seela, or Red-Water, the camp's soothsayer, made a lengthy speech extending thanks to this newcomer from the "Meneaska," as they called the white men.

One day during a lull in the search for buffalo, Parkman's hope of witnessing Indian warfare — at least on a minor scale — revived when a young brave named White Shield assembled a party of 10 followers, painted himself, donned a war bonnet fashioned from the feathers of three eagles, and announced that he would take the warpath against the Snakes the next morning. But again the historian was doomed to disappointment. During the night White Shield came down with a cold, and Parkman became the astonished witness to a total collapse of warlike resolution. White Shield took to his tipi, wretched, sneezing and downcast. "When he feels himself attacked by a mysterious evil, before whose assaults his manhood is wasted, the boldest warrior falls prostrate at once," Parkman noted.

Parkman was also surprised, having heard much of Indian stoicism, to find the encampment engagingly merry when not busy with war or the hunt. "When the sun was yet an hour high," he wrote, "it was a gay scene in the village. The warriors stalked sedately among the lodges or along the margin of the stream, or walked out to visit the bands of horses. Half the population deserted the close and heated lodges and betook themselves to the water, and here you might see boys and girls and young squaws splashing, swimming, and diving with merry screams and laughter."

Still, no matter how warmly the band seemed to accept him, he never felt entirely secure when alone with a single Indian—particularly if that Indian happened to be young and eager to build his reputation as a warrior. He had been watching the emergence into manhood of a bashful lad named Hail Storm. The boy's hunting successes affected him like an aphrodisiac. He took to wearing his blanket rakishly over his left shoulder, and he became boldly flirtatious with girls. Soon the young historian felt certain that Hail Storm had succeeded with the other sex well beyond the stage of flirtation. It now occurred to Parkman that such a feisty youth was likely to harbor ambitions larger than girls alone. "I have no doubt that the handsome, smooth-faced boy burned with desire to flesh his scalping knife, and I would not have encamped alone with him without watching his movements with a suspicious eye."

Returning to Massachusetts after six months in the field, Parkman organized his notes for publication—but at the time he considered the work no more than a narrative of a combined vacation jaunt and research expedition. Not until later did he acknowledge it to be true history, an "image of an irrevocable past." Its intimate prose-picture of Indian life was, in fact, incomparable. "Great changes are at hand," he wrote. "With the stream of emigration to Oregon and California, the buffalo will dwindle away, and the large wandering communities who depend on them for support must be broken and scattered. The Indians will soon be abashed by whisky and overawed by military posts; so that within a few years the traveler may pass in tolerable security through their country. Its danger and its charm will have disappeared together."

All the literary giants who went to the West, including essayist-historians like Irving and Parkman, were to some degree gentle liars, giving less—or perhaps more —than the whole truth, simply because their craft required them to select, highlight, rearrange. But when the creative imagination went further, testing and finally immersing itself in the waters of fiction, a very special kind of literary invention was at work. In the opinion of much of the 19th Century reading public, the supreme frontier practitioners of this art were Bret Harte and Samuel Clemens, better known as Mark Twain. They were contemporaries in the West, colleagues and close friends for a time, enemies at the end. Their professional lives as writers began on newspapers, but they used journalism only as a springboard, a tool to fashion brilliant—and very different—views of the trans-Mississippi realm.

Harte, who arrived first, had never much wanted to see the West, never ceased feeling out of place in it, escaped it as quickly as he could—and yet would have been the first to admit that it was an indispensable elixir for his career. But then nearly everything about the life of Francis Bret Harte was a paradox.

Harte could count among his paternal forebears five Connecticut governors and a grandfather who was the wealthy secretary of the New York Stock Exchange. However, a shadow hung over his heritage: the brilliant grandfather, born in London of a family of English Jews, had migrated to New York City and there contracted a youthful misalliance. He secretly married a gentile girl, Bret's grandmother, then left her soon after the birth of Bret's father, Henry. That abandonment seemed to dog the life of the luckless son, who was to become a scholarly but often impoverished schoolteacher. Henry Harte died when Bret was nine.

Bret was born in Albany in 1836, a delicate and sickly child who early became bookish and began reading Dickens—his lifelong hero—at seven. By his teens he had absorbed everything in Defoe, Fielding, Goldsmith, Cervantes, Washington Irving and the elder Dumas; he also knew Latin, some chemistry, some Greek, and had pretty well determined that he would become a famous writer. Possibly as a defense against his chronic penury and the gibes of more robust contemporaries, he began to cultivate a fastidious and rather haughty manner. Later a business associate described him as "a dainty man, too much of a woman," and Mark Twain once said stingingly that "his gait was of the mincing sort but was the right gait for him, for an

When historian Francis Parkman was in St. Louis preparing for his Western fact-finding trip, he obtained two invaluable aids from P. Chouteau, Jr. & Co., the city's dominant fur-trading firm. One was guide Henry Chatillon *(left),* a trapper whose ties with the Oglala Sioux would provide an entree to tribal life. The other was a letter *(below)* to "Any person or persons in our employ in the Indian Country," assuring Parkman and Quincy Shaw, his cousin and traveling companion, a friendly reception at all the company's wilderness outposts.

Saint Louis 25 April 1846

To any person or persons in our employ in the Indian Country, —

This will be presented by our friends Mr. F. Parkman and Mr. Quincy A. Shaw, who visit the interior of the country for their pleasure & amusement, and whom we beg to recommend to your kind & friendly attention —

If these Gentlemen shall be in need of anything in the way of supplies &c. you will oblige us by furnishing them to the extent of their wants, as also to render them any & every aid in your power, of which they may stand in need

Very truly yours &c
P. Chouteau Jun & Co.
Brm Clapp

Signature of Mr F. Parkman — F. Parkman
do Quincy A. Shaw — Quincy A. Shaw

unaffected one would not have harmonized with the rest of the man and his clothes."

Thus endowed, pale of brow, with an aristocratic nose and a wispy mustache, dressed as high in fashion as scant means would allow, he was poorly equipped to face bawdy San Francisco when he stepped ashore in 1854. He had come to join his mother, who had married an Oakland politician. He was not yet 18, a dude and an automatic target for derision.

Harte spent his first four years in the West accomplishing very little in a curious variety of ways. He dug fence postholes incompetently, had a brief job as a pharmacist's assistant, taught a country school, tutored the sons of a rancher, tried his hand at mining, and for an incongruous month or two rode shotgun on a Wells Fargo stage. Once, broke and traveling on foot—hobbling, rather, for his patent leather shoes had cracked and were crippling his feet—he was given overnight shelter by a charitable prospector named Gillis. Learning that he was destitute, Gillis sent him on his way with a $20 gold piece. Years later on a San Francisco street, Gillis recognized and greeted Harte, grandly dressed with a high astrakhan collar on his coat. Harte snubbed him: he was always casual about borrowing and even more casual about repaying a loan.

His first real break—though he failed to realize it then—came in 1858 when he was hired as printer's devil on the *Northern Californian,* a weekly in the town of Union on Humboldt Bay. Before long, editor S. G. Whipple began printing squibs of poetry and comment by his lowly assistant. From there, Harte graduated to running the paper when the editor was absent. "Mr. Harte has frequently contributed to our columns and is a graceful and easy writer," wrote Whipple in sanction of his substitute. Soon he was describing Harte as his "junior," or associate editor.

This meteoric rise was brought to an abrupt halt when Harte committed an uncharacteristic act of courage and compassion. But perhaps not so uncharacteristic after all; an experienced underdog himself, he had a deep, lifelong sympathy for the weak and helpless. In 1860—during one of Whipple's absences—a gang of white hoodlums from the nearby town of Eureka massacred a peaceful village of Digger Indians. Harte was infuriated and spoke his mind in an editorial that concluded, "We can conceive of no palliation for woman and child slaughter. We can conceive of no wrong that a babe's blood can atone for." The offended Eurekans responded by threatening Harte with the same treatment they had accorded the Digger Indians. Wisely, Harte resigned and headed for San Francisco.

There, a literary magazine, the *Golden Era,* took him on as a printer, and soon he was contributing verse and sketches. His style was pretentiously literary, but a freshness of view caught the eye of San Francisco's foremost patroness of the arts, Jessie Benton Frémont, daughter of Senator Thomas Hart Benton and wife of the Great Pathfinder, John Charles Frémont. She made him a regular Sunday guest at her salon and dinner table. Harte was exalted by her favor, awed by her intellectual circle, and much helped by the friendly literary criticism he received in her home.

The Frémonts were ardent abolitionists, and Harte too became an eloquent drumbeater for the Union cause. But when the Civil War began, he did not enlist. Instead he did something ultimately more perilous: in 1862 he married a woman named Anna Griswold. They had been introduced by the Reverend Thomas Starr King, a leading member of the Frémont abolitionist circle and the pastor of the First Unitarian Church, where Anna, who had a fine contralto voice, sang in the choir. The match was opposed by family and friends on both sides—which only served to speed the courtship and hasten an unhappy marriage. She was five years Harte's senior, humorless, demanding, domineering and scornful of his literary ambition. When their rented house needed new wallpaper she told him, "You might do it yourself after office hours, instead of writing, and you'd save money by it." He was now working days as a clerk in the U.S. Surveyor's office and earning only $1 a column for his freelance contributions to the *Era.*

Harte patiently bore with her forbidding presence. Though he called himself a bohemian, he never caroused, dutifully coming home to dinner every evening. He even submitted when, as he tried to write at night, she petulantly demanded that he put out the lights.

Through influential friends of the Frémonts, Harte was granted a patronage sinecure at the mint that paid him a salary of $180 a month, eventually raised to a lordly $270. This supported his family, his expensive taste in raiment and his writing. In 1864, with the

Era slowly failing, Harte became a partner in a new literary magazine, the *Californian.*

At about that time he met Sam Clemens, who had just crossed the Sierra from the *Territorial Enterprise* in Virginia City and was temporarily a reporter on the San Francisco *Morning Call,* which had its offices in the same building as the mint. Clemens often dropped in to talk to his new acquaintance, whom he grew to consider the best writer in San Francisco. Clemens had only recently begun to call himself Mark Twain and his mining-camp journalism was both roughshod and roughhewn. But Harte liked him—they were almost of an age, Twain being a year older—and felt he had promise. He encouraged Twain to contribute to the *Californian* and appointed himself editor of the newcomer. Though Twain came to despise his mentor, he nevertheless acknowledged his debt with grace. "Bret Harte trimmed and trained and schooled me patiently until he changed me from an awkward utterer of coarse grotesquenesses to a writer of paragraphs and chapters that have found a certain favor."

Harte's own writings of the *Californian* period were polished and versatile, and he was gaining a reputation as a humorist and satirist, generally at the expense of California and the state's pride in its recent forty-niner past. He was put off by the cultural pretensions of top-hatted, tail-coated San Franciscans who, only a little more than a decade earlier, had been illiterates clumping through the Sierra foothills in hobnailed boots and red flannel shirts. Prideful terms like "Argonaut" aroused his ire, and he zestily took on the influential Society of California Pioneers, suggesting that what the West needed instead was a "Society for the Suppression of Local Pride." Even that sacred article of faith, the California weather, did not escape his razor-edged barbs. One of his odes concluded:

Then fly with me, love, ere the summer's begun,
And the mercury mounts to one hundred and one;
Ere the grass now so green shall be withered and sere,
In the spring that obtains but one month of the year.

Although plainly gifted, Harte had not yet stumbled on the writing formula that would endear him to millions. That great revelation sneaked up on him largely unawares in 1868 when Anton Roman, a former miner turned bookseller and publisher, approached him with a proposal to edit a new magazine to be called the *Overland Monthly.* Roman's ideas ran diametrically counter to much of what Harte stood for: he wanted a magazine that would glorify California's past and bejewel its future. But Roman also felt that Harte was the only man on the scene with the ability to edit a magazine good enough to attract a national audience.

Acting on that conviction, the publisher labored for three months to persuade Harte of the virtues of a more positive editorial stance; in particular he stressed the wealth of literary possibilities in the still untold saga of California's early mining days. And in the end, he won Harte over, for the arguments did not fall on totally unprepared soil. Years earlier, during his days on the *Era,* the still-callow Harte had written a few pieces that evoked mining-camp life—notably a story called "The Work on Red Mountain," which was ignored at the time but would one day, exhumed and revived as "M'liss," become hugely popular.

Even so, the appearance of "The Luck of Roaring Camp" in 1868 in *Overland's* second issue signaled a stunning departure from Harte's former worship of gentility and Eastern cultivation. The story's realistic depiction of the often crude miners of the gold rush was so shocking that the issue was held up for a while when a lady proofreader objected to its subject matter and language. Still more daringly, Harte displayed these specimens of low life as human beings capable of occasional decent and good-hearted behavior. Small wonder that, in a world still ruled by Victorian morality, "The Luck of Roaring Camp" was an international sensation within weeks. Bret Harte was made.

The tale was simplicity itself. A raddled prostitute, Cherokee Sal, is brought to childbed in Roaring Camp, a horny-handed community of a hundred miners and gamblers. Sal dies, perhaps because of the unskilled obstetrics of a prospector who is dragooned as midwife because he is the only certified father present. The bewildered men are confronted with a baby boy and take up a collection to ensure his future. In this scene Harte unveiled the secret of his artistic glory, a golden formula of pathos mixed with humor.

"A silver tobacco box; a doubloon; a navy revolver, silver mounted; a gold specimen; a very beautifully embroidered lady's handkerchief (from Oakhurst the gambler); a diamond breastpin; a diamond ring (suggested

The barbaric, elegant world of Ramona's ranch

Perhaps the most perennially popular work in Western literature was Helen Hunt Jackson's novel *Ramona.* Much of the book's appeal lay in its setting on a 19th Century ranch in California. It was a world, Mrs. Jackson wrote, "half barbaric, half elegant, wholly generous"—and also facing extinction as the *Yanquis* took over California.

The novel's atmosphere was inspired by a ranch called Camulos, visited by Mrs. Jackson in 1882 while she was collecting material for some *Century* magazine articles. It had been owned by one family since 1839, when Antonio del Valle was granted 48,000 acres northwest of Los Angeles. After the Mexican War of 1846, the U.S. government challenged the del Valle title, and litigation coupled with disastrous drought reduced the domain to 2,000 acres. Even so, Mrs. Jackson was impressed, and when she began writing *Ramona* 18 months after her visit, she recalled Camulos in detail.

Ramona is the half-Indian foster daughter of the Moreno family. She is attracted to Alessandro, an Indian who comes to the Moreno ranch to shear sheep. As their love blooms amid grape arbors, they decide to elope. Tragically, white homesteaders drive them from their land; their baby dies; and at last Alessandro is killed by a rancher. At that point Felipe, scion of the Moreno family, shows up to take Ramona home with him. In the end, he sells the ranch to the Americans and he and Ramona go off to find happiness in Mexico.

A saccharine tale, but oddly prophetic. As the debts of the del Valles mounted, Camulos passed into American hands—and a uniquely colorful and carefree life style passed from the West.

The family chapel at Camulos was tucked into a corner of the garden. Periodically, just as in *Ramona,* a Franciscan priest from one of the nearby missions administered the sacraments to the entire household.

Much of the action in *Ramona* takes place on the veranda of the main compound at Camulos. This photograph was made two years after Helen Hunt Jackson paid a call on the ranch; she stayed only a few hours.

Canadian artist Henry Sandham pictured the star-crossed lovers eloping on horseback as the frontispiece of *Ramona*. Earlier, he had been commissioned to illustrate Mrs. Jackson's articles for *Century* magazine.

Among Ramona's most precious possessions were a jewel box and the Indian baskets Alessandro gave her — both depicted by Sandham.

by the pin, with the remark from the giver that he 'saw that pin and went two diamonds better'); a slung-shot; a Bible (contributor not detected); a golden spur; a silver teaspoon (the initials I regret to say were not the giver's); a pair of surgeon's shears; a lancet; a Bank of England note for £5; and about $200 in loose gold and silver coins.... As Kentuck bent over the candle-box half curiously, the child turned and, in a spasm of pain, caught at his groping finger and held it fast for a moment. Kentuck looked foolish and embarrassed. Something like a blush tried to assert itself in his weather-beaten cheek. 'The d---d little cuss!' he said."

As with many of Harte's most effective stories, "The Luck of Roaring Camp" ends starkly. A flash flood engulfs the community, and the child is later found downstream in the arms of Kentuck; the boy is dead and Kentuck, dying, says, "He's a-taking me with him. Tell the boys I've got The Luck with me now."

The cornucopia of Harte's new formula now spilled itself. Next came "The Outcasts of Poker Flat," a story of gamblers, robbers, drunkards and whores driven from town to die heroically in a blizzard while trying to save the life of an innocent maiden. It was followed by such classics as "How Santa Claus Came to Simpson's Bar," the tale of how Dick Bullen rides 50 miles through a storm, survives a flood and a shoot-out with a highwayman to fetch a few toys to a sick boy who had never had a "Chrissmiss." In "An Heiress of Red Dog," a homely hotel maid inherits $3 million on condition she *never* share it with anybody she loves—and then has the foul luck to fall in love with a conscienceless, consumptive gambler.

So it went, story after story, book after book. Harte never abandoned the essential ingredients: unabashed sentiment, bedizened whores with hearts of gold, chivalry and nobility deep under the case-hardened crusts of uncouth and wicked men, primal innocence rediscovered. His stories—applauded by Dickens, admired and emulated by Kipling—were the prototypes of the countless "Westerns" that would follow. He was the first to stake out the fictional territory that later writers like Owen Wister would cultivate to fresh advantage.

By 1871 his fame had grown bright enough to beckon him East—where he felt he belonged and truly wanted to be. But there, unaccountably, he abused his warm welcome. In Chicago he failed to appear at a banquet in his honor and offered neither explanation nor apology. In Boston, New York and Newport he borrowed from leading citizens and neglected to repay them. Invited to Cambridge to deliver a commencement poem at Harvard, he showed up wearing bright green gloves and read a set of comic verses that, in the opinion of one Brahmin, "did not recognize the dignity of the occasion." His Eastern publishers cooled when he failed to meet his deadlines or turned in inferior material, and they did not renew his contract when it expired.

Rejected in America, he retreated to Europe and England. The English respected him as a gifted man of letters, and his work, almost always on American Western themes, found a ready audience. England possessed still another advantage: he had left his shrewish wife behind. He never lived with Anna again—though he sent her most of his earnings. In 1902 he died at 65 of cancer in the Surrey home of a Belgian gentlewoman who had sheltered him for years.

His former pupil, Twain, came East in his turn and at the Players Club in New York was once asked by the novelist Henry James, "Do you know Bret Harte?" Twain replied, "Yes, I know the son of a bitch."

Samuel Langhorne Clemens' own journey west began in 1861. He was 25 at the time and for two and a half years had been piloting Mississippi steamboats between St. Louis and New Orleans. On April 14, the fall of Fort Sumter caught him at the downriver end of his beat. Sam drew his back pay and took passage on the last steamer to make the trip to St. Louis before the war closed the river to civilian traffic.

Back home in Hannibal, Missouri, he found the town in a fever of war excitement, with volunteers ready to fight for both sides. Sam signed up with the Marion Rangers—a small group of Confederate partisans—and was elected a second lieutenant. There followed two weeks of maneuvers during which he fell out of a hayloft and sprained an ankle, nearly drowned when his mule foundered in a swollen river and was chased by Union forces led (he found out later) by Colonel Ulysses S. Grant. He resigned his commission, citing "fatigue through persistent retreating."

Finished with war, he journeyed to Keokuk, Iowa, to visit his older brother Orion, who had opted for the Union side and had just been appointed secretary to

the territorial government of Nevada. Orion was broke, so Sam offered to pay the fare for both if Orion would take him to Nevada in some official capacity.

The Clemens brothers set out by Overland Mail stage on a 20-day trip to the new territorial capital in Carson City. Limited to 50 pounds of baggage, they sent home trunkloads of clothing but took along a *Webster's Unabridged Dictionary* that could easily have been bought in San Francisco. "It weighed about a thousand pounds and was a ruinous expense," wrote Sam. "We could have kept a family on what that dictionary cost in the way of extra freight." Moreover,

"every time we avalanched from one end of the stage to the other, the dictionary would come too, and every time it came it damaged somebody."

Learning in Carson City that the territory had no funds for a "secretary to the Secretary," Sam came down with a case of the get-rich-quick fever raging in the area; the world's greatest silver strike, the Comstock Lode, had been made in western Nevada four years earlier. It took little to infect him for, all his life, Clemens yearned to outprofit Croesus. His first effort was a trip to Lake Tahoe to stake out a timber claim. This, obviously, would turn the trick in short order;

the towns of the lode were growing madly and, as soon as a sawmill could be built, Sam would be rolling in wealth. Unfortunately, the partners fell so in love with the lake, camping and lazing beside its crystal depths, that they neglected their campfire, which set off a forest fire and sent the timber claim up in flames.

Sam also tried prospecting in Nevada's mountainous Esmeralda mining district, where winter was so severe, he wrote, that "as a general thing when a man calls for a brandy toddy, the bartender chops it off with a hatchet and wraps it up in paper, like maple sugar."

Because Orion's boss was a convivial politician and frequently absent from his post, Orion often found himself burdened with all the cares of the governor's office. Sam frequently had to give up his scramble for a new El Dorado and return to Carson City to assist the harassed Orion. A particularly distressful ordeal arose when Orion called on him for help in organizing, paying, herding, feeding and lodging the first session of the Nevada Territorial Legislature.

More than 20 years later, after huge fossil footprints were uncovered in a quarry near Carson City, Sam took his revenge for this Augean labor. A heated scientific dispute arose over the contention that some of the tracks might have been left by a giant primeval human. Sam settled the argument in an article published in the Sacramento *Daily Record-Union:* "It may be all very well to talk about the Carson footprints, and try to saddle them onto primeval man and others who are gone and cannot defend themselves, but it is not *moral.* They were made by the First Nevada Territorial Legislature and I was there when it was done. The Speaker went first. He made large tracks —the ones that are eight inches broad and eighteen inches long. He was a prime man in two or three ways, and evil in 40, but he was not the primeval man. . . . These scientists are in an ill-concealed sweat because they cannot tell *why* there are so many tracks, and all going one way, all going north. It was a large legislature, dear sirs, and the saloon was north."

During his first year in the Far West, Sam continued to pursue the chimeras of gold and silver, staking claims and swapping "feet" on rocky ledges staked by others. Once he thought he had hit high-grade ore, and throbbing with excitement, fetched home pocketfuls of a shining mineral; it turned out to be the classic

Miners sluice gold along the Calaveras River in the Sierra Nevada foothills — the setting for two short stories that earned instant ranking as gems of Western literature: Bret Harte's "The Luck of Roaring Camp" and Mark Twain's "The Celebrated Jumping Frog of Calaveras County."

Judging from these illustrations, *Roughing It* was a somewhat overstated title for Mark Twain's 1871 book on his Western experiences. To be sure, the bronco he got in Carson City was a tough customer, but as an onlooker tartly commented: "Any child could have told you he'd buck."

INNOCENT DREAMS

DRINKING SLUMGULLION

prospector's delusion, iron pyrites, known to oldtimers as fool's gold. Finally his money petered out, and Sam admitted that he had been guilty of magnifying his prospects with "40-horse microscopic power."

For some time he had been submitting letters of mining-camp comment to the *Territorial Enterprise* in Virginia City. In July of 1862, with his fortunes at rock bottom, he received a message from Joseph Goodman, the paper's publisher, offering him a reporter's job at $25 a week. He hiked 90 miles to Virginia City and arrived in the *Enterprise* office with wisps of hay sticking to his clothing, reminders of the stacks in which he had bedded on the way. Thus began Sam Clemens' professional writing career.

As a reporter, Sam never let a fact get in the way of a good story. He fabricated outright hoaxes and, when his disfavor was aroused, wrote more with a truncheon than a pen; all his life Sam Clemens was a good man with a grudge. While working on the *Enterprise* he decided to adopt a prudent custom of local journalists,

who mostly used *noms de plume*. He hit upon "Mark Twain"—the cry of a Mississippi riverboat leadsman to indicate that there were two fathoms of water under the keel. Later he said he had borrowed it from a former river news writer for the New Orleans *Picayune*. "He died in 1863 and as he could no longer need that signature, I laid violent hands upon it without asking permission of the proprietor's remains."

It was Twain's carefree style that brought about his final removal from the Comstock Lode country in 1864. A popular civic effort that year was raising money for the Sanitary Fund, a Red Cross-like organization that aided sick and wounded Union soldiers. One stunt involved the auctioning off of a 50-pound bag of flour and another was a charity ball put on by the women of Carson City. From some private well of orneriness or, at the kindest, misplaced waggishness, Twain singled out both for editorial comment. He raised no objections to the Sanitary Fund or the flour auction as such, but he did accuse the employees of the

UNEXPECTED ELEVATION

AS CITY EDITOR

rival *Union* of reneging on their pledges to the auction fund and he did assert that the proceeds of the Carson City ball had been diverted to a "Miscegenation Society" back East. Vastly unamused by these sallies, the offended parties had nearly cornered Twain into fighting not one but two duels when the Governor mercifully sent word that anyone breaking the local anti-dueling law would get two years in jail. He advised a secret and early departure by stagecoach. Twain gratefully left for San Francisco the next morning.

There he went to work for the *Morning Call*, discovering to his dismay that routine reporting was the worst sort of "drudgery," and there too he began writing for, and learning from, Bret Harte and his *Californian*. He achieved his first national attention in late 1865—to his own surprise as much as anyone's, since he didn't think that much of the yarn—when the *Saturday Press,* a New York weekly, published "The Celebrated Jumping Frog of Calaveras County." It was based on a tale that Twain had heard at Jackass Hill in Angels Camp, in the California mining country.

In the words of an amiable and rambling old man he used as narrator, Twain told of miner Jim Smiley, who would bet on either side of any proposition ("why, if there was two birds setting on a fence, he would bet you which one would fly first"), and his trained frog, Dan'l Webster, jumping champion of the area until the day he was foully disabled by a competitor. That rival, behind Jim Smiley's back, stuffed Dan'l Webster so full of buckshot "he couldn't budge; he was planted as solid as a church, and he couldn't no more stir than if he was anchored out." Twain's opinion of this yarn was to rise considerably when James Russell Lowell, a nabob of Eastern letters, called it "the finest piece of humorous writing yet produced in America."

Twain's virulent dislike of Harte, the origin of which he never explained, may have begun at this time. A book of Twain stories featuring the famous jumping frog appeared in May 1867—but only after it had been rejected by G. W. Carleton, an Eastern publisher

Joaquin Miller, "the Byron of the Rockies"

Moving in the same circles as Mark Twain and Bret Harte was a flamboyant character named Joaquin Miller who grandly referred to himself as "The Byron of the Rockies"—a title he even had printed on his calling card. While some critics might have questioned the literary merits of the comparison, none could deny that Miller shared with the famed English poet a genius for living with a magnificent theatrical flair.

The son of an Oregon schoolteacher, Miller took a fling at California gold mining, then returned to his home to try working as a newspaper editor and later as a county judge. But all the while, the muses were beckoning. In 1870, at the age of 32, he embarked for the town of San Francisco and the literary life, bidding adieu to his spouse with the lines: "When I should have said, Farewell,/I only murmur'd, 'This is hell.'"

Gregarious and charming, Miller was an immediate hit in San Francisco's salons. He regaled fellow writers with tall tales of frontier heroics, and recited poetry that was deemed to have a certain rough-hewn quality.

Before long, Miller set sail for England and broader fields to conquer. With typical panache, he arrived there with a laurel wreath to place on Byron's grave; London in turn took him to its bosom. British publishers clamored for his poetry. He became the literary lion of Mayfair, where he appeared at dinner parties in a red flannel shirt, high boots with jingling spurs, a belt filled with bowie knives and a bearskin cape.

Dress was only part of his act. Once while reciting an epic, "Kit Carson's Ride," ("Room! Room to turn round in, to breathe and be free,'' it began./"To grow to be giant, to sail as at sea") Miller fell to the floor in a sort of creative frenzy and began

Posing against a suitably romantic studio backdrop in 1888, Miller adopts a faraway look.

biting the ankles of the women around him—in order of rank, it was reported, starting with a duchess.

For two years, Miller toured Europe playing the Wild Westerner while reaping profits from his books. In 1886, nearing 50, he returned for good to a 100-acre estate overlooking San Francisco Bay. Some critics hooted at such poems as "Columbus" ("The good mate said: 'Now must

we pray,/for lo! the very stars are gone./Brave Adm'r'l, speak; what shall I say?'/'Why, say: "Sail on! sail on! and on!"'"). But others applauded, and to an adoring public, Joaquin Miller was nothing less than poet laureate. It was a role he relished to the end. Shortly before his death at 75, he protested to a physician who was prescribing medication, "Doctor, I am a poet. It is not poetic to take pills."

who soon thereafter issued a volume of Harte's stories. Mark Twain was a man of many virtues, but immunity to jealousy was not among them. His resentment was surely exacerbated if Harte, as is logical to assume, borrowed from him and failed to repay, for Twain never forgave anyone who did him out of money.

Twain left California for Hawaii in March 1866, sent by the Sacramento *Union* to roam the islands and file dispatches on whatever struck his fancy. When he returned five months later, he began a fabulously successful career lecturing on—what else?—the strange and comical adventures of Mark Twain.

His major contribution to the literature of the Old West came in 1872 with the book *Roughing It,* an often hilarious mix of tall tale, sober reportage and unforgettable imagery that told the story of Twain's years in the Far West—from the stage ride across the plains to his days as a journalist and tyro lecturer. Of a Nebraska settler living in a sod hut, he commented that it was "the first time we had ever seen a man's front yard on top of his house." As he crossed South Pass, "a number of peaks swung into view with long claws of glittering snow clasping them." Reporting a San Francisco earthquake, he told how "a lady sitting in her rocking and quaking parlor saw the wall part at the ceiling, open and shut twice, like a mouth, and then drop the end of a brick on the floor like a tooth." Lake Tahoe struck him as a spot so serene that three months there "would restore an Egyptian mummy."

Occasionally in *Roughing It,* he resorted to a meatax approach, as in a passage defending the Chinese: "They are a kindly disposed, well-meaning race, and are respected and well treated by the upper classes all over the Pacific coast. No California *gentleman or lady* ever abuses or oppresses a Chinaman, under any circumstances, an explanation that seems to be much needed in the East. Only the scum of the population do it—they and their children; they, and, naturally and consistently, the policemen and politicians, likewise, for these are the dust-licking pimps and slaves of the scum, there as well as elsewhere in America."

Roughing It went into 10 printings in the United States between 1872 and 1900. The work received probably its finest accolade from William Dean Howells, editor of the *Atlantic Monthly.* "A thousand anecdotes, relevant and irrelevant, embroider the work," Howells wrote. "Excursions and digressions of all kinds are the very woof of it; everything far fetched or near at hand is interwoven, and yet the complex is a sort of 'harmony of colors' which is not less than triumphant." Twain's freewheeling style, concluded Howells, produced "a better idea of life of the recent West" than could possibly be found elsewhere.

The crowning achievement in shaping the literary image of the Old West fell to Owen Wister, whose 1902 novel, *The Virginian,* turned the American cowboy into a legendary hero. Wister was as paradoxical a fabricator as any of his predecessors. He was born in Philadelphia in 1860, one more adornment on a family tree emblazoned with a signer of the Constitution, a famed Shakespearean actress, merchant princes, eminent physicians and officers of the United States Navy. The least expected of the male offspring of such forebears was that he should become a distinguished gentleman. Owen Wister did his best and succeeded—in a totally unorthodox way.

As a young boy he was schooled in Switzerland and England. At exclusive St. Paul's prep school in New Hampshire he contributed poetry to the literary magazine, joined the choir and, discovering a bent toward music, decided to become a composer. He majored in music at Harvard, where he wrote both the score and libretto of an Offenbach-like operetta for the Hasty Pudding Club. After graduating *summa cum laude* in 1882, he went to Bayreuth, Germany, and played his own compositions for the approving Franz Liszt. But he soon drifted away from music and took a job in a Boston bank where he was thoroughly bored—but at a loss as to what to do about it.

A momentary respite came in 1885, when he suffered a spell of indifferent health. On the advice of Teddy Roosevelt, a close friend of Harvard days who had already tested the West and found it salubrious, he decided to spend a summer on a Wyoming ranch owned by family friends. From the outset, the experience was, as he confided to his diary, "much more than my most romantic dream could have hoped." The air he pronounced "delicious. As if it had never been in anyone's lungs before." He slept in a tent, took a bath every morning in Deer Creek, and learned to stay on a bronco. He helped at roundups, watched calf-

Visiting Wyoming in search of inspiration, novelist Owen Wister sits stiffly astride a range pony. With characteristic admiration for all things Western, he said the mount had "a wit sharper than a street Arab's."

branding, rode to Medicine Bow to collect freight, all the while stirred by the awesome beauty of his surroundings. "This existence is heavenly in its monotony and sweetness," he wrote. "I'm beginning to feel I'm something of an animal and not a stinking brain alone."

He returned home, entered Harvard Law School and was admitted to the Philadelphia bar in 1890 —only to find that he detested practicing law. Since that summer in Wyoming, he had regularly fled to the West for a vacation given to exploring the big-sky country, shooting bear and stalking mountain sheep. At last he admitted his condition to himself.

"One autumn evening of 1891, fresh from Wyoming and its wild glories, I sat in the club dining with a man as enamored of the West as I was. From oysters to coffee we compared experiences. Why wasn't some Kipling saving the sage-brush for American literature, before the sage-brush and all that it signified went the way of the California forty-niner? What was fiction doing, fiction, the only thing that has always outlived fact? Must it be perpetual teacups? Was Alkali Ike in the comic papers the one figure which the jejune American imagination could discern in that epic which was being lived at a gallop out in the sage-brush? 'To hell with teacups and the great American laugh,' we two said. . . . The claret had been excellent. 'I'm going to try it myself!' I exclaimed. 'I'm going to start this minute.'" And so, that night in the library of the Phil-

adelphia Club, Lawyer Wister wrote most of his first Western story, which he called "Hank's Woman" and sold at once to *Harper's Magazine.*

In this first story appeared a cowboy called only "the Virginian" and an unidentified narrator (Wister's stand-in), who together function as witnesses and commentators on the tragedy unfolding before them. At the grand tourists' hotel in newly opened Yellowstone Park, a lady's maid is unjustly discharged by her touring employers from the East. Hank, with an eye to the wages she has just collected, woos and weds her and takes her over the mountains on horseback to a remote mining camp. There her misery and mistreatment, relieved only by a staunch religious faith that Hank de-

rides, finally resolves itself in murder. After Hank drunkenly shoots a hole in a crucifix she has hung on one wall of their rude cabin, she kills him with the ax from the woodpile, then drags his body to Pitchstone Canyon, heaves him over the edge and either jumps or falls to her own death.

A somber tale, it already gave evidence that Wister, admittedly a romantic, was no false prettifier of the West. On the contrary, he set down its cruelty and bloodiness and blunt talk—and its shiftlessness and incompetence, when he found them—as forthrightly as his editors would let him. During the summer of 1891, Wister had watched, "dazed with disgust and horror," as a Wyoming rancher deliberately gouged out the eye of a horse that displeased him. Three years later this incident turned up in the short story "Balaam and Pedro," also published in *Harper's Magazine*, and still later it would become a chapter in Wister's book *The Virginian*—but somewhat toned down. Theodore Roosevelt, to whom Wister dedicated that novel, asked the author to omit the description of the actual gouging from the book. "Roosevelt was almost fierce about it," Wister recalled later. "We argued about it for several years."

With the success of "Hank's Woman" and the stories that followed it, Wister could abandon the hated grind of the law. Thereafter he haunted the West from Oregon to Texas, but lingered longest with his first love, the plains and mountains of Wyoming. He would spend six months at a spell beyond the Missouri and then go home to Philadelphia and write in an office on Chestnut Street. In all he made 15 Western journeys, and in his passion for accuracy crammed 15 diaries with anecdotes, descriptions, Western idioms, customs and details of trades and occupations. He came to know soldiers, Indians, prospectors, gamblers, cattle kings and cowpokes. The lonely saddle tramp filled him with an admiration close to awe; he thought him a worthy descendant of King Arthur's knights errant. When a cowboy friend pressed him to accept a set of chaps as a gift, he modestly demurred, explaining, "I have always been shy of wearing or owning these garments, as being not enough of a frontiersman to be entitled to them."

Out of Owen Wister's enchantment with the West emerged his masterpiece, *The Virginian*. Laid in Wyoming between the years 1874 and 1890, it tells the love story of a cowhand—never named except as "the Virginian" (he is the same character that appeared in "Hank's Woman")—and Molly Wood, a fastidious and spirited schoolmarm from Vermont. The cowboy dominates the book. He is recognizably a human being; he drinks and can get drunk, plays fiendishly ingenious practical jokes, outsmarts a band of mutinous cowhands, fights and even, under great duress, takes part in a vigilante lynching and kills a man in a gun duel. Wister sets up his hero for good in *The Virginian*'s first long paragraph:

"I noticed a man who sat on the high gate of the corral, looking on. For he now climbed down with the un-dulations of a tiger, smooth and easy, as if his muscles flowed beneath his skin. The others had all visibly whirled the rope, some of them even shoulder high. I did not see his arm lift or move. He appeared to hold the rope down low, by his leg. But like a sudden snake I saw the noose go out its full length and fall true; and the thing was done. . . . The captured pony walked in with a sweet, church-door expression."

Against a man of that stature, the schoolmarm Molly Wood stands nary a chance, although she holds out for a couple of hundred pages. Neither does the villain, a slimy drifter and sometime cowpuncher named Trampas, who badly misjudges the Virginian at their first meeting over a poker game in a Medicine Bow saloon. The Virginian is winning, and Trampas's mood turns ugly. ("Trampas don't enjoy losin' to a stranger," says an onlooker.) When the Virginian pauses a moment before making a crucial move, Trampas snarls: "Your bet, you son-of-a------."

"The Virginian's pistol came out, and his hand lay on the table, holding it unaimed. And with a voice as gentle as ever, the voice that sounded almost like a caress, but drawling a very little more than usual, so that there was almost a space between each word, he issued his orders to the man Trampas:

"When you call me that, *smile!*"

Trampas, forced either to back down or "draw his steel," chooses to back down. But he never forgets his public humiliation, and years later he challenges the Virginian to a gun duel at sundown in that same town. In the exchange of shots, only Trampas is hit; he dies almost instantly.

The Virginian became more than a bestseller. It was the archetype that fixed the myth of the West. So perfect a creation was its tall, lank, drawling hero that countless imitations would never surpass the original. Wister received many tributes, including mistaken avowals from Westerners that they knew the person on whom the Virginian was modeled. (Wister always insisted that the Virginian was a fictional creation.) But probably no tribute pleased Wister more—or was more prophetic of the book's future—than the comment of the typist who helped him prepare the final draft of his manuscript for the publisher. "I'm sorry," she confessed one day to Wister with a smile, "that I didn't meet the Virginian before Molly Wood did."

" ' When you call me that, smile.' "

The arduous art of the pioneer photographer

The photographers who roamed the American West in the latter half of the 19th Century were pioneers twice over. Not only did these intrepid souls explore a wild land, they did so while practicing a science just a-borning.

William Henry Jackson, one of the most accomplished landscape photographers to take aim at the Old West, confessed that he "prayed every time the lens was uncapped." But prayers would go only so far. Successful "viewing"—as Jackson called his embryonic art—"meant labor, patience and moral stamina," and it also required the man with a camera to be "something of a chemist as well as an artist."

After 1850, most photographs were made by the so-called wet-collodion method, yielding glass negatives that could subsequently produce prints on paper. (In the earlier daguerreotype system, fragile—and unreproducible—images were registered on metal plates.) To sensitize a glass plate, the photographer had first to coat it with collodion—a syrupy solution of guncotton in alcohol and ether. Then, in darkness, he would dip the plate into a bath of silver nitrate. Next, with the plate still wet (it lost sensitivity when dry), he had to load his camera, check composition and take an educated guess at the proper exposure period. Since the resultant images would become less clear as the collodion hardened, he had to develop it on the spot, still wet, coping with problems of dust and light.

All this chemistry required photographers to cart around virtually a complete portable studio, including a "dark tent." The actual picture-taking equipment added mightily to their burden. Since no efficient means existed for making enlargements, a print could be only as big as the negative; if a photographer wanted a richly detailed, panoramic landscape, he had to use huge glass negatives and cameras to match.

Jackson's gear weighed close to 300 pounds. And most of it had to be unpacked several times a day. "When hard pressed for time," said Jackson, "I have made a negative in 15 minutes, from the time the first rope was thrown from the pack to the final repacking. Ordinarily, however, half an hour was little enough time to do the work."

Most of the Western landscape photographers were employed by government survey teams, plotting transportation routes and taking inventory of natural resources. But now and again some of them got a chance to work for themselves. The surveys coincided with the flowering of the great American craze for the stereoscope, a device whose two eyepieces blended a pair of photographs into a single image with a realistic three-dimensional effect. And so, along with their ponderous field cameras that were designed to serve the cause of geography, most survey photographers carried stereo cameras and earned extra income by providing images of the West for armchair travelers.

Designed to accommodate 17-by-19-inch wet-collodion plates, this 1873 field camera had a bellows construction that allowed it to be telescoped for easier transport, but it weighed a backbreaking 70 pounds.

Perched coolly on Glacier Point above a 3,254-foot drop, William H. Jackson composes a panorama of the Yosemite Valley.

F. Jay Haynes, who later became official photographer of the Yellowstone National Park, had this stereoscopic portrait of himself made in 1880 at the Great Falls of the Missouri River in Montana Territory.

On a picture-making tour of California in 1853, an apprentice daguerreotypist, Isaac W. Baker, stands arms akimbo in the entrance of the whimsically named rolling studio of his boss, Perez M. Batchelder.

210

No. 59

U. S.

Engineer Department.

Geological Exploration.

Fortieth Parallel.

T. H. O'Sullivan, Photographer.

John K. Hillers studies negatives made on an exploration of the Colorado in 1872. On the expedition as a boatman, Hillers manned the camera when the official photographer became sick and went on to take the first pictures of the Grand Canyon.

On an 1872 mission to make the first photographs of the Teton Range, William H. Jackson and his assistant, Charley Campbell, set up their dark tent on a rocky escarpment west of the mountains. The Grand Teton rises behind Campbell's head.

214

Alexander Gardner, a former Civil War photographer, shows his assistant a botanical specimen before a picture-taking session in Kansas in 1867. The aide holds a lens; chemicals can be seen in the dark tent.

Members of an 1870-1871 survey of the Rocky Mountain region cinch a load to the packsaddle of a mule. The photograph was taken by William Jackson, who later lost a precious carton of exposed plates when a fractious mule slipped its pack.

Standing in the shadow of Utah Territory's
Wasatch mountains, an unknown photographer trains his camera along the shoreline
of the Great Salt Lake in the 1870s.

William Bell, attached to an 1872 expedition of the Army Corps of Engineers, sets up gear for a shot of the Grand Canyon's Kanab Wash in Arizona Territory.

"The camera told the truth"

The hard-won photographic trophies brought back from the West never lacked for an appreciative audience. Mass-marketers of stereoscope photographs gobbled up thousands of images of natural and man-made wonders, Indians and miners, remote ranches and mountain hamlets. Many of the pictures received international exposure; one set riveted the attention of the public at the Paris Exposition of 1867 and another was shown at the Vienna Exhibition of 1873. The United States government was an almost insatiable collector of pictures of its Western birthright, and it put many of them to excellent use. Federal geologists helped persuade Congress to declare Yellowstone a national park by presenting each legislator with a selection of William Henry Jackson's regional studies. Said one observer: "The photographs were of immense value. Description might exaggerate, but the camera told the truth; and in this case the truth was more remarkable than exaggeration."

The 200-year-old Hopi pueblo of Walpi stands at the edge of a craggy mesa in northeastern Arizona Territory, in this 1875 panorama by William H. Jackson. The apartment-like adobe dwellings, some as high as four stories, overlook terraced sheep corrals and the desert 800 feet below.

An Army officer, scouts and a white family pose with local Indians at Fort Mohave, Arizona Territory, in 1868. Built nine years earlier, the fort had served as the base for successful campaigns against the Mohave and Paiute tribes, and its garrison also managed to subdue hostile Walapais at about the time Alexander Gardner took this picture.

Prospectors pause in their labors along boulder-strewn Weber Creek near Placerville, California, in 1851. Miners often commissioned such communal portraits from itinerant photographers and sent them to friends back East — thus creating a veritable mother lode of images of the gold rush.

The 1,200-foot-high palisades of Arizona Territory's Canyon de Chelly loom over photographer Timothy H. O'Sullivan's tent camp *(left)* in 1873. Carved by the wind and water from sand dunes that had been compressed into stone more than 200 million years ago, the ancient canyon became a best-selling subject for many a travel photograph.

224

Prairie homesteader James Pierce and his family line a hill-
ock near their home in an 1886 portrait — one of 1,500
made by Solomon Butcher for a history of pioneering in
Custer County, Nebraska. Their four-room house, built of
thick slabs of sod, doubled as a post office for the region.

Guided by a rider feeling out the river bottom, a mule team hauls a wagon across a ford of the Little Colorado River in 1885. Even at that late date, observed photographer Frederick Monsen, northern Arizona still remained "a land undiscovered and unfrequented by all save soldiers from frontier army posts, or occasional cowboys or prospectors."

At a camp in Kansas, an Arapaho family holds still for photographer William Soule. Many of his pictures of Indians were acquired by the Bureau of American Ethnology, organized by Congress in 1879 to study the Western tribes. By the turn of the century, the bureau's archives at the Smithsonian Institution held about 15,000 negatives.

230

Sightseers overlook the plains spreading out from their gla-
cier-sculpted aerie nearly half a mile above Green River
City, Wyoming Territory. The town of 2,000 was just a
few months old when Andrew Russell made this picture
in 1868 for a Union Pacific travel-promotion campaign.

TEXT CREDITS

For full reference on specific page credits see bibliography.

Chapter 1: Particularly useful sources for information and quotes in this chapter: Horace Greeley, *An Overland Journey from New York to San Francisco in the Summer of 1859,* new edition, ed. by Charles T. Duncan, Alfred A. Knopf, 1964; Samuel Bowles, *Our New West: Records of Travel Between the Mississippi River and the Pacific Ocean,* new edition, Arno Press, 1973; Albert Deane Richardson, *Beyond the Mississippi,* American Publishing Co., 1866; Henry Villard, *The Past and Present of the Pike's Peak Gold Regions,* new edition, Le Roy Hafen, ed., Princeton University Press, 1932; 24-25 — Gregory Gulch report quotes, *New-York Tribune,* June 27, 1859; Byers quotes, Perkin, p. 119. Chapter 2: Particularly useful sources: Robert F. Karolevitz, *Newspapering in the Old West,* Superior Publishing Company, 1965; Richard E. Lingenfelter, *The Newspapers of Nevada, 1858-1958,* John Howell Books, 1964; John Myers Myers, *Print in a Wild Land,* Doubleday & Co. 1967; Elizabeth Wright, *Independence in All Things, Neutrality in Nothing,* Miller Freeman Publications, Inc., 1973; 66 — wedding story, Turnbull, p. 473; Santa Fe shooting story, Stratton, p. 176; 68 — earthquake headlines, Lee, p. 15; 69 — Greeley quote, Dick, p. 54; 74 — Colton on V-less alphabet, Bruce, p. 5; 77 — exchange between King of William and Casey, Bruce, p. 45; 78 — Bill Nye letter, Chaplin, pp. 83-85; 81 — Mark Kellogg message and Lounsberry quote, *Tribune Extra,* July 6, 1876. Chapter 3: Particularly useful sources: John C. Ewers, *Artists of the Old West,* Doubleday & Co., 1965; Harold McCracken, *The Charles M. Russell Book, the Life and Work of the Cowboy Artist,* Doubleday & Co., 1957; Harold McCracken, *Frederic Remington, Artist of the Old West,* J. B. Lippincott Company, 1947; Robert Taft, *Artists and Illustrators of the Old West, 1850-1900,* Charles Scribner's Sons, 1953; Thurman Wilkins, *Thomas Moran, Artist of the Mountains,* University of Oklahoma Press, 1969;

94 — Durand quote, Hills, p. 6; 97 — Peale's steamboat quote, Weese, pp. 149-150. Chapter 4: Particularly useful source: Robert G. Athearn, *Westward the Briton,* University of Nebraska Press, 1953; 144-151 — Dunraven quotes, *The Great Divide;* 144 — Sienkiewicz quote, *Portrait of America,* p. 69; Simonin quote, *The Rocky Mountain West in 1867,* p. 21; 149 — English traveler quote, Burton, p. 1; 152 — Paul Wilhelm quotes, *Travels in North America;* 156-158 — Burton excerpts, *The Look of the West, 1860;* 157 — Möllhausen quotes, Barba, p. 87; 161-166 — Bird excerpts, *A Lady's Life in the Rocky Mountains;* 163 — train robbery story, London *Graphic,* August 8, 1891; 164-165 — Eagle Joe story, *Illustrated London News,* Summer Number, 1891; 166-169 — Simonin excerpts, *The Rocky Mountain West in 1867;* 172-173 — Sienkiewicz excerpts, *Portrait of America;* 173 — Bryce quotes, *The American Commonwealth,* Vol. II, pp. 890, 892, 899; 174, 176 — Kurz quotes, *Journal,* pp. 1, 38, 176. Chapter 5: Particularly useful sources: *The Best Short Stories of Bret Harte,* Robert N. Linscott, ed., The Modern Library, 1947; Washington Irving, *A Tour on the Prairies,* edited with an Introductory Essay by John Francis McDermott, University of Oklahoma Press, 1956; Helen Hunt Jackson, *A Century of Dishonor,* with Introduction by Andrew F. Rolle, Harper Torchbooks, Harper & Row, 1965; Richard O'Connor, *Bret Harte,* Little, Brown and Company, 1966; Francis Parkman, *The Oregon Trail,* Mason Wade, ed., The Heritage Press, 1943; Robert Taft, *Photography and the American Scene,* Dover Publications, 1964; Mark Twain, *Roughing It,* New American Library, 1962; Fanny Kemble Wister, ed., *Owen Wister Out West: His Journals and Letters,* University of Chicago Press, 1958; 203 — William Dean Howells in praise of *Roughing It,* Howells, pp. 95-96; 206 — quotes from *The Virginian,* pp. 2-3, 28-29.

PICTURE CREDITS

The sources for the illustrations in this book are shown below. Credits from left to right are separated by semicolons, from top to bottom by dashes.

Cover — Paulus Leeser, courtesy Rare Book Division, The New York Public Library, Astor, Lenox and Tilden Foundations. 2 — Harrison Putney, from the Collection of David R. Phillips. 6,7 — William Henry Jackson, courtesy U.S. Geological Survey. 8,9 — Courtesy Union Pacific Railroad Museum Collection. 10,11 — Courtesy National Archives, #111-SC-82307. 12,13 — Joseph E. Smith, from the Collection of David R. Phillips. 14,15 — From the personal collection of Robert A. Weinstein. 16 — Courtesy Library of Congress. 17 — No credit. 18,19 — Courtesy The Bancroft Library. 20 — Courtesy Western History Department, Denver Public Library. 23 — No credit; Charles Roscoe Savage, courtesy Historical Department, Church of Jesus Christ of Latter-day Saints. 26,27 — Courtesy Library of Congress. 28 — Courtesy Oregon Historical Society. 31 — Courtesy Library of Congress. 32 — Courtesy Culver Pictures. 34,35 — Courtesy Greeley Municipal Museum, Greeley, Colorado, except bottom right, courtesy Western History Department, Denver Public Library. 38,39 — Courtesy General Research and Humanities Division, The New York Public Library, Astor, Lenox and Tilden Foundations. 40 — Frank Lerner, courtesy of The New-York Historical Society. 41 — Courtesy General Research and Humanities Division, The New York Public Library, Astor, Lenox and Tilden Foundations. 42 through 49 — Courtesy General Research and Humanities Division, The New York Public Library, Astor, Lenox and Tilden Foundations. 50,51 — Courtesy Kansas State Historical Society, Topeka. 52, 53 — Solomon D. Butcher, courtesy Solomon D. Butcher Collection, Ne-

braska State Historical Society. 54,55 — Courtesy Western History Research Center, University of Wyoming. 56,57 — From the collection of the Arizona Historical Society. 58 — *The Yankton Press, Tri-Weekly Democrat, The Kansas Adviser, Helena Herald,* Frank Lerner, courtesy of The New-York Historical Society. *Thomas County Cat, The Pottawatomie Chief, The Scalping Knife,* courtesy Kansas State Historical Society, Topeka. 60,61 — Courtesy Collections of Greenfield Village and the Henry Ford Museum; courtesy Columbia University Libraries. 62 — Courtesy Western History Research Center, University of Wyoming. 63 — Courtesy Oregon Historical Society. 64,65 — W. F. Boyd, courtesy Photography Collection, Special Collections, University of Washington Library. 67 — Courtesy The Huntington Library, San Marino, California — courtesy The Thomas Gilcrease Institute of American History and Art, Tulsa, Oklahoma. 70,71 — Courtesy California Historical Society, San Francisco. 72,73 — Courtesy Western History Department, Denver Public Library. 74 — Courtesy The Bancroft Library. 75 — N. R. Farbman, TLPA, courtesy University of Nevada, Reno. 76 through 81 — Courtesy Kansas State Historical Society, Topeka. 82 through 93 — Joseph E. Smith, from the Collection of David R. Phillips. 94,95 — Eadweard Muybridge, courtesy California Historical Society, San Francisco; Henry Beville, courtesy Private Collection. 96 — Courtesy Library of Congress. 99 — Henry Beville, courtesy Maryland Historical Society — courtesy American Philosophical Society. 100,101 — Courtesy American Philosophical Society. 103 — Eugene Mantie, courtesy National Portrait Gallery, Smithsonian Institution, Washington, D.C. — courtesy Rare Book Division, The New York Public Library, Astor, Lenox and Tilden Foundations. 104,105 — Courtesy American History Division, The New York Public Library, Astor, Lenox and Tilden Foundations — courtesy of National Collection of Fine Arts, Smithsonian Institution (4). 106,107 — Courtesy National Gallery of Art, Washington. Collection of Mr. and Mrs. Paul Mellon. 108,109 — Courtesy The Thomas Gilcrease Institute of American History and Art, Tulsa, Oklahoma — courtesy Northern Natural Gas Company Collection, Joslyn Art Museum, Omaha, Nebraska; Henry Baskerville, TLPA, courtesy Joslyn Art Museum, Omaha, Nebraska. 110,111 — Courtesy The Walters Art Gallery. 112,113 — Benschneider, courtesy Western History Research Center, University of Wyoming. 114,115 — Courtesy Western History Department, Denver Public Library. 117 — Paulus Leeser, courtesy Collection of Mr. and Mrs. Albert M. Turner, Orono, Maine, except bottom left, Eadweard Muybridge, courtesy The Bancroft Library. 119 — Courtesy East Hampton Free Library — No credit; courtesy Library of Congress. 120,121 — Courtesy of National Collection of Fine Arts, Smithsonian Institution. 122 — Courtesy National Park Service. 123 — Herb Orth. 125 — Courtesy Remington Art Museum, Ogdensburg, New York — courtesy Remington Art Museum, Ogdensburg, New York, all rights reserved; Eric Schaal, TLPA, courtesy Amon Carter Museum, Fort Worth, Texas. 126,127 — Courtesy General Research and Humanities Division, The New York Public Library, Astor, Lenox and Tilden Foundations. 128,129 — Courtesy The Metropolitan Museum of Art, Gift of Several Gentlemen, 1911. 130,131 — Linda Lorenz, courtesy Amon Carter Museum, Fort Worth, Texas — courtesy City of Great Falls, Park & Recreation Department. 132,133 — Courtesy Montana Historical Society, Helena, Montana. 134,135 — Mark Edgar Hopkins Hawkes, courtesy the B. Hay Collection. 136,137 — Frank Lerner, courtesy Collection of Jones Library, Amherst, Massachusetts. 138,139 — Courtesy of The Rockwell Foundation, Corning, New York. 140,141 — Courtesy Western History Department, Denver Public Library. 142,143 — Courtesy The Thomas Gilcrease Institute of American History and Art, Tulsa, Oklahoma. 144,145 — Derek Bayes, courtesy Earl of Meath. 146 — Courtesy The Bancroft Library. 148 through 151 — Derek Bayes, courtesy Earl of Meath. 152 through 155 — Indian artifacts, courtesy Völkerkunde Museum der Staatliche Museen Preussischer Kulturbesitz, Berlin-West. Animal watercolors, courtesy Staatliches Museum für Naturkunde Stuttgart from Herzog Paul Wilhelm von Württemberg Atlas, vol. I & II. Photo Hanns E. Haehl. 157 — From *Baldouin Möllhausen: the German Cooper* by Preston A. Barba, copied by Henry Groskinsky, courtesy General Research and Humanities Division, The New York Public Library, Astor, Lenox and Tilden Foundations. 159 — *Great Salt Lake City, Utah, 1853,* courtesy Museum of Fine Arts, Boston. 160 — Courtesy The Bettmann Archive. 161 — Courtesy General Research and Humanities Division, The New York Public Library, Astor, Lenox and Tilden Foundations. 162 through 165 — Courtesy General Research and Humanities Division, The New York Public Library, Astor, Lenox and Tilden Foundations. 167 — Photo Bibliothèque nationale, Paris; Photo Bibliothèque nationale, Paris, by courtesy of Cabinet des Estampes, Bibliothèque nationale, Paris. 168 — Henry Beville, by courtesy of Cabinet des Estampes, Bibliothèque nationale, Paris. 170

— Courtesy Union Pacific Railroad Museum Collection (3) — David F. Barry, courtesy Western History Department, Denver Public Library. 171 — Henry Groskinsky, courtesy General Research and Humanities Division, The New York Public Library, Astor, Lenox and Tilden Foundations. 174 through 179 — Yves Debraine, courtesy Kurz Collection, Historisches Museum, Bern. 180 — Courtesy The Huntington Library, San Marino, California. 181 — Courtesy of The New-York Historical Society — Bradley & Rulofson, courtesy Silverado Museum, St. Helena, California; courtesy The Bettmann Archive. 182 — Bradley & Rulofson, courtesy California State Library, Sacramento — Bradley & Rulofson, courtesy Mark Twain Papers, The Bancroft Library, University of California, Berkeley; courtesy Shuffler Collection, Photography Collection, Humanities Research Center, The University of Texas at Austin. 183 — Courtesy Western History Research Center, University of Wyoming. 184 — Courtesy Henry W. and Albert A. Berg Collection, The New York Public Library, Astor, Lenox and Tilden Foundations and Sleepy Hollow Restorations. 188 — Courtesy The Huntington Library, San Marino, California. 191 — George M. Cushing, Jr., courtesy Colonial Society of Massachusetts — George M. Cushing, Jr., courtesy Massachusetts Historical Society. 194,195 — John Calvin Brewster, courtesy of Ventura County Historical Museum, Ventura, California; courtesy of The Mercantile Library of New York City — John Calvin Brewster, courtesy of Ventura County Historical Museum, Ventura, California; courtesy of The Mercantile Library of New York City (2). 197 — Courtesy California State Library, Sacramento. 198,199 — *Washing Gold, Calaveras River, California,* copied by P. Richard Eells, courtesy Museum of Fine Arts, Boston. 200,201 — Henry Groskinsky, courtesy General Research and Humanities Division, The New York Public Library, Astor, Lenox and Tilden Foundations. 202 — Mora Studio, New York, courtesy University of Oregon Library. 204,205 — Courtesy Western History Research Center, University of Wyoming. 207 — Henry Groskinsky, courtesy General Research and Humanities Division, The New York Public Library, Astor, Lenox and Tilden Foundations. 208 — Paulus Leeser, courtesy Collection of Mary and Weston Naef. 209 — Courtesy Western History Department, Denver Public Library. 210 — Courtesy Collection of Allen and Hilary Weiner — Lent anonymously to The Oakland Museum. 211 — T. H. O'Sullivan, courtesy The Bancroft Library. 212 — Courtesy National Archives, #57-PS-809. 213 — Courtesy National Archives, #57-HS-172. 214 — William Henry Jackson, courtesy Western History Department, Denver Public Library. 215 — Courtesy Library of Congress. 216 — Courtesy Collection of Allen and Hilary Weiner. 217 — Courtesy Library of Congress. 218,219 — William Henry Jackson, courtesy Smithsonian Institution, National Anthropological Archives. 220,221 — Alexander Gardner, courtesy International Museum of Photography at George Eastman House. 222,223 — William Shew, courtesy The Bancroft Library. 224,225 — T. H. O'Sullivan, courtesy International Museum of Photography at George Eastman House. 226,227 — Solomon D. Butcher, courtesy Solomon D. Butcher Collection, Nebraska State Historical Society. 228,229 — Frederick Monsen, courtesy The Huntington Library, San Marino, California. 230,231 — William Soule, courtesy Smithsonian Institution, National Anthropological Archives. 232,233 — Andrew J. Russell, photograph courtesy of The Oakland Museum.

ACKNOWLEDGMENTS

The index for this book was prepared by Gale L. Partoyan. The editors also acknowledge the assistance of the following persons: Dave Basso, Sparks, Nev.; Kenneth J. Carpenter, Univ. of Nevada Library; David Crosson, Western History Res. Center, Univ. of Wyoming; Mrs. Loretta Davisson, Mrs. John Bret-Harte, Arizona Pioneer Historical Society; Eugene Decker, Robert W. Richmond, Joseph Snell, Kansas State Historical Society; Lawrence Dinnean, The Bancroft Library, Univ. of California, Berkeley; Mrs. Elizabeth Wright Freeman, Borrego Springs, Calif.; Eleanor M. Gehres, A. D. Mastrogiuseppe, Western History Dept., Denver Public Library; Juliane Greenwalt, Detroit, Mich.; James Gregory, The New-York Historical Society; Villette K. Harris, Washington, D.C.; Matthew Isenberg, Hadlyme, Conn.; Dorothy T. King, Long Island Coll., East Hampton Free Library; Richard Lingenfelter, Manhattan Beach, Calif.; Kenneth Lohf, Rare Book Div., Butler Library, Columbia Univ.; Terry Wm. Mangan, Gary Kurutz, Calif. Historical Society; Harriett Meloy, Montana Historical Society; Maud D. Cole, Rare Books Div., Joe Halpern, Genealogical Div., John Miller, and the Staff of the American History Div., The New York Public Library; Arthur Olivas, Museum of New Mexico; Dick Perue, Saratoga *Sun;* Paula Richardson, National Anthropological Archives, Smithsonian Institution; Prof. James Shenton, Columbia Univ.; Milton Thompson, Jefferson National Expansion Memorial; Dr. Evan Turner, The Philadelphia Museum of Art; Mr. and Mrs. Henry H. Villard, New York City; Nelson Wadsworth, Salt Lake City; Prof. Robert C. Warner, Univ. of Wyoming; Robert G. Wheeler, Kenneth Wilson, Greenfield Village and Henry Ford Museum; Janice Worden, Oregon Historical Society.

BIBLIOGRAPHY

Andrews, Ralph W., *Picture Gallery Pioneers.* Superior, 1964.

Athearn, Robert G., *Westward the Briton.* Univ. of Nebraska Press, 1953.

Bancroft, Hubert Howe, *The Works of Hubert Howe Bancroft,* Vol. 39. Arno Press.

Barba, Preston Albert, *Baldouin Möllhausen — The German Cooper.* Univ. of Pennsylvania Press, 1914.

Bird, Isabella, *A Lady's Life in the Rocky Mountains.* Ballantine Books, 1971.

Bowles, Samuel, *Our New West.* Arno Press, 1973.

Brooks, Van Wyck, *The World of Washington Irving.* Blakiston, 1944.

Bruce, John, *Gaudy Century, The Story of San Francisco's Hundred Years of Robust Journalism.* Random House, 1948.

Burton, Sir Richard, *The Look of the West, 1860.* Univ. of Nebraska Press, 1963.

Butcher, Solomon D., *Pioneer History of Custer County, Nebraska.* Sage Books, 1965.

Catlin, George, *Letters and Notes on the Manners, Customs, and Condition of the North American Indians,* 2 vols. Ross & Haines, 1965.

Caughey, John Walton, *Hubert Howe Bancroft, Historian of the West.* Univ. of California Press, 1946.

Chaplin, W.E., "Some Wyoming Editors I Have Known." *Annals of Wyoming,* Vol. 18, 1946.

Curry, Larry, *The American West, Painters from Catlin to Russell.* The Viking Press, 1972.

Darrah, W. C., *Stereo Views, A History of Stereographs in America and Their Collection.* Times and News Publishing Co., 1964.

Dick, Everett, *The Sod-House Frontier 1854-1890.* Johnsen, 1954.

Doughty, Howard, *Francis Parkman.* Macmillan, 1962.

Dunraven, Earl of, *The Great Divide.* Univ. of Nebraska Press, 1967.

Ellsworth, Henry Leavitt, *Washington Irving on the Prairie.* S. T. Williams and B. D. Simison, eds. American Book Co., 1937.

Ewers, John C., *Artists of the Old West.* Doubleday, 1965.

Farwell, Byron, *Burton.* Holt, Rinehart and Winston, 1963.

Gallegly, J. S., "Background and Patterns of O. Henry's Texas Badman Stories." *Rice Institute Pamphlet,* Vol. 42, No. 3, Oct. 1955.

Gernsheim, Helmut, in collaboration with Alison Gernsheim, *The History of Photography.* McGraw-Hill, 1969.

Greeley, Horace, *An Overland Journey.* Alfred A. Knopf, 1964.

Greever, W. S., *The Bonanza West.* Univ. of Oklahoma Press, 1963.

Hale, William Harlan, *Horace Greeley.* Harper & Bros., 1950.

Hendricks, Gordon, *Albert Bierstadt.* Harry N. Abrams, 1973.

Henry, O., *The Complete Works of O. Henry.* Garden City Publ., 1937.

Hernandez, Richard A., "Frederick Marriott: A Forty-Niner Banker and Editor Who Took a Flier in Pioneering American Aviation." *Journal of West.* Morrison & Morrison, Oct. 1963.

Hills, Patricia, *The American Frontier, Images and Myths.* Whitney Museum of American Art, 1973.

Hogarth, Paul, *Artists on Horseback.* Watson-Guptill, 1972.

Howells, William Dean, *My Mark Twain.* Louisiana Univ. Press, 1967.

Howes, Cecil, "Pistol-Packin' Pencil Pushers." *Kansas Historical Quarterly,* May 1944.

Irving, Washington:

The Adventures of Captain Bonneville U.S.A. Putnam, 1868.

Astoria, Edgeley W. Todd, ed. Univ. of Oklahoma Press, 1964.

The Sketch Book with an introduction by Harry Hansen. Dodd, Mead, 1954.

A Tour on the Prairies. Univ. of Oklahoma Press, 1956.

Jackson, Helen Hunt:

A Century of Dishonor. Harper & Row, 1965.

Ramona. Little, Brown, 1928.

Jackson, William H., *Time Exposure.* Cooper Square Publ., 1970.

Jackson, William H., and Howard R. Driggs, *The Pioneer Photographer.* World Book Company, 1929.

Journal of Rudolph Friederich Kurz, transl. by Myrtis Jarrell, edited by J. N. B. Hewitt. Univ. of Nebraska Press, 1970.

Kaplan, Justin, ed., *Great Short Works of Mark Twain.* Harper & Row, 1967.

Karolevitz, Robert F., *Newspapering in the Old West: A Pictorial History of Journalism and Printing on the Frontier.* Superior, 1965.

Langsdorf, Edgar, and R. W. Richmond, eds., "Letters of Daniel R. Anthony." *Kansas Historical Quarterly,* Vol. 24, 1958.

Lee, W. Storrs, *The Sierra.* Putnam, 1962.

Leonard, J. Joseph, "On the Trail of the Legendary Dave Day." *The Denver Brand Book:IX,* 1953.

Lingenfelter, R. E., *The Newspapers of Nevada.* John Howell, 1964.

Linscott, Robert N., ed., *The Best Short Stories of Bret Harte.* The Modern Library, 1947.

Long, E. Hudson, *O. Henry, The Man and His Work.* Univ. of Pennsylvania Press, 1949.

Mack, Effie Mona, *Mark Twain in Nevada.* Scribners, 1947.

Marberry, M. M., *Splendid Poseur, Joaquin Miller — American Poet.*

Thomas Y. Crowell, 1953.

Martin, D. D., *Tombstone's Epitaph*. Univ. of New Mexico Press, 1951.

McCracken, Harold:
The Charles M. Russell Book, The Life and Work of the Cowboy Artist. Doubleday, 1957.
Frederic Remington, Artist of the Old West. J. B. Lippincott, 1947.
George Catlin and the Old Frontier. The Dial Press, 1959.
Portrait of the Old West, McGraw-Hill, 1952.

McDermott, John Francis, ed., *The Western Journals of Washington Irving*. Univ. of Oklahoma Press, 1944.

Meserve, John Bartlett, "Chief William Potter Ross." *Chronicles of Oklahoma*, March 1937. Oklahoma Historical Society.

Miller, Joaquin, *The Complete Poetical Works of Joaquin Miller*. The Whitaker & Ray Company, 1904.

Miller, Nyle H., and Joseph W. Snell, *Great Gunfighters of the Kansas Cowtowns, 1867-1886*. Univ. of Nebraska Press, 1963.

Miller, Nyle H., Edgar Langsdorf and Robert W. Richmond, *Kansas in Newspapers*. Kansas State Historical Society, 1963.

Monsen, Frederick I., *With a Kodak in the Land of the Navajo*. Eastman Kodak Company.

Morison, Samuel Eliot, *Francis Parkman*. Massachusetts Historical Society, 1973.

Mott, Frank Luther, *American Journalism, A History: 1690-1960*. Macmillan, 1962.

Myers, John Myers, *Print in a Wild Land*. Doubleday, 1967.

Naef, Weston J., in collaboration with James N. Wood, *Era of Exploration, The Rise of Landscape Photography in The American West*. Albright-Knox Art Gallery and The Metropolitan Museum of Art, 1975.

Newhall, Beaumont and Diana E. Edkins, *William H. Jackson*. Morgan and Morgan, 1974.

Nye, W. S., *Plains Indian Raiders*. Univ. of Oklahoma Press, 1968.

O'Connor, Richard, *Bret Harte*. Little, Brown, 1966.

Odell, Ruth, *Helen Hunt Jackson*. D. Appleton-Century, 1939.

Pabor, W. E., *Greeley in the Beginning*. Greeley Museums, 1973.

Paine, Albert Bigelow, *Mark Twain* (Vol. I). Harper & Bros., 1912.

Parkman, Francis, *The Oregon Trail*. Mason Wade, ed. The Heritage Press, 1943.

Perkin, Robert L., *The First Hundred Years: An Informal History of Denver and the Rocky Mountain News*. Doubleday, 1959.

Poesch, Jessie, *Titian Ramsay Peale and His Journals of the Wilkes Expedition*. The American Philosophical Society, 1961.

The Portable Mark Twain, selected and introduced by Bernard DeVoto. The Viking Press, 1946.

Powell, Lawrence Clark, "Flumgudgeon Gazette in 1845 Antedated the Spectator." *Oregon Historical Quarterly*, Vol. 41, 1940.

Quiett, Glen Chesney, *Pay Dirt*. D. Appleton-Century, 1936.

Ray, Grace Ernestine, "Early Oklahoma Newspapers." *University of Oklahoma Bulletin*, June 15, 1928.

Renner, F. G., *Charles M. Russell, Paintings, Drawings, and Sculpture in the Amon G. Carter Collection*. Univ. of Texas Press, 1966.

Richardson, Albert D., *Beyond the Mississippi*. American Publishing Co., 1867.

Rosa, Joseph G., *They Called Him Wild Bill*. Univ. of Oklahoma Press, 1975.

Ross, Marvin, *The West of Alfred Jacob Miller*. Univ. of Oklahoma Press, 1951.

Sedgwick, Henry Dwight, *Francis Parkman*. Houghton, Mifflin, 1904.

Sienkiewicz, Henry, *Portrait of America: Letters of Henry Sienkiewicz*, edited & translated by Charles Morley. Columbia Univ. Press, 1959.

Simonin, Louis L., *The Rocky Mountain West in 1867*, transl. and annotated by Wilson O. Clough. Univ. of Nebraska Press, 1966.

Smith, Avery, *Joseph E. Smith, Photographer, Socorro, New Mexico* (unpublished).

Smith, C. Alphonso, *O. Henry Biography*. Doubleday, Page, 1916.

Smith, Wally, "The Camulos Story." *The Ventura County Historical Society Quarterly*, Vol. 3, No. 2, Feb. 1958.

Sprague, Marshall, *A Gallery of Dudes*. Little, Brown, 1967.

Stevenson, Robert Louis, *From Scotland to Silverado*. The Belknap Press of Harvard Univ. Press, 1966.

Stewart, George R., Jr., *Bret Harte, Argonaut and Exile*. Houghton Mifflin, 1931.

Stratton, Porter A., *The Territorial Press of New Mexico, 1834-1912*. Univ. of New Mexico Press, 1969.

Taft, Robert:
Artists and Illustrators of the Old West. Scribners, 1953.
Photography and the American Scene. Dover, 1964.

Tilden, Freeman, *Following the Frontier with F. Jay Haynes, Pioneer Photographer of the Old West*. Knopf, 1964.

Turnbull, George S., *History of Oregon Newspapers*. Binfords & Mort, 1939.

Twain, Mark, *Roughing It*. New American Library, 1962.

Villard, Henry, *The Past and Present of the Pike's Peak Gold Regions*. Princeton Univ. Press, 1932.

Vorpahl, Ben M., *My Dear Wister*. American West Pub. Co., 1972.

Voss, Arthur, *The American Short Story*. Univ. of Oklahoma Press, 1973.

Wade, Mason, ed., *The Journals of Francis Parkman*. Harper, 1947.

Wagenknecht, Edward, *Washington Irving: Moderation Displayed*. Oxford Univ. Press, 1962.

Walker, Franklin, *San Francisco's Literary Frontier*. Knopf, 1939.

Weese, A. O., ed., "The Journal of Titian Ramsay Peale, Pioneer Naturalist." *Missouri Historical Review*, Jan. 1947.

The West of Owen Wister, Selected Short Stories with Introduction by Robert L. Hough. Univ. of Nebraska Press, 1972.

White, G. Edward, *The Eastern Establishment and the Western Experience*. Yale Univ. Press, 1968.

Wilkins, Thurman, *Thomas Moran, Artist of the Mountains*. Univ. of Oklahoma Press, 1969.

Wilkinson, Kristina, "Frederick Monsen, F.R.G.S., Explorer and Ethnographer." *Noticias*. Santa Barbara Historical Society, Vol. 15, No. 3, Summer 1969.

Willard, James F., ed., *The Union Colony of Greeley, Colorado — 1869-1871*. Univ. of Colorado, 1918.

Willison, G. F., *Here They Dug the Gold*. Reynal & Hitchcock, 1946.

Wister, Fanny Kemble, ed., *Owen Wister Out West: His Journals and Letters*. Univ. of Chicago Press, 1958.

Wister, Owen, *The Virginian*. Grosset & Dunlap, 1929.

Wood, Richard G., *Stephen Harriman Long, 1784-1864: Army Engineer, Explorer, Inventor*. The Arthur H. Clark Company, 1966.

Wright, Elizabeth, *Independence in All Things, Neutrality in Nothing*. Miller Freeman, 1973.

Württemberg, Paul Wilhelm, Duke of, *Travels in North America 1822-1824*, transl. by W. Robert Nitske, ed. by Savoie Lottinville. Univ. of Oklahoma Press, 1973.

Printed in U.S.A.